Prelude to
Revolution

Indiana University International Studies

Prelude to
Revolution

The Petrograd Bolsheviks and the July
1917 Uprising

ALEXANDER RABINOWITCH

INDIANA UNIVERSITY PRESS

BLOOMINGTON   LONDON

To My Parents
and Janet

Contents

List of Illustrations

Preface

The core of this book was originally prepared as a doctoral dissertation for the Department of History, Indiana University. Its point of departure was a conversation with Philip E. Mosely in the summer of 1962. At Indiana work on my dissertation was guided by John M. Thompson. Dr. Thompson's rigorous standards of scholarship, seemingly inexhaustible energy, and lively disposition have been an inspiration to his students; his continuing support and always apt advice were of inestimable value to my research and writing. Along with John Thompson, I am particularly indebted to my wife and colleague, Janet Rabinowitch, and to the late Menshevik leader and historian, Boris I. Nicolaevsky. Since 1963 my wife has permitted the Petrograd Bolsheviks and the "July Days" to dominate our intellectual lives in spite of her interest in nineteenth-century Russian intellectual history and, this not enough, she has willingly read, reread, and typed an endless stream of barely legible drafts. Whatever merit this study possesses is due in no small part to her patience and perceptive observations. As for Boris Nicolaevsky, I had the good fortune of knowing him from childhood and owe my interest in the study of Russian history to many happy summers together in the Green Mountains of Vermont. Without materials from Boris Ivanovich's library and archive, without the profound insight and encyclopedic knowledge which he generously shared with me, and perhaps most

ix

of all, without his encouragement, it is quite likely that this study would not have been completed. Piecing together a detailed picture of Bolshevik Party history without the benefit of unpublished archival materials is often frustrating, and Boris Ivanovich's frequently asserted conviction that enough information could be gleaned from available sources for a meaningful contribution to historical literature was a constant source of inspiration.

A grant from the Foreign Area Fellowship Program enabled me to conduct doctoral research in the Slavonic Division of the New York Public Library, at the Columbia University Library, and at the Hoover Institution, Stanford, California. In addition, ten sometimes frustrating but profitable months were spent studying in Soviet libraries under the auspices of the Inter-University Committee on Travel Grants. Some supplementary research expenses were provided by the University of Southern California, and a fellowship from the International Affairs Center, Indiana University, made it possible for me to spend the summer of 1966 revising the dissertation for publication.

It is a pleasure to acknowledge my debt to the staffs of the Columbia University and the University of Southern California Libraries, the Slavonic Division of the New York Public Library, and especially to Anna M. Bourguina and Marina Tinkoff of the Hoover Institution, for their help in locating and obtaining many of the sources upon which this study is based. I am grateful to them and also to Samuel H. Baron, Václav L. Beneš, Paul E. Burns, Robert F. Byrnes, Robert Feldman, Eugene Rabinowitch, Robert C. Tucker, and S. V. Utechin, who read and commented on all or parts of this study. Few of the above, as well as John Thompson, my wife, and Boris Nicolaevsky, were not uncritical of individual portions of this work, and their comments and suggestions were very helpful in preparing the final manuscript. They have done all they could. I alone am responsible for those shortcomings which have not been eliminated.

The system of transliteration employed in this work is the one used by the Library of Congress with a few modifications. Thus, proper names are in most cases spelled in their more familiar English forms. All dates are given according to the Julian calendar, employed in Russia until 1918, rather than the Gregorian calendar of the West. In 1917 the former was thirteen days behind the latter.

Finally, it should be mentioned that the present study is contemplated as the first portion of a two-part history of the Petrograd Bolsheviks in 1917. A companion volume, on the Petrograd Bolsheviks in the October revolution, is currently in preparation.

ALEXANDER RABINOWITCH

Los Angeles, California
March, 1967

Prelude to

Revolution

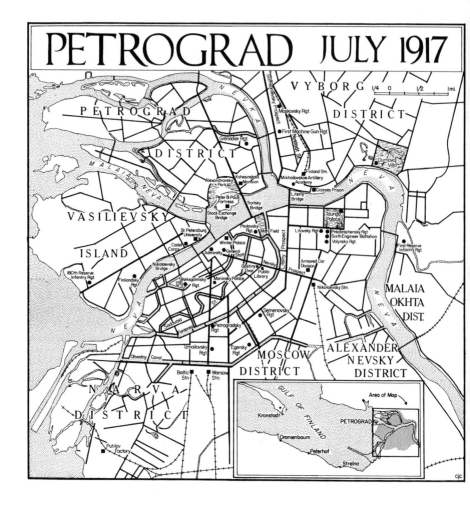

PETROGRAD JULY 1917

VYBORG

PETROGRAD

DISTRICT

DISTRICT

1/4 0 1/2 1mi.

Moskovsky Rgt.

First Machine Gun Rgt

Grenadier Rgt.

Durnovo Villa

Finland Stn.

Mikhailovskoe Artillery Academy

Alexandrovsky Park

Ksheshskaia Mansion

Peter & Paul Fortress

Litetny Bridge

Crosses Prison

Stock Exchange Bridge

Troitsky Bridge

Tauride Palace

VASILIEVSKY

St Petersburg University

Pavlovsky Rgt

Mars Field

Litovsky Rgt

Preobrazhensky Rgt
Sixth Engineer Battalion
Volynsky Rgt.

First Reserve Infantry Rgt.

ISLAND

Caden Corps

Winter Palace

Admiralty

General Staff

Nevsky Prospect

Gostiny Dvor

Public Library

Armored Car Division

Nikolaevsky Bridge

180th Reserve Infantry Rgt

Finliandsky

Keksgolmsky Rgt.

Mariinsky Palace

Nikolaevsky Stn.

MALAIA OKHTA DIST.

Sadovaia

Fontanka

Semenovsky Rgt.

Petrogradsky Rgt.

ALEXANDER NEVSKY DISTRICT

Izmailovsky Rgt.

Egersky Rgt.

MOSCOW DISTRICT

Obvodny Canal

Baltic Stn.

Warsaw Stn.

N A R V A

DISTRICT

GULF OF FINLAND

Area of Map

Kronstadt

PETROGRAD

Oranienbaum

Putilov Factory

Peterhof

Strelna

NEVKA

NEVA

MALAIA NEVA

NEVA

NEVA

cjc

Prologue

On June 10, 1917, a little less than four months after the overthrow of the Russian monarchy, a protest march of Petrograd workers and soldiers, organized in secret by the Bolshevik Party Central Committee and directed against the Provisional Government, was cancelled as a result of last minute intervention by the First All-Russian Congress of Soviets. Barely four weeks later, in early July, at the time of the political crisis caused by the break-up of the first coalition cabinet of the Provisional Government, mass demonstrations broke out in the streets of Petrograd. At the height of the uprising frequent armed clashes occurred between sailors from the nearby Kronstadt naval base, factory workers, and garrison regiments demonstrating in behalf of the transfer of all power to the Soviets, on the one hand, and supporters of the Provisional Government, on the other. Although led by rank-and-file Bolsheviks, the July disturbances were apparently only very belatedly sanctioned by the party Central Committee. The Provisional Government and the Soviet proved totally incapable of controlling the situation, and the demonstrations were quelled only after loyal troops had been summoned from the battle zones and the Bolshevik leadership had been publicly discredited as supposed agents of the German government, At the time, both events—the abortive protest march of June 10 and the chaotic street demonstrations of early July—were widely believed to have been part of a Leninist plot to seize power.

The swing to the right discernible among many Russian liberal democratic and moderate socialist leaders beginning in mid-July was in large measure a response to the Bolshevik scare produced by the disruptions that took place in the capital during the July days.

The official Soviet interpretation of the abortive June demonstration and the July uprising is that both were essentially peaceful, spontaneous expressions of dissatisfaction and impatience with the "counterrevolutionary" Provisional Government, to which the Bolshevik Party only gave organization and direction. A steadily growing number of Soviet studies of the June-July period focus attention on the growth of discontent among Petrograd workers and soldiers but add very little to our knowledge of the Bolshevik Party at this time.[1]

For their part, most non-Soviet students of Russian history acknowledge that the June and July crises were a watershed in the development of the Russian revolution. Nonetheless, these events and particularly the relation of the Bolshevik Party to them remain one of the most confused chapters in Western historiography on the Provisional Government period. With the possible exception of W. H. Chamberlin's path-breaking two-volume history of the Russian revolution,[2] there exist no detailed Western historical studies of the subject, and interpretations of the June and July demonstrations in general non-Soviet works on the revolutionary period are divided. Some writers adhere to the view that the abortive June 10 demonstration was organized by the Bolsheviks in response to mass pressure and that the July demonstrations broke out against the will of the party. Others accept the notion, largely based on N. N. Sukhanov's disclosures in his memoir history of the revolution, *Zapiski o revoliutsii*,[3] that the July uprising and particularly the abortive June 10 demonstration were directly associated with unsuccessful plans by Lenin for seizing power. Still a third group of writers appears to acknowledge the immense confusion surrounding the Bolshevik relation to the June 10 demonstration and to the organization of the July uprising by skirting discussion of these subjects almost entirely.

The aim of this study is to examine in greater depth and detail than heretofore the causes of the Petrograd June and July demonstrations of 1917 and the role and aims of the Bolshevik Party in their organization and development. I should note that the focus of the study is almost exclusively on developments in Petrograd, where by mid-summer mass unrest and support for the Bolsheviks were far more advanced than in the provinces and at the front. Attention is also centered on the attitudes and activities of local Bolshevik party organizations at least as much as on Lenin and the party Central Committee. Early in the course of research I became convinced that the key to an understanding of Bolshevik policy in June and July was not to be found in the discovery of some preconceived revolutionary plan of Lenin's and that much of the confusion surrounding this subject stemmed from a tendency, promoted by Soviet historians, to think of the Bolshevik Party as a nearly monolithic instrument subservient to Lenin's will. Western scholarship has been quick to recognize the significant differences in outlook between internal Bolshevik Party factions immediately following the February revolution and in the October period, but slow to apply the concept of a divided party to developments in mid-summer. Yet in Petrograd at this time there existed three distinct Bolshevik Party organizations—the Central Committee, the All-Russian Military Organization, and the Petersburg Committee—each with its own responsibilities and interests.

The Central Committee, at the pinnacle of the Bolshevik organizational hierarchy, was responsible for formulating over-all policy and coordinating party activities throughout Russia. In political attitude the nine-man Central Committee, as elected in late April, 1917, was far from homogeneous; generally speaking, it was about evenly split between individuals who usually could be counted on to follow Lenin and more moderate or "right" Bolsheviks of L. B. Kamenev's persuasion. The influence of this moderate group, as well as the Central Committee's natural concern lest events in the capital outstrip developments in the provinces and at the front, account for its relatively cautious posture in the pre-July period.

The Bolshevik Military Organization was created in March, 1917, by the city party organization for the purpose of conducting revolutionary activity in the Petrograd garrison and at the Kronstadt naval base. In April the organization was placed directly under the Central Committee and given the task of winning the support of the armed forces at the front and in the rear and of organizing them into a reliable, disciplined revolutionary force. From its inception, the Military Organization enjoyed a surprisingly large measure of autonomy. Moreover, because of the uniformly radical spirit of its leadership, the mass pressure from garrison followers desperate lest the socialist revolution occur too late to save them from death at the front, and the confidence inevitably inspired by substantial armed force, the Military Organization tended as a rule to stand to the left of the Central Committee on questions regarding the development of the revolution.

The Petersburg Committee, headed by a small Executive Commission and composed of representatives from district party committees, was responsible for directing Bolshevik activities in Petrograd. However, the presence of the Central Committee in the capital and the enormous significance of developments in Petrograd for the rest of the country made the authority of the Petersburg Committee ambiguous and led to continuous friction between the two bodies. Strains between the Central Committee and the Petersburg Committee increased as the untempered extremism of district and unit level party leaders, the restlessness of the Petrograd masses and their responsiveness to Bolshevik slogans, and finally, the Provisional Government's apparent weakness, made party members in the capital overwhelmingly impatient for revolutionary action.

A major theme of the present study is that the revolutionary policy of the Petrograd Bolsheviks in the June-July period was a product of the often quite different responses of these three organizations to the prevailing situation and of the varying interpretations which they gave to Lenin's conception of the revolution. Looked at with this in mind, Bolshevik activities in the pre-July period and the role of the party in the organization and development of the June and July demonstrations become somewhat more intelligible.

The problems involved in conducting detailed research on Bolshevik Party history are well known. Working on the party in the revolutionary era and particularly at such a supersensitive time as the early and mid-summer months of 1917 is especially difficult. Pertinent government and party archives are closed to Western scholars (and to most Soviet specialists as well), many important published sources are by no means easy to locate, and relevant secondary and even many documentary Soviet studies are of limited value. On the other hand, a significant amount of important historical literature, little investigated as yet by Western scholars, is available to non-Soviet students of the Russian revolution. A bibliography of the materials upon which this study is based appears at the end of the book. At this point I should like only to caution that the results of my research, subject to all the pitfalls of overdependence on non-documentary sources, are necessarily tentative and involve a certain amount of educated guessing. In writing, I have at all times attempted to separate fact from speculation and to label the latter clearly.

1

The Historical Background

Russia and the Outbreak of World War I

"His Majesty orders the army and navy placed on a war footing and reservists and horses called up . . . 18 July will be counted the first day of mobilization."[1] The historic telegram which made World War I a reality was dispatched from the central telegraph office in St. Petersburg to the far reaches of the Russian Empire early on the evening of July 17, 1914. By dawn the following morning, St. Petersburg police had already begun delivering call-up notices to the homes of reservists, and groups of anxious citizens were huddled around the red, starkly phrased mobilization proclamations that had been posted at every street corner during the night. "By His Majesty's order . . . rank-and-file reservists . . . will report to their local police stations on the second day of mobilization, Saturday, 19 July, at 6:00 A.M. for transfer to appropriate assembly points." The shattering command threw transportation services, businesses, and factories into confusion as thousands of reservists, with less than twenty-four hours in which to settle their affairs, appeared at their places of work to receive their final pay.[2]

The response of the Russian population to mobilization in 1914, at least on the surface, was such as to hearten Tsar Nicholas II. True, in the Russian countryside the peasants accepted the call to the colors fatalistically and with little enthusiasm. But in urban areas such as St. Petersburg and Moscow, the citizenry reacted to mobilization with the same outburst of patriotism that greeted news of the war's outbreak in the other capitals of Europe. During the first days after activation of the reserve the main streets of St. Petersburg were alive with parades and demonstrations supporting the war, and relatively few people attempted to avoid military service. On Sunday, July 20, the day after Germany's declaration of war, several thousand court, civil, and military dignitaries, dressed in their most splendid uniforms, assembled in the Winter Palace. They listened as Nicholas II, standing before the "miraculous" icon of the Virgin of Kazan, repeated the vow taken by Alexander I in 1812, not to make peace while a single foreign soldier remained on Russian soil. During the colorful ceremony a cheering throng of students, townspeople, and even workers, carrying flags, banners, icons, and portraits of the Tsar, waited outside on the Palace Square, where protesting workers had been massacred by government troops on another Sunday nearly a decade earlier. The British historian of pre-revolutionary Russia, Sir Bernard Pares, writes that upon sighting Nicholas II on the balcony of the palace the crowd fell to its knees and sang "God Save the Tsar" as it had not been sung before.[3]

Few Russians sensed the full implications of war for their country in that fateful summer of 1914. True, in a letter to Maxim Gorky in January, 1913, Lenin had written: "What we need right now is a war, but I am afraid Franz Joseph and little Nicholas won't do us the favor."[4] And at the opposite end of the political spectrum, in February, 1914, the conservative former Minister of the Interior, P. N. Durnovo, warned in a remarkably prophetic memorandum to the Tsar that the main burden of a war between the Entente and the Central Powers would fall on Russia, that militarily and industrially Russia was by no means prepared for such a war, and that "social revolution in its most extreme form" and "hopeless anarchy, the issue of which cannot be foreseen, would be the inevitable consequences of a losing struggle."[5] Moreover, on the eve of the war Count Witte, the capable architect of Russian industrialization, also spoke out, warning that Russia was then less prepared for war than she had been in 1904.[6] But as the military conflict in Europe began, such realism was as rare in Russia as it was in the other nations of Europe.

The outbreak of World War I came at a particularly inopportune moment in Russia's economic and social development. Although in 1914 Russia was already on the road to becoming a modern industrial nation, her economy was not equipped to support a prolonged war under modern conditions. While sweeping agricultural reforms inaugurated by Prime Minister Stolypin in 1906 constituted a significant effort to deal with Russia's centuries-old agrarian problem, the production and distribution of foodstuffs had yet to be placed on an efficient and fully dependable footing. Moreover, the beginning of the war found Russian society in the process of fundamental change. The social and economic importance of the landed gentry had been declining since the emancipation of the serfs in 1861, but the middle class upon which a modern industrial society would have to be based was still comparatively weak. The stable class of independent farmers envisioned by Stolypin had yet to become established in the countryside, and the mushrooming Russian proletariat had not achieved the meaningful economic gains that had tempered the revolutionary ardor of the western European worker in the late nineteenth and early twentieth centuries. Significant in the latter connection is the fact that the lull in the Russian strike movement that followed the revolution of 1905 came to an end with the Lena gold fields massacre in the spring of 1912, and from then until the outbreak of war the monarchy was faced with a mounting upsurge of industrial unrest. Indeed, a few weeks before the war began, a general strike which had begun in Baku was expanded to St. Petersburg by the Bolsheviks. For several days almost all factories and commercial enterprises in the capital were shut down, and pitched street battles broke out between rioting workers and government forces. Not until July 15, four days before the outbreak of the war, was order fully restored in the industrial districts of St. Petersburg.[7]

World War I came at an equally critical juncture in the political modernization of Russia. About the turn of the century intolerable political, social, and economic conditions had contributed to the formation within the Russian intelligentsia of the Social Democratic, Socialist Revolutionary, and liberal movements, each dedicated to the task of promoting revolutionary change. The aspirations of these three groups for the future of Russia differed significantly; in fact, even within each of the movements there was little unanimity in regard to how the coming revolution was to be brought about and what it was to achieve. Thus on the eve of 1905, the Marxist Social Democratic movement was already split by differences between the more orthodox Mensheviks and the ideologically flexible, more radically inclined Bolsheviks. Analogous right and left factions also existed among the neo-populist Socialist Revolutionaries and the liberals. Yet the diverse groups and subgroups that composed the Russian political opposition in the opening years of the twentieth century were united by one element—antipathy to the preservation of the autocracy.

In the wake of the disastrous military conflict with Japan which began in 1904, the Russian intelligentsia was for the first time able to combine with peasants and factory workers for a concerted attack on the government. However, the revolution of 1905 did not result in a clear victory for either the government or the Russian public. Although the revised Fundamental Laws of April, 1906, transformed the Russian political system into a limited constitutional monarchy with a popularly elected legislature (the Duma), the power of the Tsar remained vast. The Tsar retained exclusive control over foreign policy, military matters, and a large portion of the budget; he had an absolute veto over all laws and he appointed the government, which was solely responsible to him. In the first two Dumas, elected on a broad but unequal and indirect franchise, the Constitutional Democratic (Kadet) Party, the leading liberal political organization, headed by the distinguished historian, Paul Miliukov, aspired to overcome these disadvantages and to establish a genuine parliamentary government on the Western model. However, the efforts of the Kadets ended in failure; in June, 1907, Stolypin dissolved the Second Duma and enacted illegal franchise restrictions which produced a Third Duma more attuned to the conservative attitudes of the monarchy.

These constitutional realities, coupled with the continued powerful influence of ultrareactionary elements upon the Russian government, especially after Stolypin's assassination in 1911, cast doubt on the degree to which the events of 1905 brought about a fundamental change in Russian political life. As disappointing as were many aspects of post-1905 political conditions to much of the Russian public, however, it would be wrong to imply that during this time Russia's political modernization was not advanced significantly. The broad civil liberties granted during the revolution of 1905 were abridged at times but never rescinded. Political parties could now function openly for the first time, and regulations governing education and censorship were liberalized. Most important, in the Duma all shades of opinion could receive a public hearing, and through its right of voting on parts of the budget and of interpellating government ministers, the Duma was able to exert a modest, though by no means insignificant, influence on the policies of the government.

There is no assurance that the peaceful modernization of Russia could have continued indefinitely. On the eve of the war, the Tsarist government was faced with a mounting social and political crisis. Impressive Bolshevik success in intensifying the political strike movement, particularly in St. Petersburg and Moscow, and in wresting control of major trade unions from the more moderate Mensheviks testified to the increasing alienation and explosiveness of Russian workers. At the same time, appalling evidence of governmental stupidity, incompetence, and paralysis and the growing influence of reactionary forces again strained the patience of the educated Russian public to the limit. Within the Fourth Duma, elected in 1912, a majority of deputies once more could be found siding with the constitutional opposition.

The immense task of finding solutions to Russia's political and social problems and of superintending the Empire's entry into the twentieth century called for the pioneering spirit and boundless energy of a Peter the Great or at least the political realism and adaptability of an Alexander II. Instead, Russia's fortunes were in the hands of a stubborn and short-sighted monarch, who maintained until the last an overriding faith in the value of autocracy for Russia and who was incapable of comprehending, let alone dealing with, the enormous problems of his time. To compound the tragedy, Nicholas II had a remarkable propensity for surrounding himself with mediocre advisors, and like many men in lesser stations, he was dominated by his wife, the Empress Alexandra, a strong-willed, blindly prejudiced, and mystically inclined woman of highly reactionary political convictions. Undoubtedly, the backward character of the Russian monarchy on the eve of the Great War reduced the possibility that Russia might have been able to modernize effectively without violent social revolution; nevertheless such a possibility cannot be excluded. What seems certain is that World War I, putting Russian society to so demanding a test at a time when many fundamental problems remained unresolved, not only sounded the death knell to peaceful reform, but, as we shall see, greatly prejudiced the nature of the revolution that was to come. In this sense, July 17, 1914, the day that Nicholas II yielded to the appeals of his military commanders and signed the ukase mobilizing the Russian army, is one of the most fateful dates in Russian history.

Opposition Policies on the War

On July 26, 1914, the deputies to the Fourth Imperial Duma gathered in the magnificent Taurida Palace built by Catherine the Great for her favorite Potemkin and dutifully authorized war credits that had been requested by the government. Of the parties represented in the Duma, only the Trudoviks led by Alexander Kerensky and the Social Democrats refused to support the Russian crown on this occasion. The Trudoviks, a caucus of unaligned, populist-oriented socialists (the Socialist Revolutionaries boycotted the Third and Fourth Dumas), summoned their followers to defend Russia. As a gesture of their opposition to the policies of the Tsarist government, however, they refused to vote in favor of war credits. The Social Democrats condemned the government and walked out of the Duma before the vote on the supplementary budget was taken.[8]

For the principal Russian opposition parties the problem of defining their attitude toward the Russian war effort was, of course, not an easy one. The popular support offered to the government at the outbreak of the war did not change the fact that the political regime then in power was one of the most backward and incompetent in Imperial history. Was it now the duty of the opposition to lend its full support to this government? Had just demands for political and social reform to be postponed until the struggle against the Central Powers had been brought to successful completion? This was precisely the view adopted at the outset of the war by the Constitutional Democratic Party. Proclaiming a moratorium on opposition to the monarchy for the duration, the Kadets joined conservative and right-wing Duma parties in pledging their unqualified support to the crown. The position of liberal deputies in the Duma was expressed by Paul Miliukov at the Duma session of July 26 with the statement: "We demand nothing and impose no conditions; we will simply place our indomitable will to victory in the scales of war."[9] When in 1915 the Tsarist government's incompetence in conducting the war against the Central Powers became fully apparent, Duma liberals attempted to exert pressure on the crown for the formation of a government "enjoying the confidence of the nation." However, even after their appeals were ignored the liberals did not encourage revolution from below, calculating accurately that an uncontrolled mass upheaval would be equally damaging to the war effort and to the cause of Russian liberalism.

For the major Russian socialist organizations—the Socialist Revolutionary (SR) Party and the Social Democratic Menshevik and Bolshevik Parties—formulating a unified policy in regard to the war proved infinitely more difficult than for the liberals. The outbreak of war confronted socialists throughout Europe with the choice between loyalty to country and allegiance to the principles of international socialism. Forsaking the latter, the Social Democratic Parties of Great Britain and France, as well as those of Germany and Austria-Hungary, succumbed to the rising tide of nationalism and war fever and quickly joined in approving their respective governments' requests for war credits. Moreover, socialist leaders such as Guesde and Sembat in France and Vandervelde in Belgium even accepted ministerial portfolios in wartime cabinets. For their part, Russian Social Democrats demonstrated no such unanimity in their attitudes toward the war, their bloc abstention from the vote on war credits notwithstanding. Indeed, for Russian socialists of all persuasions the war issue was so thoroughly divisive that it cut across traditional alignments, making former allies the bitterest of enemies and former enemies into allies.

Speaking generally, within each of the more important Russian socialist parties there emerged "defensist" factions, whose support for the war was analogous to that proclaimed by most western European socialists, and "internationalist" factions, whose positions on the expanding struggle were more in accord with the peace-keeping principles approved by the Stuttgart Congress of the Second International in 1907. The defensist current was undoubtedly stronger among the Mensheviks and SR's than among the Bolsheviks. In the late summer of 1914, as the armies of the Entente and Central Powers confronted each other in eastern and western Europe, quite a number of prominent SR's and Mensheviks abroad, many of them long-time veterans of Tsarist prisons, called for the suspension of revolutionary activity until Prussian militarism had been crushed. They rallied to the Russian war effort as spiritedly as did the liberals. The astonishing Germanophobia and staunch patriotism displayed by them at this time is mirrored in the comment which the venerable father of Russian Marxism, G. V. Plekhanov, is said to have made soon after the war began to Angelica Balabanoff, then a prominent member of the Italian Socialist Party: "So far as I am concerned, if I were not old and sick I would join the army. To bayonet your German comrades would give me great pleasure."[10] Taking Plekhanov at his word, hundreds of SR's and Mensheviks abroad volunteered for service in the French army. Moreover, the immediate aspirations of the defensist wings of the SR and Menshevik Parties now coincided so closely that elements within these heretofore irreconcilable groups were able to cooperate in several journalistic enterprises.[11]

The émigré internationalist factions of the Russian revolutionary parties also took shape almost immediately upon the outbreak of war. At first relatively isolated, these factions tended to gain strength as early enthusiasm for the war began to wane. The chief theorists of the internationalists within the SR and Menshevik camps, respectively, were Victor Chernov[12] and Iu. O. Martov. Both were unequivocal in their condemnation of the military struggle in Europe; both viewed the triumph of either of the warring sides as equally damaging to the cause of international socialism and sought to stimulate a mass, worldwide peace movement on behalf of an immediate peace without victors or vanquished.

Not surprisingly, however, the most radical of the Russian socialist anti-war programs was advanced by the Bolshevik leader, V. I. Lenin. In 1903 Lenin had permanently shattered the unity of the Russian labor movement with his fanatic insistence that only a small, professional, and highly centralized revolutionary organization was capable of leading the Russian proletariat in a socialist revolution, this at a time when many Russian Social Democrats desired a more democratically organized, broadly tolerant, mass Marxist party. In the latter stages of the 1905 revolution Lenin had demonstrated his tenacious radicalism by working to keep the revolutionary cauldron boiling and to prepare for another popular insurrection well after the Russian masses had become apathetic to revolutionary appeals and the more moderate Mensheviks had lost faith in the efficacy of further immediate direct action. Still later, during the period of reaction before the war, Lenin had striven to preserve the conspiratorial character and revolutionary militancy of the Russian workers' movement at a time when many Mensheviks had shifted their attention to the building of a broadly based workers' party and the achievement of meaningful economic reform through legal parliamentary and trade union activity. Now, in the last days of August, 1914, from Berne, Switzerland, Lenin, in his "Theses on the War," condemned the leaders of the Second International for their "betrayal of socialism" and proposed the fomenting of social revolution in all countries as an immediate Social Democratic slogan. Moreover, he set himself squarely apart from all other Russian internationalist groups by arguing that Russia's defeat at the hands of Germany was desirable as a means of weakening the monarchy.[13] In its bitter repudiation of the Second International, in its emphasis on civil war rather than on peace, and in its espousal of defeatism for Russia, Lenin's program was shockingly extreme. It was criticized with equal vigor by defensists and by Menshevik and SR internationalists. Indeed, even many subsequently important Bolsheviks stood closer to Martov's more moderate internationalism than to Lenin's brand of intolerant radicalism. Moreover, Leninist resolutions on the war were rejected at international socialist conferences at Zimmerwald in August, 1915, and at Kienthal in April, 1916, in favor of less extreme anti-war resolutions.

Socialist leaders remaining in Russia were as divided on the war issue as their colleagues abroad. According to Oliver Radkey, historian of the SR's, attitudes of SR leaders in Russia were fairly well distributed between defensism and moderate and radical internationalism.[14] Among Menshevik leaders in Russia there were some influential supporters of limited defensism. But a majority of party figures, including the Menshevik Duma faction, pursued a policy of moderate internationalism. Formally opposed to the war and increasingly open in their hostility to the Tsarist government, they nonetheless refrained from obstructing the Russian war effort. The anti-war position of Bolsheviks in St. Petersburg was symbolized in late August, 1914, by their decision to remain the "Petersburg Committee" after the official name of the Russian capital was hastily changed from the German sounding St. Petersburg to Petrograd.

From the fall of 1914 a number of underground Bolshevik committees, loosely directed by Lenin through the Russian Bureau of the Central Committee, attempted to foment popular opposition to the war and the Tsarist government and to organize the renewal of strike activity. But in the initial months of the war the only consequence of such efforts was severe government repression.[15] Like their counterparts throughout Europe, Russian workers—rank-and-file SR's, Mensheviks, and Bolsheviks among them—were supporting their country's war effort.

Russia at War

The outbreak of hostilities in 1914 found the Russian army woefully unprepared to withstand the test of war against the Central Powers. A seemingly inexhaustible supply of manpower and a generous measure of courage could not compensate for critical shortages of guns and ammunition, primitive supply and medical systems, a disorganized and at least in part incompetent high command, and perhaps most important, an appalling incapacity to institute necessary improvements. To be sure, Russia's initial mobilization went more quickly than the enemy expected or Russians dared hope. And the rapid invasion of East Prussia in mid-August, 1914, was undoubtedly of importance in enabling France to win the crucial first battle of the Marne that saved Paris. But in late August and early September, 1914, occurred the devastating Russian defeats in the battles of Tannenberg and the Masurian Lakes. A simultaneous Russian offensive southward into Galicia was more successful. The onset of winter, 1915, found Tsarist forces at the southern slopes of the Carpathians. However, the following spring the Austro-German armies launched a massive offensive of their own that ended in the fall of 1915 with the whole front having been pushed back an average of two hundred miles. Moreover, while the initial results of the imaginative Brusilov campaign of 1916 in Galicia were encouraging, huge Russian losses (more than a million men) far outweighed the meager strategic gains.

In view of the foregoing, it is by no means surprising that by the fall of 1916 the patriotic ardor of Russian soldiers for further battle was largely spent, and the disintegration of the army was already well advanced. Thanks to improvements in military procurement the Russian army was better equipped than before. But the thousands of regular officers and noncoms who had been sacrificed in the early stages of the conflict could not be replaced. The bulk of the huge Russian war machine was by then composed largely of hastily trained and undisciplined recruits, largely from among the peasantry, who had little interest in the cause for which they were asked to fight.[16] As early as the winter of 1914 refusals to fight, desertions, and mass surrenders to the enemy handicapped the Russian war effort. In the wake of the 1915 disasters such incidents reached immense proportions, and in the aftermath of the demoralizing Brusilov offensive, the bulk of the Russian army was overwhelmingly tired of war, critical of its leadership, distrustful of its government, and generally ripe for rebellion. "Among the soldiers [at the front] dissatisfaction with and distrust of officers is growing," reported a leading Russian general to M. V. Rodzianko, President of the Fourth Duma, in January, 1917. "The army is gradually becoming demoralized, and discipline threatens to collapse completely. Under these circumstances," the general concluded, "it may easily be that during the winter the army . . . may just abandon the trenches and the field of battle."[17]

Disintegration of the same kind was taking place among troops of the Petrograd garrison. From 1683, when Peter the Great created the first unit of the Household Guards, the Preobrazhensky Regiment, these elite, specially trained forces had been a traditional bulwark of the crown. As a young Grand Duke, Nicholas II had himself served in a guards regiment, and during the revolution of 1905 the guards had been employed to crush rebellion not only in the capital, but in Moscow, the Baltic borderlands, and installations of the Imperial fleet as well.[18] However, as World War I entered its third year, the soldiers stationed in and around the capital, including those in regiments of the guard, were almost exclusively

wartime recruits, mostly peasants, to whom military discipline was
foreign and whose greatest desire was to return home as quickly as
possible. Continuing contact both with troops at the front and with
restless factory workers further served to undermine their spirit.
As early as December, 1915, police officials at the Kronstadt naval
base were reporting that "troops [of the garrison] would not be
willing to oppose the workers and instead would help square accounts with the government."[19] A definite sign that the Petrograd
garrison was no longer the reliable arm of the monarchy that it had
been in 1905 appeared in mid-October, 1916, when several hundred
soldiers of the 181st Reserve Infantry Regiment quartered in the
Vyborg factory district helped striking workers from the "Reno"
automobile plant fend off the police. That the association between
soldiers and disgruntled factory workers was undermining the
reliability of the garrison did not escape the notice of the Petrograd
authorities, and at the end of December, 1916, the 181st Infantry
Regiment was transferred from the capital. However, contact between workers and remaining units of the Petrograd garrison continued.[20]

It is worth recalling that after nearly three years of war acute
demoralization was not peculiar to the Russian army. The spirit of
the British and French armies was similarly shattered by the futile
blood-letting of 1916 at Verdun and on the Somme. What made the
Russian situation more tragic was that sinking morale at the front
was combined with increasing political paralysis and economic disintegration in the rear. In Russia there emerged no Lloyd George or
Clemenceau to stifle a growing spirit of defeatism and to marshal
the people for a decisive national effort. It will be remembered that
upon the outbreak of war in 1914 a broad segment of Russian public
opinion declared a moratorium on political opposition and rallied
loyally to the support of the government. "This second war for
national survival," recalled Kerensky, "gave the Tsar a unique opportunity to extend the hand of friendship to the people, thereby
ensuring victory and consolidating the monarchy for many years
to come."[21] If this was indeed the case it was a chance that was

ignored from the outset. Tending to view every expression of public initiative as subversive, the Russian government, under the decrepit and increasingly senile I. L. Goremykin, did its best to stifle such worthwhile endeavors as those of the All-Russian Union of Zemstvos and the All-Russian Union of Towns to further the war effort through the mobilization of industry, refugee relief, and the reorganization of the medical services. This in itself need not have been disastrous had the policies of the monarchy been in any measure successful. But as the staggering reverses at the front and the obvious mismanagement in the rear became widely recognized, the government began to be criticized openly not only by the old political opposition, but by conservative Duma deputies who previously had been among its staunchest supporters.

In his *History of the Second Russian Revolution*, Paul Miliukov suggests that among Duma leaders great skepticism in regard to the actions of the monarchy first emerged openly after a meeting with government ministers on January 25, 1915.[22] Criticism of the government inevitably became more widespread as the military debacle of 1915 began to unfold. In the spring of 1915 the government made some concessions to public demands for reform, acquiescing in the establishment of a network of private War Industries Committees to assist the government's war effort and Special Councils to coordinate government and private endeavors in the fields of national defense, transportation, fuel, and food supply. Moreover, in June popular pressure secured the ousting of four of the most reactionary Tsarist ministers and their replacement by significantly better qualified individuals. But Goremykin stayed on as Prime Minister, a development at least partly responsible for the formation in the summer of 1915 of a coalition of center parties in the Duma (the so-called Progressive Bloc) which adopted as its primary demand the appointment of a government "enjoying the confidence of the nation." The Progressive Bloc's moderate program (apart from the call for changes in the government, it included demands for a more tolerant religious and ethnic policy, an amnesty for political prisoners, and an end to restrictions on trade unions) was undoubtedly supported by the bulk of Russian public opinion. Indeed, it did not seem unreasonable to the more forward thinking government ministers. But it was obstinately opposed by Goremykin, who in September, 1915, obtained the crown's approval for the proroguing of the Duma.

The mobilization of public opinion against the government was not the only significant result of the Russian military reverses of 1915. From the outbreak of the war the Russian army in the field had been commanded by the Tsar's uncle, the Grand Duke Nikolai Nikolaevich. There seems little doubt that the Grand Duke was not equal to the immense responsibilities of supreme command. But infinitely worse in its consequences was Nicholas II's solution to the problem. Ignoring all advice save that of his wife and the unscrupulous faith healer Rasputin, in late August, 1915, he departed from the capital to take personal command of his retreating troops. The result of this doubly unfortunate step was that while the Tsar now left himself wide open to criticism for the rapidly deteriorating military situation, the fate of the government was left in the hands of a reactionary court camarilla headed by the Empress and Rasputin, her closest advisor. The scandalous political machinations which now became the order of the day in Petrograd are unparalleled in modern history. At the discretion of the Empress and Rasputin, government ministers shuffled on and off stage with bewildering frequency; "ministerial leapfrog" was the term used by the rightist Duma deputy, V. M. Purishkevich, to describe the phenomenon. Among the first ministers to go were all but one of the relatively competent department heads appointed the previous June; they were replaced by a procession of nonentities and adventurers. In January, 1916, Goremykin was finally relieved of his post as Prime Minister, but his successor was the notorious Boris Sturmer, a puppet of the court, whose "character, mental condition, and intellectual equipment," according to a close associate, "prevented him from directing anything."[23]

What made this increasingly ludicrous political situation all the more tragic was that it was coupled with rapidly deteriorating economic conditions. To Petrograd, Moscow, and other industrial centers the war brought critical shortages of housing, food, clothing, and fuel, which grew particularly acute in the last months of 1916. To some extent these shortages were caused less by insufficient production than by distribution problems. Russian railroads were inadequate to meet both civil and military needs. In the case of grain, the peasants, finding it impossible to procure manufactured goods, refused to part with their produce for rapidly depreciating paper money. As the scarcity of goods increased, the gap between wages and the rising cost of living widened. Workers were hardest hit by the resulting inflation, and in the period from 1915 to 1917 their growing bitterness was mirrored in a renewed burst of strike activity. However, inflation seriously affected the urban middle class as well. Although economic conditions in the countryside were significantly less critical than in the cities, the peasantry, who had borne the brunt of the war losses, was overwhelmingly impatient for an early end to hostilities. Hence by the winter of 1916, much of the Russian population had reached the breaking point—the thoroughly demoralized soldier, as well as the worker trying desperately to keep his head above water financially, the peasant seeking by any means to avoid the draft, and the urban housewife waiting endlessly in the bitter cold, often without success, to buy bread and other necessities of life.[24]

The government was well aware of the growing popular indignation. Unable to cope with the expanding economic crisis, it did its best to strengthen its own defenses. The gravity of the developing situation was also abundantly clear to progressive circles in the Duma, but fearful of provoking a popular explosion, they were helpless to do much about it. The crying need for a political change was acknowledged by everyone, and the possibility of a palace coup was freely discussed in the court, the Duma, and the command of the army. Indeed, from 1916 on it was something of a race as to which would come first—a palace coup or a revolution from below.

Members of the Duma were again affronted in September, 1916, by the appointment of A. D. Protopopov, Rasputin's candidate, as Minister of the Interior. On the verge of insanity at the time of his appointment, Protopopov, a member of the right, liberal Octobrist Party and a former vice-chairman of the Duma, was virtually unable to express himself coherently. The Empress and Rasputin were universally despised, and amid the ever worsening news from the battle zones, unfounded rumors that the court was selling out to the Germans gained increasing credence. The sessions of the Duma from November 1 to December 16, 1916, witnessed attacks on the government unprecedented in their directness. Thus, on the day the Duma opened Paul Miliukov bitterly recounted the government's failures, mentioning the Empress and Sturmer by name and concluding each indictment with the caustic question, "Is this stupidity or is this treason?" The powerful speech, although censored out of the newspapers, was reproduced in millions of copies and circulated throughout Russia.[25] In response the crown had the good sense to dismiss Sturmer as Prime Minister, but his replacement, the strongly conservative A. F. Trepov, was no real improvement. Rasputin's murder in December by members of the nobility was cause for celebration by everyone except the Empress. But it did little to ease the unbearable tension in Petrograd. The unusually cold Christmas holidays, 1916, came and went, and still the government maintained its suicidal course as if in a daze. "Everyone knew then," remembered Miliukov, "that the country was living on a volcano."[26]

The Fall of the Monarchy[27]

The year 1917 began the way 1916 ended, with plunging temperatures and sky-rocketing prices, with strikes and food riots, and with renewed efforts on the part of the Petrograd Military District to alert and prepare the garrison and police for possible riot duty. Elaborate plans for suppressing any major outbreaks were drawn up, and machine guns were positioned at strategic locations throughout the city. In an impressive display of working class solidarity more than one hundred fifty thousand Petrograd workers went out on strike on January 9, the anniversary of Bloody Sunday. Some of the factories shut down that day were struck for the first time since 1905, and, equally significant, soldiers watching demonstrating workers were observed tipping their hats and cheering as red banners bearing revolutionary slogans were carried by. On February 14, the day the Duma opened, workers in some sixty Petrograd factories joined in a political strike, and hundreds of university students, ignoring threats by the police, marched down Nevsky Prospect singing revolutionary songs. On February 22 thirty thousand workers were left in desperate straits when a lockout of indefinite duration was announced at the mammoth Putilov metalworking plant. And then on the twenty-third, International Women's Day, disturbances which broke out among long lines of housewives waiting for bread developed into spontaneous street demonstrations calling for the overthrow of the monarchy and an end to the war. Neither planned nor even expected by any of the Russian revolutionary parties, the popular eruption had begun.

In trying to visualize the revolutions of 1917 in Petrograd one must remember that during the more than two hundred years since its founding by Peter the Great, the Russian Imperial capital, like Paris, had become divided into rather sharply defined socioeconomic districts. Generally speaking, the central sections of the city, encompassing the southern parts of Vasilievsky Island and the so-called "Petersburg side" on the right bank of the Neva, and much of the left bank extending from the river to the Obvodny Canal, were the domain of the upper and middle classes, while most factory workers lived and worked in the outer industrial suburbs.

The central sections boasted the luxurious rococo and neoclassical palaces of the royal family and high aristocracy, the massive edifices that served as headquarters for Imperial officialdom, the imposing Isaac and Kazan Cathedrals, and the granite river and canal embankments which together made Petrograd one of Europe's most beautiful capitals. Here, too, were concentrated such centers of Russian culture as the Royal Mariinsky Theater, home

of the opera and the famed Imperial ballet; the Royal Alexandrin-
sky Theater, where the best in European drama and comedy alter-
nated with the classics of Gogol, Turgenev, and Tolstoy; and the
Petersburg Conservatory, on whose stage the greatest musicians of
the time performed. Also located in this central area on the left
bank of the Neva were the capital's banks, offices, and better resi-
dential neighborhoods, changing as one went further from the Admiralty—the hub of the city—from aristocratic palaces through
professional apartment houses to the tenements of the lower middle
class. Originating at the Admiralty and dominated by its needle
spire was Nevsky Prospect, Petrograd's broadest and finest avenue
with the city's most fashionable shops, while across the Neva to
the north, the embankment at the eastern end of Vasilievsky Island
was lined by the distinctive buildings of the University of St. Petersburg, the Russian Academy of Sciences, and the Academy of
Fine Arts, three symbols of Russian intellectual and artistic achievement, and by the columned façade of the Stock Exchange.

The major factories of Petrograd were located in the suburbs
surrounding this central area—in the Narva, Moscow, and Alexander Nevsky Districts on the left bank of the Neva, and in the
more remote areas of Vasilievsky Island and the Okhta and Vyborg
Districts on its right bank. These outlying districts were developed
during the initial phases of Russian industrializaton in the late nineteenth century, when land close to rivers and canals was still relatively cheap and plentiful. Here, in often filthy and crowded,
hastily constructed multilevel brick barracks and wooden hovels
sandwiched between soot-gray factories, lived the bulk of Petrograd's approximately three hundred fifty thousand workers, a large
percentage of them recent arrivals from the countryside.

Only rarely did the populations of the two parts of the capital
mix. The Petrograd proletariat first gave vent to its resentment toward the privileged classes by invading the central sections of the
Russian capital during the revolution of 1905. Now, on February 23
and 24, 1917, like a massive tidal wave, their crimson banners aloft,
the workers circumvented guarded bridges and swarmed across the

frozen Neva by the thousands to demonstrate once again in the central sections of the capital. By the twenty-fifth the popular explosion had become general. Newspapers ceased publication, streetcar traffic halted, and university students dropped their studies to join the street marches.

The situation became really menacing to the government when Cossacks sent to quell the disturbances instead demonstrated sympathy for the rebelling workers. In response to a cable from the Tsar at army headquarters in Mogilev "to suppress all disorders in the streets beginning tomorrow," General S. S. Khabalov, commander of the Petrograd Military District, issued an order to his forces to fire on crowds which refused to disperse. The following day, Sunday, February 26, a company of the Pavlovsky Regiment mutinied in response to this order. The garrison Volynsky Guards fired on the crowds, but back in their barracks these same soldiers declared their unwillingness to participate in further attacks on the population. The government, evidently unaware of its glaring weakness in the prevailing situation, chose this moment to prorogue the Duma until April. But the following morning the Duma deputies, showing a more realistic perception of the growing chaos in the streets, refused to disperse. Instead, they formed a Provisional Committee, made up of members of the Progressive Bloc and two deputies to the left of it, the Trudovik Alexander Kerensky and the Menshevik leader N. S. Chkheidze, to restore order.

About the same time on February 27, some members of the labor group of the Central War Industries Committee, who had just been released from prison (eleven labor representatives on the committee were arrested on January 26, 1917, for alleged revolutionary activity), several socialist Duma deputies, and some representatives of the trade union and cooperative movement, met in another hall of the Taurida Palace. Initiating steps to reestablish a Soviet on the 1905 model, they selected a committee to arrange the convocation of a Soviet of Workers' Deputies in Petrograd. Announcements of a session of the Soviet to be held the same evening were immediately dispatched to the factories, and it was at this meeting on the night of February 27 that the Petrograd Soviet of Workers' and Soldiers' Deputies and its Executive Committee formally came into being. In succeeding months similar institutions of popular self-government were set up throughout Russia.

The decisive moment of the February events came on this same day, February 27, when first the Volynsky and then elements of the Preobrazhensky and Litovsky Guards Regiments joined what had by now developed into a full-blown revolution. For their part, those troops supposedly still obeying the government simply melted away upon contact with rebelling elements, and only individual groups of officers and police offered serious resistance. The desertion of the garrison units marked the crucial difference between the outcome of the February, 1917, events and the revolution of 1905. By the evening of the twenty-seventh almost all of Petrograd, including the main arsenal and the Peter and Paul Fortress, was in the hands of insurgents. A few thousand troops, still obeying General Khabalov, held out in the area of the Admiralty and the Winter Palace, waiting for support from military forces expected from Mogilev and from the northern front. But neither reached the capital, and when Khabalov's troops quietly dispersed the next day, the February revolution in Petrograd was all but over. February 28 was the turning point in Moscow and at Kronstadt, the naval base at the approach to the capital in the Gulf of Finland, where sailors settled old scores by slaughtering the port commander and fifty of his most hated officers. [28] Nowhere did any serious resistance to the overthrow of the old order emerge, so thoroughly bankrupt had the Tsarist regime by now become.

At first some Duma liberals, including the Kadet leader Paul Miliukov, hoped to preserve a semblance of continuity with the past by establishing a constitutional monarchy with a popularly elected parliamentary government, but the revolution had already progressed too far for that. On March 2, Nicholas II, yielding to the inevitable, abdicated the Imperial throne in favor of his brother, the Grand Duke Michael. Whether vainly hoping to save his own life or correctly sensing the futility of preserving the monarchy,

Michael rejected the throne at least until the convocation of a Constituent Assembly, and the more than three hundred year reign of the Romanovs came to an inglorious end.

From the outset the Executive Committee of the Petrograd Soviet contented itself with acting as guardian of the revolution and demonstrated no interest in challenging the Provisional Committee of the Duma as the lawful government of Russia. In part this was for doctrinal reasons—the Mensheviks who dominated the Executive Committee remained committed to the orthodox Marxist assumption that a "bourgeois revolution," which the overthrow of the autocracy appeared to represent, had necessarily to be followed by an indefinite period of bourgeois, liberal rule. For their part, representatives of the Socialist Revolutionary Party in the Executive Committee, while not rigidly prevented by ideology from taking power into their own hands, for the most part shared with many Mensheviks an awareness of their own organizational weaknesses and a corresponding desire to utilize all of Russia's energies in the interests of the defense effort and as a bulwark against counterrevolution. Consequently, on March 1, a majority of the Petrograd Soviet's Executive Committee agreed to authorize the Duma to organize a Provisional Government, provided certain political conditions were met. At the same time it was also decided that the socialists should not betray their principles or prejudice their standing with the masses by accepting ministerial portfolios in a liberal government.

The next day the Duma's Provisional Committee and the Executive Committee of the Soviet were able to hammer out a compromise political program, and the former appointed a Provisional Government headed by the president of the Union of Zemstvos, Prince G. E. Lvov, as Premier, and including Miliukov as Foreign Minister, the Octobrist leader A. I. Guchkov as War and Naval Minister, and the inexhaustible and eloquent Kerensky as Minister of Justice. (In accepting the post, Kerensky, a Trudovik, disregarded the Soviet Executive Committee's decision against socialists serving in the government.) The program agreed upon on March 2 and adopted by the new government provided for, among other things, full amnesty for political prisoners, broad civil liberties, and legal equality for all. Preparations for a Constituent Assembly, which would determine Russia's future form of government and which would be elected by universal suffrage, were to begin immediately. Troops taking part in the revolutionary movement were not to be disarmed or removed from Petrograd, and all soldiers were to be guaranteed full civil rights when off duty. A declaration embodying this program was published late on the evening of March 2, but it did not touch on such vital issues as the war and the redistribution of land, primarily because the Duma deputies and the socialists in the Soviet could reach no agreement on these questions. However, the new government's intention soon became clear: a settlement of the land question was among the basic reforms to be postponed until the convocation of the Constituent Assembly, while the war was to be pursued "to a victorious conclusion."

That there would be divisions between the Provisional Government and the Soviet on the land question and the war should not be surprising. The Provisional Government was composed for the most part of liberals, leading representatives of the moderate stream in the Russian opposition, many of whom had distinguished themselves in the Zemstvo institutions of local self-government created by Alexander II and in the Imperial Duma. Dedicated Russian patriots, they also felt a natural kinship for the Western democracies, whose political system they hoped to emulate. Thus, it is not strange that the maintenance of revolutionary Russia's commitments to the Entente was a matter of great importance to them, or that they had a very serious concern for creating the future Russian political system legally and with care lest it be swept away by the tide of revolution. The Petrograd Soviet and later the All-Russian Congress of Soviets were dominated by moderate socialists, either SR's or Mensheviks (the Bolsheviks did not win a majority in the Petrograd Soviet until late summer). While they were convinced of the need for an indefinite period of liberal rule, they were nonetheless impatient for fundamental social reform. Moreover, although the vast majority of SR's and Mensheviks ultimately supported a defensist policy as regards the war, "revolutionary defensism" as the policy was now called, they remained significantly more internationalist in spirit than the liberals and continued to exert pressure on behalf of an immediate negotiated peace without victors or vanquished.

Although the Provisional Government established on March 2 received the Soviet's formal support, in point of fact the more radically inclined Executive Committee of the Petrograd Soviet, under constant pressure from its constituents, acted as a watchdog over the Provisional Government's affairs, on occasion even usurping the latter's authority. The arrangement was unstable because, while the Lvov cabinet was recognized as the formal government, the Soviet, although unwilling to take power into its own hands, was far and away the stronger force by virtue of the confidence which it commanded among industrial workers and politically conscious portions of the armed forces. The result of this awkward state of affairs was a virtual paralysis of governmental authority, aggravated by the many basic political, social, and economic problems which could not await the convocation of a Constituent Assembly, by the impossibility of continuing a war effort not supported by the bulk of the population, and by the increasingly disruptive activities of the Bolshevik Party.

II

The Struggle Begins

The Petrograd Bolsheviks and the
February Revolution

The Bolsheviks no less than other Russian revolutionary parties
were taken unaware by the February days. That party membership
at the time of the Tsar's overthrow was insignificant is admitted
even by some Soviet historians.[1] Local party organizations were
either very weak or nonexistent, and most of the figures destined
to play important roles in the October revolution had emigrated or
were in prison or exile. To name but a few, Lenin and his closest
associate, G. E. Zinoviev, were in Zurich, Switzerland, Nikolai
Bukharin and Leon Trotsky were in New York, and J. V. Stalin,
Ia. M. Sverdlov, and L. B. Kamenev were in Siberia. In Petrograd
the party's skeleton organization was directed by the Russian Bureau of the Central Committee composed of A. Shliapnikov, V. M.
Molotov, and P. A. Zalutsky. There also existed a stunted Bolshevik
Petersburg Committee, but it was all but wiped out on February 26,
when five of its number were among a hundred suspicious persons
arrested by the Tsarist police. Indeed, in the last days of February
the Petersburg Committee was so decimated by arrests that it became necessary to transfer its functions temporarily to the healthier
Vyborg District Bolshevik Committee.[2]

In the days immediately following the revolution, the Bolshevik
organization in Petrograd turned its attention to the practical matters of establishing itself on a legal basis and organizing a party

newspaper. At a meeting on March 2, the day of the Tsar's abdication, the Russian Bureau of the Central Committee entrusted Molotov with the latter task, and on the same day a number of party members gathered in the attic of the Central Labor Exchange and formed a temporary Petersburg Committee to serve until convocation of a city party conference.[3] Shortly afterward the Petersburg Committee moved into the spacious and elegant mansion of the Tsar's mistress, the ballerina M. F. Kshesinskaia, and at about the same time several district party organizations came into being. On March 5, *Pravda*, theoretically a joint organ of the Bureau of the Central Committee and the Petersburg Committee, made its initial appearance. A further significant step was taken on March 10, when the Petersburg Committee created a Military Commission to lay the groundwork for a permanent Bolshevik Military Organization.

Apart from organizational matters, among the immediate problems facing the Petrograd Bolsheviks in the aftermath of the February revolution was the formulation of a position on such key issues as relations with the Provisional Government and continued Russian participation in the war. Lenin set forth his views on these questions in a set of theses prepared jointly with Zinoviev in Switzerland on March 4, and in a series of "Letters from Afar," written between March 7 and March 12. Here Lenin took the clear-cut position that the "bourgeois" Provisional Government should by no means be supported and that the party's absolute opposition to the "imperialist" war remain unchanged. His views on the government question and the war were succinctly summarized in correspondence with Bolshevik feminist Alexandra Kollontai at this time. "This first stage of the revolution . . . will not be the last. . . . Of course we shall continue to oppose the defense of the fatherland," he wrote on March 3. The next day he commented: "Now on the agenda is . . . organization of the masses . . . and preparation for the conquest of power by the Soviets of Workers' Deputies. Only such a power can give bread, peace, and liberty."[4] In yet another message of the same period, to a group of Bolsheviks leaving

Stockholm for Russia, Lenin declared: "Our tactics: no trust in and no support of the new government; Kerensky especially suspect; the arming of the proletariat is the only guarantee."[5]

In March, 1917, however, direct communications between Lenin in Zurich and party organizations in Russia were all but nonexistent, and in any event no degree of effective coordination of party policy was possible. On the war issue the Bolshevik leadership in the capital was generally in agreement with Lenin. A meeting of the Bureau of the Central Committee on March 7 concluded that "our attitudes [toward the war] have not changed since the war is an imperialist one and remains so." A formal resolution passed on this occasion declared that "the basic task of the revolutionary social democracy is, as before, the struggle for the transformation of the present anti-peoples' imperialist war into a civil war of peoples against their oppressors—the ruling classes."[6] The Petersburg Committee, meeting the same day, adopted a similar position. On the government question, however, the Petrograd Bolsheviks demonstrated no such unanimity. Very generally, while the attitude of the Bureau of the Central Committee under Shliapnikov was close to Lenin's categorical opposition to the Provisional Government, the position of the majority of the Petersburg Committee was not very different from that adopted earlier by the majority socialist leadership of the Soviet. Meanwhile, to the left even of Lenin and the Bureau of the Central Committee was the Vyborg District Bolshevik Committee, which on its own initiative began to appeal for the immediate seizure of power by the workers.

The government question was discussed by the Vyborg District Bolshevik Committee at its first legal meeting on March 1. There a resolution was adopted calling for the immediate seizure of power by the workers and the abolition of the Duma's Provisional Committee. A proclamation to this effect was printed and circulated before the Bureau of the Central Committee succeeded in putting a stop to such activities.[7] According to Shliapnikov, the only argument the Bureau had with the Vyborg District Committee on the matter was that it considered preparation and organization necessary before giving battle.[8] On March 2 the Bureau introduced in the Petrograd Soviet a resolution which declared that the Provisional Government, as the "representative of the grand bourgeoisie and big landowners, was incapable of realizing the basic revolutionary aims of the people," and which consequently appealed for the "initiation of a struggle for the creation of a Provisional Revolutionary Government,"[9] presumably to be controlled by socialists.

The Soviet, of course, rejected this position. On March 3 the Bureau of the Central Committee brought the same resolution before its own Petersburg Committee, which after heated debate voted it down as well and adopted the following "semi-Menshevik" resolution:

> The Petersburg Committee of the RSDLP [Russian Social Democratic Labor Party], considering the resolution of the Petrograd Soviet of Workers' and Soldiers' Deputies on the Provisional Government, declares that it does not oppose the Provisional Government as long as its policies are consistent with the interests . . . of the people, but it declares its intention of conducting the most relentless struggle against any Provisional Government attempts to reestablish a monarchic government in any form whatsoever.[10]

The Bureau of the Central Committee tried again to win the Petersburg Committee to its position on the government question two days later. At a meeting of the Petersburg Committee on March 5, Molotov introduced a resolution which stated: "Finding that the Provisional Government is made up of representatives of the monarchist grand bourgeoisie and big landowners [and] that it is basically counterrevolutionary, the Petersburg Committee cannot support this government and adopts as its task the struggle for the creation of a Provisional Revolutionary Government." However, this motion, too, was rejected, and instead the Petersburg Committee reaffirmed its position of March 3.[11]

In the first half of March, *Pravda* mirrored the opposition of the Bureau of the Central Committee and the Petersburg Committee to the war. The Bureau's call for the immediate creation of a new Provisional Revolutionary Government was also a dominant *Pravda* theme during this period.[12] But all this changed in the middle of March with the return from Siberia of Kamenev, Stalin, and M. K. Muranov and their subsequent seizure of control of *Pravda*. Beginning with the March 14 issue the central Bolshevik organ swung sharply to the right. Henceforth articles by Kamenev and Stalin advocated limited support for the Provisional Government, rejection of the slogan, "Down with the war," and an end to disorganizing activities at the front. "While there is no peace," wrote Kamenev in *Pravda* on March 15, "the people must remain steadfastly at their posts, answering bullet with bullet and shell with shell." "The slogan, 'Down with the war,' is useless," echoed Stalin the next day. Kamenev explained the mild attitude of the new *Pravda* editorial board to a meeting of the Petersburg Committee on March 18, where it met with approval.[13] Obviously, this position contrasted sharply with the views expressed by Lenin in his "Letters from Afar," and it is not surprising that *Pravda* published only the first of these and with numerous deletions at that. Among crucial phrases censored out was Lenin's accusation that "those who advocate that the workers support the new government in the interests of the struggle against Tsarist reaction (as do the Potresovs, Gvozdevs, Chkhenkelis, and in spite of all his inclinations, even Chkheidze [all Mensheviks]) are traitors to the workers, traitors to the cause of the proletariat, [and] the cause of freedom."[14] Lenin might have applied this accusation to Kamenev and Stalin as well.

Lenin's Return and the "April Theses"

Such were the views prevailing among Bolshevik leaders in Petrograd when, on April 2, they received word that Lenin, after his celebrated sealed train ride through Germany, was to arrive in the capital the next evening. Thus alerted, they set about to insure that their returning chief would receive a proper welcome. Not only would a triumphal reception demonstrate Lenin's popularity among the masses and hence serve as a counterweight to inevitable criticism of his travel through enemy Germany; it would also provide Lenin with an immediate opportunity to gauge Bolshevik strength in the capital. While a small group of top Bolshevik leaders prepared to meet Lenin's party at the Beloostrov railway station on the Russian border, lower ranking party functionaries hurried to mobilize factories and garrison military regiments throughout the capital for a massive homecoming celebration at the Finland station.

According to the Kronstadt Bolshevik leader, F. F. Raskolnikov, who was among the welcoming group at Beloostrov, Lenin wasted no time and minced no words in voicing his displeasure with the conservative line pursued by *Pravda.* Turning to Kamenev as soon as the Bolshevik traveling party was ensconced in its coupe, Lenin burst out: "What's this you're writing in *Pravda?* We have seen several issues and really swore at you."[15]

Arriving at the Finland station in the heart of the Vyborg factory district shortly after 11:00 P.M. on April 3, Lenin was greeted by a cheering crowd of workers and soldiers. In the imperial waiting rooms formerly reserved for the Tsar, the Mensheviks N. S. Chkheidze and M. I. Skobelev officially welcomed Lenin in the name of the Petrograd Soviet, and Chkheidze wishfully invited Lenin to join with the rest of the revolutionary democracy in defending the revolution from within and without. Ignoring the plea, Lenin declared to the assembled throng that the February revolution had not solved the Russian proletariat's fundamental problems, that the working class of Russia could not stop half-way, and that in alliance with the soldier masses, the Russian proletariat would turn the bourgeois democratic revolution into a proletarian, socialist revolution.[16] A sharper break with the policies of the moderate socialists in the Soviet could scarcely be imagined.

Lenin reiterated his appeal for continued revolution, coupling it with a vehement attack on the policy of conditional support for the Provisional Government and the war effort at an informal gathering of Bolshevik party leaders held later the same evening in the white-columned drawing room of the Kshesinskaia mansion. W. S.

Woytinsky, nominally a right Bolshevik but about to transfer his allegiance to the Mensheviks, was present at the historic gathering and recalled in his memoirs that Lenin concluded his speech with an appeal for organization, suggesting that the party's former "discipline" and "unity of thought" were missing.[17] Woytinsky also remembered that for the most part the audience responded to Lenin's words with stunned silence.[18] Another spectator, N. N. Sukhanov, recorded Kamenev's reaction to Lenin's "anarchist ravings": "Wait, just wait!"[19]

Lenin's arrival in Petrograd coincided with the last sessions of a gathering of Bolshevik delegates from all over Russia, held in conjunction with the First All-Russian Conference of Soviets, which met in the capital from March 29 to April 3. Before Lenin's appearance at the Bolshevik meetings[20] Stalin had succeeded in winning unanimous approval for a resolution calling for "vigilant control" over the activities of the Provisional Government and support for the Petrograd Soviet as the "beginning of a revolutionary power."[21] This was so close to the SR-Menshevik position that the Bolsheviks were able to support the majority resolution on the Provisional Government passed at the Conference of Soviets.[22] The moderate views of Stalin and Kamenev on the war had also been accepted by the Bolsheviks, and it was agreed that disorganizing activities at the front should be suspended. In addition, the Bolshevik gathering decided to begin exploratory discussions on unification with the Mensheviks. Only when viewed against the background of temperance and détente prevailing among the Bolsheviks at this time can the explosive effect of the unequivocal program now proposed by Lenin be understood.

On the afternoon of April 4, Lenin addressed the Bolshevik delegates to the Conference of Soviets as they were preparing to attend a joint meeting with the Mensheviks to discuss reunification. It was on this occasion that Lenin read his celebrated "April Theses" in their entirety for the first time. In contrast to the Kamenev-Stalin position on the war, the theses reaffirmed Lenin's previous call for total repudiation of "revolutionary defensism" and advocated fraternization at the front. They defined the "current moment" not as the "bourgeois-liberal" stage of the revolution in Russia, as had the Mensheviks and the Bolsheviks of Kamenev's persuasion, but as the transition between the first "bourgeois-liberal" stage, which presumably had been completed, and the second, "socialist," stage, during which power would be transferred into the hands of the proletariat. As regards the Provisional Government, Lenin's theses rejected the "limited support" formula of the Soviet and Kamenev and the "no opposition" pledge of the Petersburg Committee and called instead for the complete rejection of the Provisional Government. Further, the "April Theses" discounted as preposterous the possibility of reunification with the Mensheviks. Finally, they projected as the immediate order of the day a struggle for transfer of all power to the Soviets, the establishment of a Republic of Soviets "from top to bottom," the abolition of the police, army, and all officialdom, the confiscation of all landlord estates, and the transfer of control over the production and distribution of goods into the hands of the Soviet.[23] (It should be borne in mind that Lenin's campaign for transfer of power to the Soviets in the spring and early summer of 1917 was a convenient means of attracting the support of the Russian masses, of weakening and perhaps destroying the Provisional Government, and most important, of preparing for the seizure of power by the revolutionary proletariat, i.e., the Bolsheviks. In the long run, government by a moderate socialist controlled Soviet was no more attractive to Lenin than rule by the liberals.)

It is small wonder that most of Lenin's listeners were thunderstruck by his ideas. To be sure, the overriding impatience for decisive action and the ideological flexibility which the theses reflect were not untypical of Lenin's outlook in the pre-revolutionary period. Then, too, much of what was said in the theses differed little from Lenin's policy in years past.[24] For example, Lenin's unequivocal position in regard to the war was precisely the one which he enunciated at the outbreak of hostilities in 1914. Similarly, a permanent aversion to liberal government was axiomatic with

Lenin from the time of the 1905 revolution. Dating from 1905 as well was Lenin's belief that the Russian proletariat, in temporary alliance with the peasantry, might seize immediate power and thereby avoid an extended bourgeois-liberal stage in the revolution; this formula grew out of Lenin's disdain for the liberals and his awareness of the relative weakness of the Russian working class. But in the past Lenin had advanced these arguments largely in long-range theoretical terms, and when circumstances warranted it, he had demonstrated a high degree of political realism and restraint. Now, when the predominant spirit in both the Bolshevik and Menshevik camps was one of moderation and reconciliation, Lenin was baldly presenting these ideas as a guide for immediate revolutionary action.

No discussion followed the initial presentation of Lenin's theses because the Bolsheviks had to hurry to their meeting with the Mensheviks.[25] Sukhanov's recollections, however, contain a few of the indignant Menshevik reactions to a second reading of the "April Theses" at the latter gathering. Evidently not atypical was B. O. Bogdanov's response: "This is the raving of a madman! It's indecent to applaud this claptrap!" A former Bolshevik, I. P. Goldenberg, took the floor to declare that "Lenin has now made himself a candidate for one European throne that has been vacant for thirty years —the throne of Bakunin! Lenin's new words echo something old— the superannuated truths of primitive anarchism." The same day the Menshevik leader M. I. Skobelev confidently assured the cabinet that Lenin was a "has-been who stands outside the ranks of the [Social Democratic] movement."[26]

Initially, Bolshevik circles were equally unresponsive to Lenin's program. At a meeting of the Central Committee Bureau on April 6, Kamenev predicted that the party would be transformed into a group of propagandists if Lenin's theses were adopted, and Stalin supported him.[27] There is no evidence of a vote on the theses on this occasion, but two days later the Petersburg Committee rejected them by a vote of 13 to 2 with one abstention.[28] According to an account by the Soviet historian E. N. Burdzhalov, the immediate reaction in many provincial party organizations was similar. On April 8 *Pravda* carried a statement entitled "Our Disagreements," signed by Kamenev but probably reflecting accurately attitudes prevailing within a large segment of the party. Emphasizing that the "April Theses" represented Lenin's "personal opinion" only, it declared that "we hope to defend our point of view as the only one possible for revolutionary Social Democrats as long as they want to remain the party of the proletarian masses." The statement concluded that "Lenin's general scheme appears to us unacceptable since it starts from the assumption that the bourgeois revolution is finished and counts on the immediate transformation of this revolution into a socialist revolution."

Yet in spite of this inauspicious beginning Lenin was able to win a large portion of the party to his side in an amazingly short time. There were probably a number of reasons for this. Among them, Lenin's intellectual superiority over his opponents was undoubtedly of key importance. "Within a certain realm of ideas . . . Lenin displayed such amazing force, such superhuman power of attack," recalls Sukhanov, "that his colossal influence . . . was secure."[29] Then, too, in the days following his return Lenin conducted an incredibly energetic campaign for support, evidently tempering his position somewhat in order to allay the more immediate apprehensions of party moderates.[30] A further factor contributing to Lenin's success was the significant change taking place at just that moment within the membership of the party at the local level. In Petrograd mass disenchantment with the revolution, partly a consequence of continued economic hardship, was just starting to set in. From the time of the February revolution requirements for party membership had been all but suspended, and now Bolshevik ranks swelled with impetuous recruits who knew next to nothing about Marxism and who were united by little more than overwhelming impatience for revolutionary action. Moreover, returning to the capital from prison, exile, and the emigration during this period were a number of party veterans who tended to be more radical than Bolsheviks who had remained in Petrograd during the war.

This transformation in the composition of the Petrograd party organization is reflected distinctly in the minutes of the Petersburg Committee for the April period and in the protocols of the First Bolshevik Petrograd City Conference, where Lenin won his initial victories over the right. Meeting in mid-April (April 14-22), the First Petrograd City Conference adopted by a decisive 37 to 3 vote Lenin's resolution condemning the Provisional Government and calling for the eventual transfer of all power to the Soviets. Kamenev attacked the resolution on both theoretical and practical grounds, claiming it would be taken to mean that the Provisional Government should be overthrown immediately.[31] True to this prediction, some members of the Petrograd party organization reached precisely this conclusion during the April crisis, which began even before the City Conference came to an end.

The April Crisis and the Seventh All-Russian Conference of the RSDLP(b)

The first major crisis of the Provisional Government broke out over the crucial war issue. On March 14 the Petrograd Soviet published a manifesto "to the peoples of the world" voicing the majority socialists' idealistic hopes for a negotiated settlement of the war based on the principle of peace without annexations and indemnities. To be sure, the document was ambiguous, attempting as it did to combine the principle of a non-predatory peace with an affirmation of revolutionary Russia's determination to defend its newly won liberty. But the Soviet set great store by it, and more importantly, thousands of war-weary Russian workers and soldiers came to view it as a significant first step toward ending hostilities. To Paul Miliukov, the Provisional Government's Foreign Minister and self-proclaimed guardian of traditional Russian national interests, however, the manifesto was anathema. Along with many other liberals Miliukov was confident that the overthrow of the autocracy had revitalized Russia and strengthened her fighting capacity. When Miliukov declared during the course of a press interview on

March 23 that Russia was fighting to unite the Ukrainian parts of the Austro-Hungarian Empire with Russia and to gain Constantinople and the Straits, the Soviet's outraged reaction was instantaneous. So great was the hue and cry that on March 27 the Provisional Government was forced to publish a statement of war aims more in keeping with the Soviet's position and later to forward the latter to its allies as an official statement of government policy.[32]

This was done on April 18. Miliukov, however, attempted to nullify the implications of the statement with a covering note affirming that the revolution would not result in any slackening of the war effort. To the contrary, he asserted, revolutionary Russia was more than ever inspired by the lofty democratic aims of the Allies and would observe all obligations toward them. The text of the Miliukov note came to the attention of the Executive Committee of the Petrograd Soviet on April 19, and was published in the newspapers the next day. The majority socialist leaders in the Soviet naturally felt betrayed, while the volatile workers and soldiers of the capital gave vent to their fury by armed protest demonstrations. On April 20 and 21 thousands of soldiers, bearing such slogans as "Down with Miliukov," "Down with annexationist policies," and even "Down with the Provisional Government," demonstrated outside the government's headquarters in the Mariinsky Palace. A few armed clashes occurred between pro- and anti-government demonstrators, and the disturbances were not ended until late on the twenty-first, when the Soviet proclaimed a two-day ban on street demonstrations and the Provisional Government published an explanation—or more accurately, a retraction—of the Miliukov note in which it reaffirmed its solidarity with the position of the Soviet. The ultimate consequence of the April days was the departure of Miliukov from the cabinet and the formation of the first coalition Provisional Government, composed of six socialists and nine "capitalists."[33] (In the aftermath of the April crisis the Executive Committee of the Petrograd Soviet voted to rescind its ban on the participation of socialists in the government in order to help restore internal order and buttress the defense effort.)

The parts played by the Bolshevik Central Committee and the

Petrograd organization of the party in the development of the April crisis were revealing and prophetic. Rank-and-file party members from garrison regiments and factories undoubtedly helped to provoke the street demonstrations in the first place, although the Bolshevik Central Committee evidently did not become involved until after the movement was well underway. On the morning of April 20, an emergency meeting of the Central Committee adopted an ambiguously worded resolution written by Lenin which condemned the Miliukov note and suggested that only by transferring all power to the Soviet was immediate peace possible, but which stopped short of inviting party followers into the streets.[34] A second resolution drafted by Lenin and adopted by the Central Committee on April 21 was more direct, calling on Bolshevik agitators to organize mass protest meetings and demonstrations at once.[35] When the Executive Committee of the Petrograd Soviet resolved to ban further demonstrations, however, Bolshevik representatives did not oppose the measure.[36]

Meanwhile, impulsive elements in the Petrograd party organization and the Bolshevik Military Organization adopted a more militant pose. On April 20, when raging mobs were gathered at the Mariinsky Palace, some district delegates at the afternoon session of the First Bolshevik Petrograd City Conference appealed for the immediate overthrow of the Provisional Government, and V. I. Nevsky of the Military Organization spoke out in favor of mobilizing troops, evidently for agitational activity in behalf of seizure of power by the Soviet. Ludmilla Stal, a long-time Bolshevik and member of the Petersburg Committee, tried to dampen this hotheadedness with the admonition that delegates "should not be further left than Lenin himself," and the conference delegates ultimately voted to call the workers and soldiers to "organized expressions of their solidarity with the resolution of the Central Committee," i.e., its cautious first resolution condemning the Miliukov note and suggesting the transfer of power to the Soviet.[37]

At a meeting of the Executive Commission of the Bolshevik Petersburg Committee late the same evening, however, the question of overthrowing the Provisional Government was reconsidered and evidently attracted increased support.[38] The only leader of this movement identified in official Soviet accounts is S. Ia. Bogdatiev, an outspoken Petersburg Committee member from the Putilov factory and candidate for the Bolshevik Central Committee at the Seventh All-Russian Bolshevik Party Conference. Bogdatiev is credited with having prepared a leaflet over the signature of the Petersburg Committee appealing for the immediate overthrow of the Provisional Government; this was widely circulated on April 21 and was primarily responsible for the sudden appearance among demonstrators of "Down with the Provisional Government" banners. In Soviet histories Bogdatiev and his supporters are also accused of having agitated for the arrest of the cabinet ministers.[39] Lenin voiced his opposition to these unauthorized activities in a statement at the Seventh All-Russian Bolshevik Party Conference on April 24. His remarks on this occasion suggest that the task of marshaling the masses for the overthrow of the Provisional Government now appeared to him more complex than it had in the days immediately following his return to Russia:

> We did not know if in this troubled moment the masses would swing in our direction; the question would have been different if they had swung sharply. We proposed a peaceful demonstration but some comrades in the Petersburg Committee injected a different slogan. We annulled it but could not stop it in time, and the masses followed the slogan of the Petersburg Committee. We acknowledge that the slogan "Down with the Provisional Government" is adventurist, that we cannot now overthrow the government. . . . We wanted only a peaceful reconnaissance of our enemy's forces and not to give battle. But the Petersburg Committee took a position "a wee bit to the left". . . . To move a "wee bit left" at the moment of action was inept. We regard this as a grave crime. . . . We would not remain in the Central Committee for a minute if we consciously permitted such a step. It occurred because of imperfections in our organizational machinery. . . . Were there mistakes? Yes, there were. Only those who don't act don't make mistakes. But to organize well—that's a difficult task.[40]

At the Seventh (April) All-Russian Conference of the RSDLP-(b), which met in Petrograd from April 24 to 29, 1917, Lenin's position on the Provisional Government won majority support despite the fact that the unauthorized activities of left Bolsheviks during the April crisis had borne out Kamenev's prediction that untempered denunciation of the Provisional Government would be interpreted as a call for its overthrow. A small right-wing faction still spoke out in favor of "watchful control" over the Provisional Government, but it no longer included Stalin. An overwhelming majority of delegates also sided with Lenin on the question of the war. The conference resolved that despite the establishment of the Provisional Government the Russian war effort remained imperialist in character, and hence the party of the proletariat could not in good faith support it. Further, the conference's declaration condemned the policy of "revolutionary defensism," insisted that the war could end with a democratic peace only after power in at least a few belligerent countries had been transferred to the proletariat, and suggested that such a transfer in Russia would pave the way for similar revolts in other countries. Finally, the declaration advocated mass fraternization at the front as a further means of stimulating revolutions abroad.[41]

Yet Lenin did not have his way on all the issues before the April Conference. His proposal to break conclusively with the Second International attracted no support. The resolution on the "current moment" adopted by the conference contained significant theoretical concessions to the Kamenev faction and even so was approved with a margin of only 24 votes. And more importantly, the right wing of the party managed to elect four of its number, Kamenev, Nogin, V. P. Miliutin, and G. F. Fedorov, to the new Central Committee chosen at the close of the April Conference (the remaining members were Lenin, Zinoviev, Sverdlov, Stalin, and I. T. Smilga), thereby ensuring its relative conservatism throughout the pre-October period. Taken as a whole, however, the resolutions of the April Conference were a summons to prepare for a socialist revolution and thus constituted a great personal triumph for Lenin.

For the moment emphasis was on the campaign for increased mass support and the winning of Bolshevik majorities in the Soviets. But the organization of technical fighting strength to be employed in the seizure of power was by no means ignored, and here the goal of winning over the Petrograd garrison assumed crucial importance.

The Bolshevik Military Organization
and the Campaign for Control of
the Petrograd Garrison

Under the Tsarist regime the Petrograd garrison was an immensely powerful military force, inevitably a major and sometimes the decisive factor in the political history of the Russian state. In the 1905 revolution it had remained loyal to the Tsar and in so doing had insured the preservation of the monarchy. In February, 1917, Nicholas II's fate was sealed when units of the garrison, one after the other, joined the side of the rebellion. Similarly, developments in the garrison were crucial to the defeat suffered by the Bolsheviks in July and to their subsequent triumph in October. Because of this strategic importance a detailed knowledge of the Petrograd garrison's numerical strength and sociological composition, as well as the process by which it was transformed from a bulwark of autocracy to an ally of popular revolt, is indispensable to an understanding of the Russian revolution. Unfortunately, relatively little work has been done on the make-up and role of the Petrograd garrison in 1917, on the Soviet side because of preoccupation with the importance of the workers during the revolutionary period, and in Western accounts because of a shortage of reliable published data.

It will be remembered that on the eve of the February revolution the originally reliable garrison troops, having suffered enormous losses in the early phases of the war, had been replaced almost entirely by undisciplined recruits from the countryside, who shared the immense social, economic, and political dissatisfactions of the bulk of the population and who were not at all attracted by the prospect of going to the front. The backbone of the garrison's strength was sixteen guards infantry regiments and six army reserve infantry regiments, quartered in Petrograd and its suburbs, whose primary task was the training of replacement companies for frontline duty. Though popularly referred to as regiments, these units were technically reserve battalions of regiments at the front. The guards infantry regiments contained between 4,500 and 7,500 men each and included the Preobrazhensky, Semenovsky, Izmailovsky, Egersky, Moskovsky, Pavlovsky, Finliandsky, Litovsky, Keksgolmsky, Petrogradsky, Volynsky, and Grenadier Regiments, all quartered in Petrograd. Also included among guards infantry units were four reserve rifle battalions, two located in Petrograd and two in Tsarskoe Selo, a village seventeen miles from Petrograd where one of the Tsar's palaces was located. The six army reserve infantry regiments contained from 10,000 to 19,000 men each and included the First and 180th Reserve Infantry Regiments in Petrograd, the Third Reserve Infantry Regiment in Peterhof, the 176th Reserve Infantry Regiment in Krasnoe Selo, the First Reserve Machine Gun Regiment in Oranienbaum (from the time of the February revolution until after the July days the bulk of the First Machine Gun Regiment was actually billeted in the Vyborg District in Petrograd), and the Second Reserve Machine Gun Regiment in Strelna. All of the above regiments were quartered within twenty miles of the capital. The remainder of the garrison was made up largely of the First and Fourth Don Cossack Regiments, spread throughout the city and its suburbs, a number of reserve units, and various military schools. Published estimates of the total number of troops stationed in and around Petrograd at the time of the February revolution vary greatly; 215,000 to 300,000 would seem to be a fair approximation, although a recent estimate by the Soviet historian V. M. Kochakov runs considerably higher.[42]

Because of its political significance a contest for influence in the garrison among the Provisional Government, the Petrograd Soviet, and the major Russian political parties was inevitable in the period immediately following the February revolution. During the first weeks of March the Provisional Government sought to reestablish the Petrograd Military District's command over the forces of the garrison, but its efforts were quickly overshadowed by those of the more broadly based Soviet. Giant steps toward assuring the allegiance of the garrison were taken by the Soviet on February 28, when army units were invited to elect representatives to participate in the work of the Soviet and on March 3, when Soviet pressure forced the Provisional Government to include in its initial proclamation a provision that troops taking part in the revolution could not be disarmed or removed from Petrograd. Even more significant was the publication at about the same time of the Soviet's Order Number One regarding behavior in the armed forces. Among other things, the order authorized the immediate election of soldier and sailor committees with broad but vaguely defined administrative authority in all military units, placed control of all weapons in the hands of these committees, announced that orders of the Provisional Government should be obeyed only if they did not conflict with the orders of the Soviet, and proclaimed full civil rights to soldiers when not on duty. The practical effect of these provisions was to make garrison units responsible to the Petrograd Soviet, and to all but destroy traditional codes of behavior in the armed forces. Moreover, the fact that the Petrograd Soviet's stand on the war corresponded more closely to the soldiers' yearning for peace than did the patriotic declarations of the Provisional Government probably contributed to the popularity of the Soviet in the initial weeks of the revolutionary period. At any rate, striking proof of the Provisional Government's impotence in the garrison was furnished as early as the April crisis, when troops responded to the authority of the Executive Committee of the Petrograd Soviet rather than to General Kornilov, then commander of the Petrograd Military District. Subsequently, in matters concerning the garrison the Provisional Government was forced to act in concert with the Soviet.

In addition, the Kadets, SR's, Mensheviks, and Bolsheviks competed among themselves for influence in the Petrograd garrison during the spring of 1917, each creating a special military organization for this purpose.[43] But more than any other party, the Bolsheviks devoted attention and an enormous expenditure of effort to this cause. Alone among the major Russian political parties, the Bolsheviks sought to challenge the Soviet as spokesman for the garrison's seething discontent. Moreover, only they set for themselves the task of obtaining absolute control of major individual garrison regiments, establishing party cells at battalion and even company levels as a means of attaining this objective. According to the Bolshevik Military Organization leader V. I. Nevsky, the party's interest in the garrison was two-fold. Most important, garrison regiments were viewed as a major element in the armed force that would be needed to overthrow the bourgeoisie, and second, the spread of Bolshevik ideas to the soldier-peasants of the garrison was seen as an important means of gaining a foothold in the countryside.[44] The significance for the Bolsheviks of the struggle for control of the armed forces (and first of all the Petrograd garrison) was summed up by Nevsky at the party's Second Petrograd City Conference in July: "No matter how well armed the working class is, the triumph of the revolution without the participation of the huge military mass is impossible."[45] In a post-revolutionary work Nevsky put the matter even more directly: "To win the Petrograd garrison was to win first place in the revolution."[46]

The sustained Bolshevik campaign for influence in the garrison began almost as soon as legal Bolshevik party organizations came into being. At the first official meeting of the Petersburg Committee an unidentified party member affirmed the immediate necessity of "influencing" and "organizing" the soldiers, and it has already been mentioned that on March 10 a special Military Commission was appointed to found a permanent Bolshevik Military Organization to direct party work in the Petrograd garrison. The original members of the Military Commission were S. N. Sulimov, S. Ia. Bogdatiev, V. I. Nevsky, and N. I. Podvoisky,[47] the last three of whom can definitely be identified as representatives of the party's extreme left wing. On March 22 the Military Commission resolved to invite representatives of garrison regiments to a Military Organization Constituent Assembly, and it was at this gathering on March 31 that the Bolshevik Military Organization was formally established.[48]

From the beginning the work of the Bolshevik Military Organization was under the direction of N. I. Podvoisky and V. I. Nevsky. Both were long-time Bolsheviks, Podvoisky having joined the party in 1901 and Nevsky in 1897. In his *History of the Russian Revolution* Trotsky recalls Podvoisky as "a sharply outlined and unique figure in the ranks of Bolshevism with traits of the Russian revolutionary of the old type . . . a man of great although undisciplined energy with a creative imagination which often went to the length of fantasy."[49] The Kronstadt Bolshevik F. F. Raskolnikov remembers that in the days immediately following the February overturn Podvoisky was the first to declare boldly that "the revolution is not over; it is just beginning."[50] Nevsky had been a student in the Natural Sciences Faculty at Moscow University and in the 1920's distinguished himself as an historian of the Russian revolutionary movement. According to Trotsky, he "attached the soldiers to him by his simplicity, sociability, and attentive kindness."[51] One suspects that Nevsky's powerful writing talents, which in 1917 were turned to the production of scathing critiques of the contemporary situation, contributed greatly to the stature which he acquired in the garrison. It should also be mentioned that both Nevsky and Podvoisky were distinguished by an independence of spirit (Soviet sources refer to it as "an unwillingness to abide by direction from the Central Committee"[52]) which could not fail to affect their leadership of the Military Organization.

Bolshevik attempts to gain a foothold in the Petrograd garrison were by no means immediately successful. In March such efforts were hampered by a shortage of trained agitators (and in any event the troops were probably content to follow the Soviet), and in early April the criticism of the Bolsheviks aroused by Lenin's return passage through enemy Germany increased the difficulty of conducting anti-war propaganda in the garrison. In this respect the April crisis and the beginning a short time later of preparations to resume active military operations at the front evidently marked something of a turning point in Military Organization fortunes. From then on the revolutionary Bolshevik program attracted a steadily increasing mass following. "Club Pravda," a "non-party" soldiers' club opened by the Military Organization in the basement of the Kshesinskaia mansion, became a magnet for the most extreme elements in the armed forces. Garrison rallies staged by the Military Organization drew crowds numbering into the thousands. *Soldatskaia pravda*, the Military Organization's special soldiers' newspaper and probably its most successful enterprise, quickly attained a circulation of 50,000, half of which was distributed in the Petrograd garrison and the remainder sent to the front.[53]

Soldatskaia pravda was founded by the Military Organization in mid-April out of a conviction that much of the Central Committee's *Pravda* was unintelligible and uninteresting to the average uneducated soldier. Advertising itself as the soldiers' own organ, *Soldatskaia pravda* focused attention almost exclusively on political issues of particular interest to the troops and on the hardships of everyday life in the armed forces. In a simple and direct style that contrasted sharply with *Pravda*, *Soldatskaia pravda* issued a steady stream of propaganda on such important aspects of the Bolshevik program as the removal of the Provisional Government, the transfer of all power to the Soviets, the confiscation of farmland, and immediate peace. *Soldatskaia pravda*'s inaugural issue launched a campaign to encourage fraternization at the front, and in subsequent articles practical ways of initiating fraternization were discussed in detail. Each day except Monday, from April 15 to July 5, *Soldatskaia pravda* articles, often written by the soldiers themselves, attacked government attempts to reestablish a minimum of discipline in Petrograd regiments and to transfer soldiers from the garrison to the front, while an endless stream of letters and resolutions from frontline soldiers sketched a disturbing, albeit distorted, picture of conditions there.

By mid-May the effect of such propaganda must already have been observable. To be sure, soldiers' committees in most units remained under the control of non-Bolshevik moderates, as they had been from the first days of the revolution, and a few regiments were still relatively free of Bolshevik influence. However, Military Organization membership in Petrograd already probably totaled well over one thousand;[54] party cells had been founded in most major units of the garrison, and these were represented in the central Military Organization. The influence of the party was particularly strong in the garrison First Machine Gun Regiment, 180th Reserve Infantry Regiment, Petrogradsky and Moskovsky Guards Regiments, and Sixth Engineer Battalion,[55] and in the radically inclined Kronstadt naval base, where the local Soviet passed a resolution rejecting the authority of the Provisional Government on May 16. (On May 24 the Kronstadt Soviet, under pressure from the Provisional Government and the Petrograd Soviet, formally reversed this decision, although for practical purposes the Provisional Government's authority in the naval base was never reestablished.) As Bolshevik Military Organization leaders readily acknowledged, efforts to organize garrison troops into a disciplined revolutionary force by no means kept pace with the striking growth in support for the Bolshevik program,[56] and the forging of Bolshevik ties with frontline troops was just beginning. Nonetheless, the Military Organization's militant new garrison converts, their discontent and apprehension for the future whipped to fever pitch, soon began demanding more than mere words.

The Abortive June 10
Demonstration

The Military Organization's Proposal

The initiative for the June 10 demonstration, primarily as an expression of mass opposition to the Provisional Government's preparations for an early military offensive, came from the Bolshevik Military Organization. It was first suggested by the Presidium of the Military Organization (the membership of the Presidium included Podvoisky, Nevsky, K. Mekhonoshin, S. Cherepanov, and P. V. Dashkevich[1]) to the Central Committee around the middle of May. At that time the Central Committee ignored the suggestion,[2] and perhaps remembering the independence exhibited by members of the Petersburg Committee and the Military Organization during the April crisis, directed that no political steps of any kind be taken without its consultation.[3]

Between the middle of May and the beginning of June the demands of individual representatives of Military Organization units in favor of an armed protest demonstration, directed primarily against Kerensky's attempts to reinstitute military discipline and against the increasing threat of transfer to the front, became more insistent.[4] At a Petrograd Military Organization meeting on May 23 it was reported that the Pavlovsky, Izmailovsky, Grenadier, and First Reserve Infantry Regiments, among others, "were ready to go out on their own if a positive decision were not adopted at the center."[5] This threat was to be used effectively by garrison Bolsheviks to influence the policies of the Military Organization throughout the pre-July period.

No one at the May 23 meeting spoke out against a demonstration, while a succession of soldier-Bolsheviks supported the idea. The leadership of the Military Organization was also favorably inclined. For the latter an imposing expression of mass support for the Bolshevik program and particularly its attitudes toward the war effort, coinciding with the opening of the First All-Russian Congress of Soviets of Workers' and Soldiers' Deputies (the Congress met in Petrograd from June 3 to June 24, 1917), was an attractive proposition. The movement, initiated as it was by the party rank-and-file, also would serve to win for the Military Organization greater influence among the increasingly restive regiments of the garrison. At the May 23 meeting the Military Organization leaders Dashkevich and Nevsky encouraged the demonstration proposal, Nevsky cautioning only that "to arrange a demonstration that would not attract a majority would be a tactical error, but if it were certain that a successful demonstration were feasible, then it could be done." The sense of this discussion, as interpreted by the chairman, was that a march should be organized. At the close of the gathering it was decided to hold a closed meeting with representation from Kronstadt before making a firm decision or setting a date for the demonstration. This meeting was held on June 1, and it voted in favor of organizing a mass garrison demonstration.[6] Forwarded by the Military Organization to the party Central Committee was a list of regiments, all told an estimated 60,000 soldiers, who presumably could be counted on to participate.[7]

The "revolutionary mood" of the more radical units in the Petrograd garrison was tested by an event that occurred on June 4, the day after the opening of the First Congress of Soviets. On that day several hundred Bolshevik-led Kronstadt sailors staged a demonstration, the ostensible purpose of which was to pay tribute to the dead heroes of the February revolution, on Mars Field in Petrograd. The Military Organization evidently viewed this event as a sort of dress rehearsal for its own prospective demonstration; for this reason and as a means of currying Kronstadt's favor, it arranged the last-minute participation of hundreds of garrison troops. Elements of the Pavlovsky, Moskovsky, Grenadier, First Machine Gun, 180th Infantry, Finliandsky, and Sixth Engineer Regiments, among others, took part, and the June 7 *Pravda*, with some justification, hailed the imposing turnout as a barometer of Bolshevik strength. F. F. Raskolnikov on behalf of the sailors, N. V. Krylenko for the Central Committee, and A. Ia. Semashko, representing the Military Organization, addressed the spirited revolutionary rally. The mood of the event is characterized by Semashko's praise of the Kronstadt Military Organization. "Following its example," he concluded in an obvious reference to Kronstadt's radicalism, "and using it for support, the Bolshevik Military Organization can become the bulwark of the revolution."[8]

Two days later, on June 6, Podvoisky and Nevsky brought up the question of a demonstration at a joint meeting of the Central Committee, Military Organization, and Executive Commission of the Petersburg Committee.[9] In a short report Podvoisky informed the expanded gathering of the results of the June 1 Military Organization meeting and urged that the Central Committee make a quick decision (i.e., to authorize a demonstration). He justified the movement on the grounds that it would "increase the influence of the party in Petrograd" and would serve "as a battering ram that would effect a breach in the Congress." The heated controversy which followed Podvoisky's proposal mirrored the sharply differing views regarding strategy and tactics that existed within the Central Committee at this time. In the debate at least two opposing factions emerged—one, led by Lenin, strongly in favor of a demonstration and the other, led by Kamenev, just as firmly opposed.

Although the published record of Lenin's remarks is fragmentary, it does reveal his obvious enthusiasm for the proposed march. "This is the will of the soldiers and the proletariat," he declared. "Their slogans are ours. Down with the capitalist ministers. . . . Let there be agreement with the proletariat and not the Kadets. Transfer power to the Soviet and it will immediately propose peace terms." Lenin suggested that a survey of forces be conducted and that a meeting be scheduled two days later to make technical decisions. In a subsequent remark Lenin emphasized the seriousness with which he viewed the offensive then in preparation by the Provisional Government and the importance which he attached to an impressive anti-government, anti-war demonstration as a means of sabotaging it. (At this point, Lenin evidently was convinced that transfer of power to the Soviet and Russia's unilateral renunciation of the struggle against the Central Powers were of crucial importance in turning the "imperialist" war into a worldwide "class war against the exploiters." In his view a successful offensive would serve only the interests of the "capitalist dominated" Provisional Government and would drastically retard the opportunity for revolution.[10])

Sverdlov, Fedorov, and Stalin supported the demonstration proposal; Sverdlov commented that "an organized outlet for the mood of the masses had to be provided." Fedorov, a party moderate, cautioned only that the demonstration should be unarmed, to which Nevsky replied that the demonstration would be "unimposing" and "amateurish" if arms were not taken. Cherepanov of the Military Organization ended this exchange with the comment that "the soldiers will not demonstrate without arms; the question is settled."

Nogin, Zinoviev, and Kamenev, on the other hand, voiced strong opposition to what they viewed as a rash and untimely proposal. Acknowledging that a conflict was brewing, they argued that the party's actual strength in the country was not yet great enough to justify an action which, in Nogin's words, was tantamount to revolution. Zinoviev suggested that the change (presumably in favor of the Bolsheviks) was just beginning and that "the party was risking its life." In any event, argued the representatives of the Central Committee's right wing, a soldiers' demonstration would give the party nothing, while among the workers there was no overwhelming urge to do battle.[11] Interestingly, even Lenin's wife, N. K.

Krupskaia, who rarely opposed her husband, expressed apprehension in regard to the proposed march. "It won't be peaceful," she declared, "and so perhaps it should not be staged."

At the end of this meeting it was agreed that a gathering of the Central Committee, Petersburg Committee, and Military Organization, with the participation of regimental, trade union, and factory representatives, would be called for June 9 in order to make a final decision on the question of organizing a mass soldier-worker demonstration.

Shortly after the Central Committee meeting, still on June 6, the full Petersburg Committee also discussed the question of a demonstration.[12] V. I. Nevsky, a representative of the Petersburg District in the Petersburg Committee as well as a Military Organization leader, reviewed the conflicting positions that had emerged at the earlier meeting and presented in some detail the case for a demonstration. He argued that there was grave unrest in the garrison for which an outlet was necessary and that, practically speaking, there would be a demonstration whether the party wanted it or not. The questions remaining were whether the Bolsheviks would lead the movement and whether the workers would take part in the soldier demonstration. In reply to comments Nevsky implied that the demonstration could result in a serious setback for the party, but emphasized that in his view this was preferable to shirking leadership. He acknowledged that the Executive Committee of the Soviet was against armed demonstrations, but added later that its interference could be avoided by keeping the demonstration secret.

The discussion of Nevsky's proposal by the Petersburg Committee (the published protocol of which is quite detailed) was fully as interesting and revealing as the earlier debate within the Central Committee. Significantly, the overwhelming majority of the Petersburg Committee was enthusiastic about the idea of organizing a demonstration and of finally taking the offensive against the "counterrevolutionary" Provisional Government. Some members were relatively pessimistic about the possibility of attracting mass worker support; a few, discounting the possibility of staging a workers' demonstration, were favorably disposed to a march of garrison units alone. But there were evidently almost no Petersburg Committee Bolsheviks who, like Kamenev, Zinoviev, and Nogin, categorically opposed the organization of an undoubtedly armed mass demonstration against the Provisional Government.

Among enthusiastic supporters of a "peaceful demonstration" were V. Volodarsky, A. Dylle, V. A. Ivanov, P. A. Zalutsky, and M. Ia. Latsis. Volodarsky, recently returned from America, expressed the apprehensions of the majority when he stated that "if we don't support the concrete demands of the soldiers, they will turn away from us." And like several others, he emphasized the absolute necessity of worker participation in any mass demonstration. Optimistic about the possibility of obtaining broad support for a protest march, Volodarsky argued that among the masses a change in mood favoring the Bolsheviks was growing, and he added that "any hour an event could occur that would spur the workers to action." Ivanov, a representative from the Vasilievsky Island District, spoke out in a similar vein, commenting that the prevailing mood among both workers and soldiers undoubtedly favored a peaceful demonstration and that such action was necessary as protection against the Bolsheviks' opponents. Zalutsky emphasized the significance of the war in the trend toward Bolshevism and pointed out the value of a demonstration in strengthening the Bolshevik position among the masses. M. Ia. Latsis, who had close ties with the First Machine Gun Regiment and who was an especially key figure by virtue of his leadership in the important Vyborg District party organization,[13] agreed with Nevsky that a military demonstration with or without Bolshevik leadership was bound to take place. As regards workers, Latsis stated that the elections to the Vyborg District Duma[14] showed that the workers were ready to go out into the streets at any moment. Thus, according to Latsis, there was hope that the demonstration would be impressive.

While most members of the Petersburg Committee, echoing Volodarsky, thought in terms of a joint worker-soldier demonstration, A. I. Plotnikov and M. Kalinin spoke out in favor of an exclusively military demonstration. "The soldiers have reason for dissatisfaction," stated Kalinin, "the workers don't. There exists a revolutionary mood among the workers, but it will take a long period of growing consciousness before it will mature." Kalinin concluded by suggesting that a march exclusively of soldiers would provide a means of ascertaining what the party had to count on.

Only one speaker, V. B. Vinokurov of the Nevsky District, is recorded as having spoken out emphatically against any demonstration whatever. Vinokurov maintained that in his district the Bolsheviks were still weak, that the soldiers would not listen to party members, but that they would respond to the Military Organization's call for a demonstration. "With this degree of influence can we direct a demonstration?" he asked realistically; "what can such a demonstration develop into?"

It is notable that during this discussion, J. V. Stalin of the Central Committee made one of his rare appearances at a meeting of the Petersburg Committee, apparently in order to lend support to the demonstration proposal. In his comments Stalin revealed just how far left he had traveled since his return to the capital in March. He suggested that the counterrevolutionary steps already taken showed that unless the coalition Provisional Government was challenged, it would soon condemn the Bolshevik Party to death. Acknowledging that the workers did not share the definitely discontented mood of the soldiers, he argued that the party "must call the masses to battle not only when the situation has reached the boiling point. Since we are an organization possessing influence, we have the duty to awaken the spirit of the masses." At the time that the Provisional Government is preparing an offensive, continued Stalin, "our duty is to repulse it. Our duty is to organize this demonstration—a review of our strength. Seeing armed soldiers," he concluded enthusiastically, "the bourgeoisie will hide."

Much more cautious were the comments of M. P. Tomsky, a member of the Petersburg Committee's Executive Commission, who combined interest in a demonstration with a measure of realism and foresight. He suggested that the important question was not whether the demonstration would be peaceful or armed, or whether it would be imposing or not, but what it would develop into:

> It is to be expected that the Executive Committee of the Petrograd Soviet will exert all of its efforts in order to prevent the demonstration and will first of all try to exert influence on the soldiers. And this won't end with applause for the ministers. The mood of class antagonism is so high . . . that it cannot be expected that the demonstration will take place peacefully. Imagine what could happen in a clash of hundreds, perhaps thousands of people; there might be more than a demonstration. We must be especially careful in taking this step. Operating on the mood of the broad masses means operating on what to some degree is an unknown.

Because of his reservations, Tomsky urged that the Petersburg Committee postpone announcing any decision until after a meeting with party rank-and-file (i.e., until after the expanded meeting already scheduled for June 9). This was evidently also the consensus of the rest of the Petersburg Committee, and so at the close of this discussion the session was adjourned without any concrete decision regarding a demonstration having been reached.

The Petrograd Federation of Anarchist-Communists

Before the convocation of the June 9 Bolshevik meeting to explore further the question of a demonstration, there occurred the catalytic incident that Volodarsky predicted would "spur the masses to action." The incident was a seemingly minor one—the threatened eviction of the Anarchist-Communists from their Durnovo villa headquarters—but it stimulated serious unrest in the explosive Vyborg factory district. Before turning to this crisis, a few general remarks must be made about the Anarchist-Communists.

The Petrograd Federation of Anarchist-Communists was the less refined, tactically more radical, and consequently the more influential of the two major anarchist organizations operating in Petrograd in the summer of 1917. The Anarcho-Syndicalists were the second group.[15] Actually, very little is known about the Anarchist-Communist organization or its principal leaders. Of the latter, among the better known in early summer, 1917 (in the factories, the garrison, and Kronstadt), were I. Bleikhman, chief Anarchist-Communist spokesman in the Petrograd and Kronstadt Soviets, Asnin, who was a familiar figure in Kronstadt and the First Machine Gun Regiment prior to his death on June 19, 1917,[16] A. Fedorov, also a member of the Petrograd Soviet, and P. Pavlov and P. Golubushkin—both of whom played key roles in stimulating the July uprising within the First Machine Gun Regiment.

The program of the Anarchist-Communists was extremely general and unsophisticated.[17] According to a pamphlet distributed in the early summer of 1917, the organization called for the immediate destruction or elimination of, among other things, all autocratic and parliamentary governments, the capitalist system, the war, the army, the police, and all state boundaries. The same pamphlet advocated the establishment of a new "totally free" communal society, without government or laws, in which individual freedom would be absolute, the peasants would own the land, and the factories would belong to the workers.[18]

There are many parallels between the future ideal societies envisioned by the Anarchist-Communists and by the Bolsheviks. In addition, their positions coincided on such immediate issues as the continuation of the war, the reestablishment of discipline within the army, institution of worker control over industry, and opposition to the Provisional Government. Instances of mutual support between Bolsheviks and Anarchists were not at all infrequent. In this regard V. N. Zalezhsky, a member of the Petersburg Committee and the Helsingfors party organization in 1917, recalls that the Anarchist-Communists had great influence in Kronstadt, but that:

> In practice the Anarchist-Communists worked arm in arm with the Bolsheviks. . . . The common practical platform which allowed the Bolsheviks to work with the Anarchist-Communists

was the struggle against the policies of the Provisional Government aimed at strengthening the capitalist system, preserving the privileges of the landlords, and pursuing the imperialist war to a victorious conclusion. Both Bolsheviks and Anarchists fought to prepare October; that is, the socialist revolution.[19]

At the rank-and-file level, particularly within the garrison and at the Kronstadt naval base, there was in fact very little to distinguish Bolshevik from Anarchist.[20] Yet, it must also be borne in mind that in addition to ideological differences, there were important practical considerations that distinguished the two groups. The major emphasis of the Anarchist-Communists was on the immediate destruction of government and society and consequently they saw little need for organization and planning. The Bolsheviks, on the other hand, were directly interested in seizing power in order to establish a dictatorship of the proletariat. Unlike the Anarchists, the Bolshevik leadership (with perhaps some exceptions) had a very real concern for the future, for the party's self-preservation, and for its ultimate capacity not only to seize but to maintain power. Tactically, these considerations meant that it was often either unable or unwilling to match the Anarchist-Communists' almost total recklessness.

Modern Soviet historians almost completely ignore the role of the Anarchists in 1917, and they are perhaps correct in maintaining that the Anarchists were a passing phenomenon and had no future (thanks in no small measure to the Bolsheviks after they seized power). But it is unjustified to say, as do Soviet historians, that the Anarchists were completely insignificant during the Provisional Government period. The Anarchist-Communists and the Bolsheviks competed for the support of the same uneducated, depressed, and dissatisfied elements of the population, and the fact is that in the extremely fluid, unstable situation prevailing in Petrograd in the summer of 1917, the Anarchist-Communists, with the support they enjoyed in a few important factories and regiments, possessed an undeniable capacity to influence the course of events. Indeed, the Anarchist appeal was great enough in some factories and military units to influence the actions of the Bolsheviks themselves. Thus, for example, the Soviet historian, P. M. Stulov, describing the unauthorized activities of Military Organization members in the First Machine Gun Regiment on the eve of the July days, makes the relevant point that "the leftism of [Bolshevik] agitators is even more understandable if we take into consideration the fact that the Anarchists had great influence in the unit. . . . I. Bleikhman, Asin [sic], and many other Anarchist-workers were just as much habitual visitors in the unit as the Bolsheviks. They provided constant political competition to the Bolsheviks with their irresponsible speeches against governmental power generally, their advocacy of the immediate expropriation of capital, the banks, etc. The masses, in their class bitterness, grabbed at these slogans and didn't want to hear anything more moderate. The [Bolshevik] leaders, not wanting to fall behind the masses, did not always take the correct tactical steps."[21]

The First Crisis over the Durnovo Villa[22]

The headquarters of the Petrograd Federation of Anarchist-Communists was the Durnovo villa, located in the Vyborg District. Formerly the suburban summer home of General P. P. Durnovo, a high government official under Nicholas II, it had been seized by revolutionary troops after the fall of the monarchy. Soon after the February revolution the Anarchists began holding daily meetings and lectures in the villa, and here they prepared a steady flow of inflammatory leaflets and newspapers.[23] In the summer of 1917, the Anarchists shared the building with, among others, the district bakers' union, an SR Maximalist group, and an Anarchist-Bolshevik dominated organization which called itself the Soviet of the Petrograd People's Militia, while the grounds of the villa were used by neighborhood residents as a park and playground.

The Anarchist-Communists really made themselves heard for the first time in early June when they suddenly decided to procure by force the services of a first class printing press. On June 5 eighty Anarchist-Communists (allegedly led by Asnin), armed with rifles, bombs, and a machine gun, seized the printing press of the right-wing newspaper, *Russkaia volia*. Two military regiments forced the Anarchists to surrender their prize the next day, but this did not end the matter. On June 7, P. N. Pereverzev, the Minister of Justice, decided to eliminate once and for all the threat to order posed by the Anarchist nest in the Durnovo villa. He issued an order giving the Anarchist-Communists twenty-four hours to vacate their headquarters. The Anarchists refused to comply and appealed to Vyborg factory workers and soldiers to support them. The next day thousands of workers went out on strike; twenty-eight factories were left idle,[24] and several minor armed demonstrations took place in the factory districts. At the same time the Anarchist-Communists, augmented by the arrival of fifty armed Kronstadt sailors,[25] prepared to defend their headquarters.

What appeared to be an inevitable clash was averted by the intervention of the Bureau of the Executive Committee of the Petrograd Soviet. At its afternoon session on the eighth it delegated L. D. Sokolov to request the Minister of Justice to rescind his ultimatum temporarily.[26] In addition, the Bureau, after having heard protests from several Vyborg worker delegations, appointed Sokolov and I. P. Goldenberg to draft an appeal to the workers to resume work —this appeal was also to reaffirm the Petrograd Soviet's opposition to independent seizures of public and private property and the impermissibility of armed demonstrations without the express authorization of the Soviet. A resolution to this effect appeared in *Izvestiia* on June 9.

The All-Russian Congress of Soviets dealt with the Vyborg District emergency at its June 8 evening session. It listened to a report on the situation by the Executive Committee of the Petrograd Soviet and a supplementary statement by A. R. Gots and V. A. Anisimov, who had just returned from conversations with Anarchist-Communist leaders. Gots, a leading SR, reported that in addition to keeping their headquarters, the Anarchist-Communists now demanded that all socialists and anarchists jailed since the February revolution be released regardless of their crimes and that three major printing presses, those of the newspapers *Novoe vremia*, *Russkaia volia*, and *Riech'*, be confiscated and turned over to the Anarchists and socialists.[27] Not long after the conclusion of this report, Menshevik E. P. Gegechkori proposed the adoption of a resolution very similar to that approved earlier by the Bureau of the Executive Committee of the Petrograd Soviet, i.e., calling on striking workers to return to work and affirming the absolute unacceptability of armed demonstrations without the specific authorization of the Petrograd Soviet. This appeal was passed by a large majority despite opposition by Kamenev for the Bolsheviks and Lunacharsky on behalf of the Interdistrict Committee (a Social Democratic organization, headed by Trotsky, which merged with the Bolshevik Party at the Sixth Congress in July). A motion by Lunacharsky to postpone the eviction of the Anarchists pending an investigation by the Congress of its justice was also adopted. Accepted by the Minister of Justice, it halted government measures against the Anarchist-Communists.

In his memoirs Menshevik leader I. G. Tsereteli attaches major importance to the unrest in the workers' districts at this time and particularly to the failure of the Congress and the government to take positive steps against the suddenly active Anarchist-Communists. "The indecisiveness exhibited by the Congress and the government on the matter of the Anarchists," he writes, "reassured the Bolshevik Central Committee, while the unrest on the Vyborg side heightened tension in the capital."[28]

The Petrograd Bolsheviks Prepare
a Demonstration

For the Bolshevik party organization, which, as we have seen, was already exploring the possibility of leading a mass protest march against the Provisional Government, the sudden explosion of Anarchist-stimulated unrest was not at all unwelcome. Indeed, the situation suddenly appeared so opportune that the joint meeting of the Central Committee, Petersburg Committee, and Military Organization with regimental, trade union, and factory representatives originally planned for June 9 was hastily rescheduled for the evening of the eighth. The consensus of this meeting was that the prevailing mood should immediately be utilized in order to stage a really impressive soldier-worker demonstration.[29] No official protocol of this important gathering has been published, but an interesting contemporary account, the reliability of which is supported by a number of other sources, is contained in the published version of a diary kept by Vyborg District Bolshevik leader M. Ia. Latsis.[30]

The June 8 meeting began with reports by factory and garrison representatives on the mood in the factories and regiments with regard to the possibility of organizing a mass demonstration.[31] Representatives of the Military Organization pledged the support of several garrison units, though apparently even now there was some disagreement over the prospect of attracting broad worker participation.[32] According to Latsis, the gathering voted on three propositions: (1) was there among the masses a mood to rush into the streets; (2) would the masses go into the streets in the face of opposition by the Soviet; and (3) should a demonstration be organized? Latsis reports that the first and second propositions passed 58 to 37 with 52 abstentions and 47 to 42 with 80 abstentions, respectively. The third proposition, that of staging a demonstration, passed overwhelmingly, 131 to 6 with 22 abstentions. Thus it appears that a significant number of Bolsheviks supported the demonstration despite doubt that the prevailing mood was to "rush into the streets" and despite uncertainty as to whether the workers would demonstrate against the wishes of the Soviet.

Soon after this expanded meeting the Central Committee (with the added votes of three representatives of the Petersburg Committee's Executive Commission) formally resolved to organize a mass soldier-worker demonstration to be held at 2:00 P.M. on Saturday, June 10.[33] The scheduling of the demonstration for June 10 left very little time, actually only a day and a half, for planning, preparation, and coordination. This was to be the joint responsibility of the Executive Commission and the Military Organization.[34] The

June sixth and eighth meetings suggested possible slogans, but among other things there were security measures to be planned, rally points and march routes to be selected, appropriate appeals to be issued to district and unit leaders, and placards and banners to be constructed and distributed. This work was begun late on the evening of June 8 and continued the next day. By agreement all this was carried out as secretly as possible; thus there was no suggestion or mention of the planned demonstration in the June 9 issues of *Pravda, Soldatskaia pravda,* or *Golos pravdy*.

According to plans worked out by the Executive Commission and the Military Organization, the first public announcements of the demonstration were not to appear in the Bolshevik press until the morning of the demonstration. At that time *Pravda* was to carry a general appeal for participation in the march on behalf of the Central Committee, Military Organization, and Petersburg Committee. More detailed demonstration directives for both factories and regiments were to appear in *Soldatskaia pravda*. Because of this, the June 10 *Soldatskaia pravda* is of particular interest in respect to both the nature of the Bolshevik appeal for support and the precise plans and preparations for the demonstration.

Almost all of the June 10 *Soldatskaia pravda* was devoted to explanations and instructions in connection with the planned march. The front page bannered the news that:

> At two in the afternoon a peaceful protest demonstration against the obviously growing counterrevolutionary [policies] of Miliukov, Rodzianko, and K[erensky] has been scheduled. The conscious and organized segment of the military and the workers will take part in the demonstration.

And it appealed for the broadest possible support:

> Comrades! Those who are for the brotherhood of all peoples, those who favor an open and honest democratic policy for an end to the war, those who oppose the capitalists who organize strikes and who force the people to starve—all who are against the curtailing of soldiers' and sailors' rights and who oppose bourgeois persecution—come out and express your protest.

This front page announcement and a Military Organization editorial in the same issue indicate the tenor of the Bolshevik appeal. The pleas focused attention on all causes of mass dissatisfaction in the capital (boiling down the most complex situations into a single catchy phrase!) and placed the blame for unresolved problems upon the "greedy capitalists and landlords" who supposedly controlled the coalition Provisional Government. The Military Organization's editorial implied that increasing garrison troop transfers (at least partly motivated by the need to support the planned offensive) were solely attempts to weaken and even destroy the strength of the revolutionary soldiers,[35] and suggested that the "capitalists and landlords" were already contemplating taking from the workers "all of the gains that had been won in the revolution." The editorial continued with a demand and an invitation:

> The country is tired of waiting—the workers and soldiers demand answers to the basic questions of their poverty-stricken lives.
>
> And since there will be no answers as long as the capitalists and landlords run the country—we demand that all power be transferred to our Soviet of Workers' and Soldiers' Deputies, that a quick end be brought to the war, that hard-labor sentences and the declaration of no rights for soldiers be abolished, and that the capitalists leave the government.
>
> We protest the reorganization of garrison regiments and invite all comrades to join our protest; we invite all soldiers and workers to a peaceful demonstration at 2:00 P.M. on Saturday.

The editorial ended with the slogan, "War to a victorious conclusion against the capitalists!"

Detailed instructions in the June 10 *Soldatskaia pravda* specified the route and order of march for all elements in the parade. These directives are interesting to the historian in that they indicate the degree to which the demonstration was carefully organized with security a major consideration. All civilian groups in the march were to be protected by armed units of the garrison. Thus, for example, the order of march from Mars Field, the first of three specified assembly points, was: (1) Armored Car Division, (2)

First Machine Gun Regiment, (3) Pavlovsky Regiment, (4) the Executive Commission, the Petersburg Committee, and the Vyborg District, (5) Moskovsky Regiment, (6) Petersburg District, (7) Grenadier Regiment, (8) Porokhovsky District, (9) Liteiny District, and (10) First Reserve Infantry Regiment.

Throughout the day of June 9 the Petrograd Bolsheviks staged district agitational and administrative meetings. Although some military units and factories rejected Bolshevik-sponsored demonstration resolutions,[36] it appears that generally the Bolshevik appeal struck a responsive chord, and many thousands of workers and soldiers were ready to participate. Because the core of the demonstration appeal was transfer of power to the SR-Menshevik controlled Soviet, and not to the Bolshevik Party itself, even supporters of the moderate socialist parties were enticed into the movement.

Among important local organizational meetings held on June 9 were a late afternoon gathering of the Vyborg District Committee with representatives from twenty-eight Vyborg factories and four Vyborg-based military units and a Military Organization meeting in the quarters of the Izmailovsky Regiment at about the same time. Both meetings voiced wholehearted support for the demonstration. Interestingly, accounts of these gatherings suggest that the Vyborg District Committee and some elements within the Military Organization were hoping that the demonstration would develop into a decisive clash and were making preparations with a view to this possibility. At the Vyborg District gathering, representatives of the First Machine Gun, Moskovsky, and First Reserve Infantry Regiments emphatically reaffirmed that, the wishes of the party leadership notwithstanding, they would not demonstrate without arms. Even factory representatives stated that workers intended to carry whatever arms they had (which was probably even then enough to equip a small army!), a position with which M. Ia. Latsis was in full agreement.[37] The same mood evidently prevailed in Kronstadt. I. P. Flerovsky remembers that nobody at the naval base slept much the night of the ninth-tenth; the sailors "cleaned their weapons, quietly talked among themselves and awaited the morning."[38]

Although the Bolsheviks foresaw that the Soviet leaders would oppose their demonstration, it could be expected that the Interdistrict Committee and Anarchist-Communists would aid the party's cause. Thus it is somewhat surprising that the Interdistrict Committee was not even informed about the plan until preparations were already well advanced. The Bolsheviks only obtained the support of Trotsky's organization at a meeting on the afternoon of June 9. At that time the Interdistrict Committee delegation in the Congress of Soviets, upon the insistence of Trotsky and against the objections of Lunacharsky, voted to join the demonstration.[39]

The Anarchist-Communists were, of course, sympathetic to any activity against the Provisional Government. On the afternoon and evening of June 9, at a meeting in the Durnovo villa allegedly attended by 123 factory and soldier representatives,[40] the Anarchist-Communists formed what they called the "Provisional Revolutionary Committee." This committee was undoubtedly related to plans for the next day, though its precise role in the organization and administration of the demonstration is difficult to determine. There is evidence that the meetings in the Durnovo villa were attended by some Bolsheviks, but the exact relationship of these gatherings to the efforts of the Bolshevik Petersburg Committee and Military Organization is far from clear.[41] Some of the demonstration directives issued on June 9 emanated from the Anarchist-Communist headquarters. Thus an appeal to the Kronstadt sailors to participate in the demonstration was signed by M. N. Gavrilov, the alleged leader of the Anarchist-Communist Provisional Revolutionary Committee. The Gavrilov invitation reads: "A conference of revolutionary soldier and worker representatives sends fraternal greetings to . . . the heroic Kronstadt [sailors] and informs them that tomorrow, June 10, at 2:00 in the afternoon revolutionary Petrograd will go out into the streets so that together with their Kronstadt comrades they may present their demands to the Provisional Government and the bourgeoisie."[42] The official Bolshevik organization, on the other hand, sent parallel announcements directly to party committees apparently over the signature of G. Boky, secretary of the Petersburg Committee.[43]

By the afternoon of June 9, Bolshevik leaflets calling for a mass demonstration (the text was written by Stalin) began to appear in garrison buildings and in the worker sections of the city.[44] Like the editorial prepared for the June 10 *Soldatskaia pravda*, the leaflets catalogued the injustices of the prevailing situation and stated:

> Comrades, it is impossible to suffer these things in silence any longer. It is a crime to be silent after all this. . . . Workers! Join the soldiers and support their just demands . . . . Everyone into the streets.

Among demonstration slogans suggested in the leaflets were: "Down with the Tsarist Duma!"; "Down with the ten capitalist ministers!";[45] "All power to the Soviets of Workers', Soldiers', and Peasants' Deputies!"; "Revise the Declaration of Soldiers' Rights!"; "Rescind the orders against the soldiers and sailors!"; "Time to end the war!"[46]

The Congress of Soviets Opposes the
June 10 Demonstration[47]

Alarming rumors of the rapidly burgeoning demonstration movement first began drifting into the headquarters of the Petrograd Soviet Executive Committee at about 3:00 P.M. on June 9. Within an hour the information was verified and the ominous news relayed to the Provisional Government and to the Presidium of the All-Russian Congress of Soviets. The former immediately issued an appeal calling for order and warning that "any use of force would be countered with all the power at the disposal of the government."[48] By evening military patrols were on duty throughout the city.

To the Executive Committee in the Taurida Palace and the Congress Presidium in the Cadet Corps building, the sudden prospect of a Bolshevik-Anarchist led, massive armed protest march against the coalition Provisional Government was fully as disturbing as it was to the Provisional Government itself. Only the day before the full All-Russian Congress of Soviets had voted by an overwhelming majority full cooperation and support to the Lvov government.

Now the Bolsheviks and Anarchists were evidently calling on the workers and soldiers of the capital to repudiate that decision.[49] Only the day before the Congress had also specifically prohibited armed demonstrations of any kind without the authorization of the Petrograd Soviet. Now the Bolsheviks apparently had allied with the Anarchists to challenge openly and brazenly the authority of the Soviet to issue such an order.

Even if, as Tsereteli remembers, there was no doubt that "with the existing correlation of forces, the attempt of the Bolsheviks to seize power had no chance of succeeding," a second more immediate consideration could not but weigh heavily on the minds of the Soviet leaders. This was in part the same consideration that Tomsky and Vinokurov had raised at the Bolsheviks' Petersburg Committee on June 6.[50] "We knew that if on the streets of Petrograd there appeared a huge crowd of armed soldiers and workers with a demand for the transfer of power to the Soviets," recalls Tsereteli, "a bloody clash would be the inevitable result. The direct consequence of this demonstration would be corpses on the streets of Petrograd, the discrediting of the democracy unable to protect the capital from such eruptions, and the strengthening of counterrevolutionary currents in the country. It was necessary no matter what to prevent the demonstration that was being prepared."[51]

In view of these considerations, the Executive Committee resolved at once to take all possible steps to prevent the demonstration from taking place. It appointed a seven-man commission to formulate jointly with the Congress Presidium methods for dealing with the movement.[52] At about the same time Chkheidze, Gots, Dan, and Tsereteli of the Congress Presidium were drafting an appeal to the population for order and were preparing to bring the emergency up for consideration at the evening session of the Congress.[53]

Meanwhile, in the Kshesinskaia mansion, preparations for the next day were going ahead full blast. Reports from the districts were generally encouraging. The organization of the demonstration was coming along well not only in Petrograd but in the immediate outlying areas as well. There was also less comforting news.

It gradually became apparent that workers and soldiers probably could not be stopped from going out into the streets armed to the teeth and poised for a confrontation. In addition, in the early evening there came definite word of the Soviets' uncompromising response and the angry opposition of even the Bolshevik Congress delegation, most of whose members had not been apprised of their own Central Committee's plans.[54] Finally, apparently unfounded rumors began circulating to the effect that Kerensky had military forces on the way to the city to crush the demonstration.[55]

At 8:30 in the evening Zinoviev, Nogin, and Kamenev, who had originally opposed the demonstration, returned to Bolshevik headquarters from the Congress and requested an immediate meeting of the Central Committee, Executive Commission, and Military Organization in order to reconsider the demonstration question in the light of the Soviets' opposition to it. In the meantime other leaders of the Bolshevik delegation at the Congress and Lunacharsky of the Interdistrict Committee sought to stall the Congress from taking any action against the demonstration in the hope that the Central Committee would itself call off the move. Soon afterward a gathering which included six members of the Central Committee (Lenin, Nogin, Kamenev, Smilga, Zinoviev, and either Sverdlov or Stalin), six members of the Petersburg Committee (including Latsis, Tomsky, Slutsky, Boky, and Volodarsky), and two members of the Military Organization (probably Nevsky and Podvoisky) was held in the headquarters of the Petersburg Committee. After some discussion, during which all of the factors outlined above were brought up and considered, the question of canceling the demonstration was brought to a vote. Apparently fourteen of the sixteen participants in the meeting, Zinoviev included, voted in favor of going ahead with the march.[56]

It appears that even at this meeting the important question of arms was not decisively confronted. To use Latsis' words, it was still "hushed up" even though Smilga urged that "the party not reject the possibility of seizing the post office, telegraph, and arsenal in the event of an armed clash." Judging by his diary, Latsis did not think this at all a bad idea. He writes that he was "not able to reconcile himself to the majority opinion," presumably in regard to the ultimate results of the demonstration, and with Semashko, nominal commander of the powerful First Machine Gun Regiment, and Rakhia, one of the more radical Petersburg Committee members, agreed that the demonstration should be fully armed and supported by the First Machine Gun Regiment and prepared, if necessary, "to seize the railroad stations, arsenals, banks, post office, and telegraph."[57] It should be noted that there is no evidence that such plans were authorized by either the Central Committee, Executive Commission, or even the Military Organization. In his *History of the Russian Revolution*, Trotsky, taking issue with Sukhanov,[58] asserts that only "individual Bolsheviks . . . 'aiming a bit too far to the left,' " to use Lenin's phrase, viewed the planned demonstration as a direct device for the seizure of power.[59] In the absence of reliable evidence to the contrary, the historian is forced to accept this interpretation.

The full Congress of Soviets began discussing the planned demonstration at 12:30 A.M. on June 10. By that time the Presidium had already approved an appeal to the population, and Congress delegates had been sent to worker districts and military barracks to get a better sense of the situation and to attempt to counteract the Bolshevik propaganda barrage. At the Congress session Gegechkori, after reading the complete text of Stalin's leaflet calling the workers and soldiers into the streets, proposed the adoption of an appeal to the masses which read in part:

> *Comrade soldiers and workers:*
> The Bolshevik Party calls you into the streets.
> This appeal was prepared without the knowledge and authorization of the Soviet of Workers' and Soldiers' Deputies, without the knowledge and authorization of the All-Russian Congress, without the knowledge and authorization of the Soviet of Peasants' Deputies and all the socialist parties. It comes precisely during the uneasy time when the All-Russian Congress has asked the workers of the Vyborg District to remember that all demonstrations during these days can bring damage to the cause of the revolution. . . .

Do not do what you are called upon to do.

In this uneasy time you are called into the streets to voice a demand for the overthrow of the Provisional Government, the support of which the All-Russian Congress has just acknowledged as necessary. And those who call you could not but know that your peaceful demonstration could develop into bloody disorder. . . .

Comrades! In the name of the Soviets of Workers' and Soldiers' Deputies, in the name of the Soviet of Peasants' Deputies, the army, and the socialist parties, we tell you:

Not a single company, not a single regiment, not a single group of workers should be on the street.

Not a single demonstration should be held today.

The Bolsheviks and the Interdistrict Committee did not participate in the Congress vote on this appeal and it was passed unanimously. With little discussion the Congress also passed a Chkheidze-sponsored resolution prohibiting all demonstrations for a three-day period and creating a joint Petrograd Soviet-All-Russian Congress committee (Bureau for Counteracting the Demonstration) to check any attempt on the part of the Bolsheviks and Anarchists to proceed with the march. After the adoption of these measures the Congress session was adjourned and the operations of the Congress were transferred from the Cadet Corps building to the Taurida Palace, where communications facilities were better.[60]

The Central Committee Cancels
the Demonstration

Not long after these actions on the part of the All-Russian Congress of Soviets, the Bolshevik Central Commitee reversed itself and resolved to cancel the planned demonstration. Historical literature published in the 1920's and in the period since the death of Stalin makes it possible to reconstruct fairly precisely the curious, yet significant, way in which this tactical change (both Tsereteli and Lenin agreed it was a retreat) was brought about.[61]

It has already been noted that the demonstration was opposed by the Bolshevik delegation in the Congress of Soviets, which either for reasons of secrecy or because of an almost unbelievable over-sight did not know of its own party's plans. Evidently, not long after news of the demonstration became generally known, an emergency meeting of this group ended in a lively debate over what should be done. At this meeting Nogin and probably Kamenev supported a resolution in favor of applying pressure on the Central Committee to cancel the demonstration.[62] The majority of the delegation was furious over the failure of the Central Committee to take the group into its confidence.[63] It also felt that a demonstration in the prevailing circumstances could only result in the party's ouster from the Soviet and consequently in its complete political isolation—a prospect which must have appeared far from attractive. Because of this the proposal won easy approval, and as we have noted, Nogin and Kamenev, armed with this mandate, tried unsuccessfully to act upon the party to reverse its position.

Evidently, at about 2:00 A.M. on the morning of June 10, not long after the Congress had adjourned, Lenin, Zinoviev, and Sverdlov met with the Bolshevik Soviet delegation and listened once again to the arguments of Nogin and Kamenev against a demonstration. Again the question of canceling the demonstration was brought to a vote, this time with only five members of the Central Committee and no representatives of either the Petersburg Committee or Military Organization participating. In these circumstances three votes were cast in favor of canceling the demonstration (Zinoviev now siding with Kamenev and Nogin), with Lenin and Sverdlov abstaining.[64] Lenin's action, despite his technical abstention, cannot be interpreted as anything but a conscious retreat, as he himself acknowledged at a Petersburg Committee meeting the following day.[65] It is evident that, had he wished otherwise, this decisive and highly irregular vote at the early morning meeting of the Soviet delegation need not have taken place at all. Lenin had wavered at the brink and backed away.[66]

Word of the cancellation was rushed to members of the Petersburg Committee, the Military Organization, and other local civilian and garrison party organizations. The message was also sent to the

Anarchist-Communist gathering in the Durnovo villa.[67] The Petrograd Bolsheviks, many of whom were bitterly critical of the Central Committee's eleventh-hour reversal, now set about to put out the fire they themselves had helped kindle. In the early morning hours of June 10 Bolsheviks added their efforts to those of Soviet and Congress delegates who had been visiting factories and military units to explain the Congress position on the demonstration and to insure that there would be no outbreaks of any kind at the appointed hour.

At about 3:00 A.M., an order to halt production and distribution of "call-out" issues was telephoned to the editorial offices of *Pravda* and *Soldatskaia pravda*. In the case of *Pravda* a front-page announcement calling off the demonstration was immediately substituted for an invitation to demonstrate, and no copies of the original edition reached the streets. There is some confusion about what occurred in the editorial office of *Soldatskaia pravda*, which distributed several thousand copies of the original edition before substituting a one-page cancellation edition. There was an apparent delay of two hours between the time when the telephoned cancellation should have been received by *Soldatskaia pravda* and the time it was put into effect, leading to speculation that the news was initially disbelieved or disobeyed.[68] In the morning, when a second one-page edition of *Soldatskaia pravda* finally was distributed to garrison troops, the announcement of the cancellation rather pointedly freed the Military Organization from any responsibility for the decision:

> *To all workers and to all soldiers of Petrograd:*
>
> In view of the fact that the Congress of Soviets of Workers' and Soldiers' Deputies and the Executive Committee of the Soviet of Peasants' Deputies have banned all, even peaceful, demonstrations for three days, the *Central Committee* of the RSDLP cancels the demonstration scheduled for two o'clock Saturday. The *Central Committee* appeals to all members of the party and its sympathizers to make this decision a reality. [Italics mine.]
>
> Military Organization under the Central Committee

The general effect of the prohibition of the June 10 demonstration upon the Petrograd masses has been the subject of some dispute.[69] There appears to be no doubt, however, that although all factories and regiments agreed not to go ahead with the demonstration plans, a significant number did not comprehend or share the Congress position. "All night long, without a wink of sleep," reported a Menshevik correspondent in the *Izvestiia* of the Moscow Soviet, "a majority of the Congress, more than five hundred members, dividing themselves into tens, traveled through the factories and shops and military units of Petrograd, urging everybody to stay away from the demonstration. . . . The Congress had no authority in a good many of the factories and shops, and also in several regiments of the garrison. . . . The members were frequently met in a far from friendly manner, sometimes hostilely, and quite often they were sent away with insults."[70] Some factories and military regiments passed formal resolutions emphasizing that they were responding to the will of the Bolshevik Party rather than to that of the Congress or the Provisional Government,[71] and at some meetings even the Bolshevik leadership itself was subject to scorn. M. Ia. Latsis noted in his diary and reported to the Petersburg Committee that there were cases of rank-and-file Bolsheviks tearing up their party membership cards in disgust.[72]

Reactions to the cancellation were apparently particularly hostile within those radically inclined military regiments which first initiated the demonstration movement and in Kronstadt, where disenchantment with both the Provisional Government and the Soviet was the most advanced. It was reported, for example, that Semashko, who controlled the First Machine Gun Regiment, had publicly attacked members of a Soviet delegation as "liars who had come to stir up the soldiers," while the soldiers insisted that in any event "they would go out into the streets in a few days to crush the bourgeoisie."[73] In his memoirs I. P. Flerovsky, a prominent Kronstadt Bolshevik, remembers that at Kronstadt news of the cancellation was greeted with disbelief and fury and that the hours immediately after word of the cancellation was received "were among the most unpleasant" of his life.[74] At the Sixth Congress he reported that "inhuman measures" were necessary to prevent the sailors from responding to Anarchist-Communist appeals (as well as those of some undisciplined Bolsheviks) and immediately rushing to Petrograd.[75] Apparently only a suggestion by Flerovsky to send a two hundred man delegation to Petrograd "to survey the situation" served to calm the impatient sailors.

A bit of the unrest prevailing at the naval base at this time is mirrored in the June 11 issues of *Izvestiia Kronshtadtskogo Soveta* and *Golos pravdy*. Both papers published this announcement on behalf of the Kronstadt Soviet:

> At the present moment the Kronstadt Soviet is sending a delegation to explore the situation in Petrograd. . . . The Kronstadt Soviet of Workers' and Soldiers' Deputies calls on all military units and all Kronstadt workers to refrain from participating in disorganized armed demonstrations without the authorization of the Soviet. Do not obey orders to demonstrate not signed by the Executive Committee of the Soviet.

At the same time the Kronstadt Soviet Executive Committee authorized a count of all small arms available in the fortress and ordered that these be distributed immediately to inadequately armed military units, with any residue to be turned over to party organizations in the event of an emergency. The June 11 *Golos pravdy* also announced an obligatory meeting of all Kronstadt Bolsheviks to be held the same day (to hear an explanation of the cancellation by Smilga of the Central Committee[76]), and appealed:

> The Kronstadt Committee of the RSDLP calls on all comrades to remain calm and patient. Victory will be possible only when we will demonstrate in an organized way alongside the whole revolutionary democracy. All isolated demonstrations help the counterrevolution.
>
> Do not yield to provocations by the bourgeoisie whose interests are served by untimely demonstrations and their submersion in rivers of blood. Don't listen to individuals. Listen only to the appeals of the revolutionary organizations. Victory comes only to those who maintain patience and revolutionary discipline.

The Congress of Soviets and the Problem
of the Bolsheviks

After the threat of the demonstration against the coalition government was ended, the Congress of Soviets was left with the immediate problem of what to do about the Bolsheviks. The June 10 experience had revealed the gulf separating Bolshevik goals from those of the Congress majority and showed the inherent danger from the left in the prevailing unstable situation. The all-important question of how best to deal with the Bolshevik-Anarchist threat, however, found the majority socialist leaders hopelessly divided. I. G. Tsereteli recalls that this was the first occasion when discussions within the Menshevik-SR leadership developed into such serious political differences.[77] Simply speaking, the Congress leadership was split between those who viewed the June 10 experience as a turning point in the revolution and wished to take decisive measures against the Bolsheviks before it was too late and a faction which tended to minimize the Bolshevik threat or at any rate to shy away from precipitous action against Lenin and his followers.

Those two viewpoints first emerged at a meeting June 11 of a special commission, made up of Mensheviks and SR's established to consider methods of dealing with threats such as the one just ended.[78] Within the commission a bitter controversy developed over a proposal by Tsereteli, who argued that the abortive June 10 demonstration was a turning point in the development of Bolshevik strategy; that the struggle had been transformed from a propaganda war into an open, armed drive for power; and hence, that the only possible course was to disarm those military regiments and units of the Red Guard under Bolshevik control. "We cannot satisfy ourselves with an ideological fight with the Bolsheviks and verbal prohibitions of armed demontrations," argued Tsereteli, "but must at the same time adopt practical measures to make it impossible for them to conduct armed attacks on the democratic system." Tsereteli was supported by A. R. Gots, M. I. Liber, and K. M. Ermolaev and bitterly opposed by F. I. Dan, B. O. Bogdanov, and L. M. Khinchuk, who argued that such a drastic measure ran counter to the mood of the "revolutionary democracy" and would only play into the hands of the Bolsheviks. They urged that the Bolshevik demonstration plans be publicly condemned and that for the future independent armed demonstrations be prohibited. These limited measures were favored by a majority of the commission, but Tsereteli refused to let the matter drop.

Thus the controversy was renewed at a special closed meeting of representatives of all Congress delegations held about 5:00 the same afternoon (June 11), also for the purpose of determining what to do about the Bolsheviks. The meeting began with a resolution by Dan that the position approved earlier by a majority of the commission (i.e., that the Bolsheviks be condemned and future armed demonstrations prohibited) be adopted. He emphasized that those parties not willing to abide by the rule against armed demonstrations would place themselves outside the democracy and would not be allowed to remain in the Soviet.[79] Soon after Dan finished presenting his resolution Kamenev (in Lenin's absence) was called upon to explain the Bolshevik position. In answer to a question regarding the background of the demonstration movement, he explained that at the beginning of the previous week evidence of mass unrest was so great that after some discussion the Bolshevik leadership adopted a resolution to organize a demonstration. What's all the clamor about? asked Kamenev. A peaceful demonstration was scheduled and there were no slogans for the seizure of power. "All power to the Soviets" was the only positive slogan, and the demonstration was canceled as soon as the Congress requested it.[80] A description of what then occurred appeared in *Pravda* on June 13.

> Tsereteli is granted the opportunity of speaking out of order. From his first words it can be felt that Tsereteli is going to say something unusual. He is as white as a sheet and very excited. Tense silence reigns in the hall.
>
> "The Dan resolution is not suitable. Such resolutions are not needed now," says Tsereteli scornfully waving his arms. "What occurred was nothing other than a conspiracy, a conspiracy to

overthrow the government and to seize power by the Bolsheviks, who know that they will never come to power any other way. The conspiracy was rendered harmless at the moment we discovered it. But tomorrow it may repeat itself. . . . The weapon of criticism is supplanted by criticism with the aid of arms. Let the Bolsheviks accuse us—we now move to different methods of warfare. We must take weapons away from those revolutionaries who do not know how to handle them with dignity. The Bolsheviks must be disarmed. The technical means they have had up to now has been too great. It cannot be left in their hands. We cannot permit a conspiracy."

The excitement in the hall rises higher and higher. One of the officers present has suffered an hysterical attack.

"Mr. Minister, if you are not throwing words into the winds, you have no right to limit yourself to a speech; arrest me and try me for conspiracy against the revolution," announces Kamenev. The Bolsheviks leave the hall. Tension reaches its highest point.[81]

After the departure of the Bolshevik delegation, Tsereteli's accusations and his proposal for dealing with the Bolsheviks were heatedly debated.[82] N. N. Sukhanov, a member of the left Menshevik-Internationalist group; A. V. Lunacharsky, a member of the Interdistrict Committee; S. Saakian, an SR; P. V. Bronzov, a Trudovik; L. G. Shapiro, a Menshevik; and Iu. O. Martov, leader of the Menshevik-Internationalists, all rose to attack Tsereteli's proposals. Sukhanov criticized Tsereteli on the grounds that there was not enough evidence to support charges of a conspiracy against the government. Lunacharsky defended the Bolsheviks with the claim that only a peaceful demonstration was intended. "The Bolsheviks," he said, "have always been against Blanquist conspiracies." Lunacharsky, among others, agreed that an attempt to disarm the Bolsheviks would serve only to alienate the masses, who would view the step as counterrevolutionary. Saakian and Bronzov suggested that Black Hundreds had mixed into the demonstration and made it look worse than it actually was. Saakian urged that the Congress take the initiative in trying to reach an amicable agreement with the Bolsheviks.

Martov denounced Tsereteli's plan, saying that it would destroy the very basis of Russia's free democratic system. "Much has been said here about Bolshevik adventurism," he remarked, "but don't forget that you are dealing not with a small group of Bolsheviks, but with the great masses of workers who stand behind them. Instead of trying to attract these masses of workers away from Bolshevik influence, you hasten to measures which will create a gulf between you and the more active part of the proletariat. . . . Instead of applying force, shouldn't we tell the workers that their dissatisfaction is justified and that the Congress will speed up the passage of reforms in the control and organization of industry?"

The right socialists in the Congress, A. F. Kerensky, N. D. Avksentiev, S. F. Znamensky, and M. I. Liber, supported Tsereteli, as did A. A. Vilenkin, a delegate from the Fifth Army. Vilenkin argued that the front was in dire need of the machine guns now being used by the Bolsheviks to threaten the government. Neither the soldiers nor our frontline democratic organizations can adjust to this situation, he maintained. Liber, a Menshevik, also emphatically favored disarming the Bolsheviks, arguing that "the destiny of the revolution could not be handed to a praetorian guard recruited by the Bolshevik Party." "The absence of resoluteness on our part in this question," he said, "will only strengthen Bolshevik prestige in the eyes of their followers. The democracy must show the masses that it will not permit the settlement of political questions by means of machine guns in the streets."

Toward the close of the debate on the Dan and Tsereteli positions, Trotsky defended the Bolsheviks and attacked the moderate socialists for participating in the coalition government. After Tsereteli and Dan defended their positions, the gathering was adjourned so that delegation discussions could be held before any votes were taken. During these discussions the SR's and Mensheviks met together, and the Dan resolution was approved by a very small majority. Tsereteli and Liber, having lost all hope of winning sufficient support for their proposal, now expressed willingness to accept the moderate Dan resolution, and it was adopted at the evening session of the Soviet Congress on June 12.

The Petersburg Committee vs. the Central Committee

The effect of the June 10 experience in creating the first serious fissures in the majority socialist bloc in the Soviet was paralleled by its impact on the Bolshevik Party organization itself in the days immediately following the abortive demonstration. At the Bolshevik Sixth Congress in late July, D. Z. Manuilsky, a former member of the Interdistrict Committee, took issue with Iu. K. Milonov, a delegate from the Samara organization, who suggested that from the provinces it looked as if the June 10 demonstration had been organized in a conspiratorial manner by the overly Petrograd-oriented Central Committee, whereas such an activity really should have been organized on an all-Russian scale. Manuilsky commented that the Central Committee's organization of the demonstration did not have a conspiratorial character: "Excuse the expression," he said, "but it had rather an hysterical character. . . . One can't adopt a decision at 10:00 in the evening and change it at 12:00. Such hysterical decisions alone comprise our central organ."[83]

This exchange illustrates critical attitudes toward the Central Committee prevailing throughout the party in the aftermath of the June 10 experience. It may be recalled that Kamenev, Nogin, and Zinoviev opposed the very idea of an armed protest march and the Bolshevik Soviet delegation offered bitter resistance when suddenly confronted with news of the party's plan to stage one. On the other hand, as might be expected, the most enthusiastic supporters of the demonstration within the Central Committee who had not been consulted about the cancellation, notably Stalin and Smilga, were not at all happy when they learned of the party's last-minute reversal.[84] Flerovsky recalls that Smilga viewed the cancellation as a "great and baseless mistake" and believed that "Lenin, in agreeing to it, was not well enough oriented to the mood of the factories and the garrison." Significantly, in an explanation of the cancellation to the Kronstadt sailors on June 11, Smilga did not emphasize the justification for the cancellation, stressing instead the need to challenge the counterrevolution. "This question," he said, "stands before every worker and soldier; it demands not words but action. . . . For each of us at Kronstadt it is bitter and sad that the demonstration was canceled, but we should be proud, conscious of our power, conscious of having obeyed the requirements of revolutionary discipline in that Kronstadt did not demonstrate by itself."[85] Both Stalin and Smilga demonstrated their dissatisfaction by submitting their resignations from the party Central Committee, though these were subsequently rejected.[86]

Potentially the most significant criticism, however, came from the ranks of the Petersburg Committee. Indeed, the differences which developed between the Petersburg and Central Committees over the cancellation issue were the most serious of the whole February to October period. These differences emerged at a June 11 emergency Petersburg Committee meeting specifically convened for the purpose of hearing an explanation by the Central Committee.[87] The detailed published protocols of the gathering mirror the initial Bolshevik reactions to Tsereteli's Congress speech, the bitterness and independent spirit of the Petersburg Committee, and the strikingly different conceptions of the June 10 demonstration held by the Petersburg Committee and the Central Committee. Lenin's personal appearance in order to defend the Central Committee's action attests to the importance of the June 11 session. His report was the first presented.

Lenin began by acknowledging that the dissatisfaction of many members of the Petersburg Committee with the cancellation was fully justified. He explained, however, that the Central Committee could not have acted otherwise because of the Soviet's formal order forbidding the demonstration and because it was learned from reliable sources that the counterrevolution intended to make use of the demonstration. "Even in simple warfare," Lenin asserted, "it happens that scheduled offensives must be canceled for strategic reasons and this is all the more likely to occur in class warfare. . . . It is necessary to determine the situation and be bold in decisions."

Judging by his speech, for Lenin as for Tsereteli the June 10 experience marked a turning point in the struggle for power. "Today

Tsereteli gave his historical and hysterical speech," said Lenin, and "today the revolution moved into a new phase of development. . . . In his speech Tsereteli showed himself to be a true counterrevolutionary. He announced that the Bolsheviks must be fought not with words, not with resolutions, but by depriving them of technical means. . . . The workers must soberly realize," continued Lenin, "that it is no longer possible to talk about peaceful demonstrations. The situation is more serious than we expected. We were going ahead with a peaceful demonstration in order to put maximum pressure on the decisions of the Congress; this is our right; but we are accused of having organized a conspiracy to arrest the government."

For the future, Lenin appealed for "maximum calm, caution, patience, and organization," bearing in mind that peaceful demonstrations were a thing of the past. "We should not give cause for attack," he said; "let them attack us and the workers will understand that they are aiming at the very existence of the proletariat itself. But reality is on our side and it is still not certain whether their offensive will succeed: at the front are troops among whom the spirit of discontent is very strong; in the rear there is the high cost of living, economic chaos, and so on. The Central Committee does not want to exert pressure on your decision," he concluded. "Your right, the right to protest against the actions of the Central Committee, is legitimate, and your decision must be a free one."

Lenin's speech was followed by some supplementary remarks by Zinoviev. It should be noted that Zinoviev was the subject of special scorn inasmuch as his changed vote formally insured that the demonstration would not take place. In his comments Zinoviev attempted to justify his action:

> About 8 o'clock Friday evening [June 9] several members of the Central Committee, Petersburg Committee, and Military Organization gathered here. We already knew that the Congress was protesting our demonstration. I voted then in favor of the demonstration. Returning to the delegation, we met a fully crystallized situation. The whole delegation was unanimously opposed

to the demonstration. I surrendered last. We were given one hour to decide. We rushed here in the thought of finding members of the Petersburg Committee on duty but were unsuccessful and were forced to decide the question independently. There were five of us: three expressed themselves in favor of canceling and two abstained from voting.

"Even if what happened yesterday [presumably the widespread dissatisfaction with the cancellation of the demonstration] had not occurred," argued Zinoviev, "we still wouldn't be the losers for having called off our demonstration. . . . We can be sure our organization will grow."

Like Martov and Lenin, Zinoviev viewed Tsereteli's proposal to disarm and break up garrison regiments as a potential boon. He suggested that this would be "going from the frying pan into the fire—spreading revolutionary fire all over Russia." And Zinoviev continued:

> Today we are in a completely new situation. When we on Thursday, numbering 150 people, discussed a peaceful demonstration, we did not know that our demonstration would be so fraught with events. If you think the demonstration should not have been canceled, you will become convinced [that it should have been] by later happenings. Yesterday we walked gropingly; today the situation is clear; now everyone will understand why there is a struggle.

Like Lenin, he closed by acknowledging the right of the Petersburg Committee to censure the Central Committee, but added: "If you had been with us at the Congress you would have voted with the Central Committee."

These speeches by Lenin and Zinoviev by no means satisfied the Petersburg Committee. If anything, it appears that their explanations served to strengthen the feeling that at best the party leadership had acted irresponsibly and incompetently and was seriously out of touch with reality. The questions put to Zinoviev upon the conclusion of his speech illustrate this. G. F. Kolomin pointedly asked whether the Central Committee foresaw the danger of a demonstration by counterrevolutionaries. Zinoviev ignored the question. I. V. Kosior asked if any agreements in connection with the demonstration had been made with the Interdistrict Committee. Zinoviev replied that there was no agreement in advance, but that this was a mistake on the part of both the Central Committee and the Petersburg Committee. Nevsky focused attention on an obvious blunder by asking whether the Bolshevik Congress delegation had been informed in advance of the scheduled march. Zinoviev replied that it had not, but that this was the fault of the Petrograd organization. A. I. Slutsky asked the final and, in the eyes of the Petersburg Committee, most pertinent question: "What arguments other than private rumor caused the Central Committee to cancel the demonstration?" Zinoviev answered that private rumors were not a factor, the matter had been taken up with the Congress Presidium.

Now it was the Petersburg Committee leadership's turn to be heard and, among others, Volodarsky, Tomsky, Slutsky, Boky, Kalinin, and Latsis availed themselves of the opportunity. Volodarsky's speech has particular significance because he had been designated to speak on behalf of the Executive Commission as a whole. He began by tracing the background of the demonstration decision:

> The Central Committee [at the June 6 Petersburg Committee meeting] asked what the Petersburg Committee could say in regard to the mood of the working masses. We did not exaggerate the mood; we said: yes, there is a change and it is to our benefit, but there is no will to rush into the streets no matter what. . . . On Wednesday [June 7] the Provisional Government decided to evict the Anarchists from the Durnovo villa; there came the explosion of strikes on the Vyborg side; it was almost impossible to hold back the Putilov factory, etc. These events showed that enough inflammatory material had been stored in the worker masses. The meeting scheduled for Friday was moved up to Thursday. At this meeting the Petersburg party workers reaffirmed that it was not possible to place very rosy expectations on the Petrograd proletariat. The representatives of the military units made a more optimistic report. The Central Committee and three delegated representatives of the Executive Commission resolved that it was necessary that the demonstration take place.

We knew that the Soviet would take all possible steps to prevent the demonstration from taking place. . . . I emphasize that the purpose of the demonstration was to protest the growing counterrevolution. . . . We prepared for the demonstration all day Friday. At 8:30 in the evening . . . [at] an emergency meeting of the Executive Commission, Military Organization, and Central Committee . . . everyone saw things so clearly that the demonstration was arranged in such a way that weak units were protected by strong military units. . . . We knew that the counterrevolution might raise its head and we said, with two members in opposition, that retreat was impossible, that the scheduled demonstration had to be made a reality.

Volodarsky, for the Executive Commission, then directly attacked the Central Committee in these words:

At 2:00 at night the Central Committee voted to cancel the demonstration. I must add that this decision was adopted by three votes, of which two were originally opponents of the demonstration and because they were able to change the vote of one comrade [Zinoviev], they were able to decide the question in the way they felt was correct in the beginning. What changed in the elapsed time between the two decisions? Exactly nothing. I repeat, we took account of everything in making our last decision. Such a situation in our party must be considered immensely dangerous. The Central Committee acted hastily and thoughtlessly, but the question is when? At the time when it decided to demonstrate or when it canceled the demonstration? What should we do? The Executive Commission offers no concrete solution. It wants to hear district reports. We must answer three questions: (1) Was it necessary to cancel our demonstration? (2) Is a situation which permits the vacillations of one man to change all decisions permissible in our party? (3) What are our next steps going to be?

M. Tomsky, also a member of the Executive Commission, who on June 6 had appealed for a thorough investigation of the demonstration question before making a final decision, was plainly not satisfied with Volodarsky's condemnation. In his remarks, Tomsky, like Volodarsky, outlined the way in which the demonstration decision had been reached and ridiculed Lenin's assertion that previously unknown factors necessitated the last-minute cancellation:

> We didn't close our eyes to how a demonstration in which the soldiers refused to participate without arms could end. We knew that all Mensheviks and socialists would come out against us; we foresaw that the Petrograd Soviet and the Congress of Soviets would take the firmest steps against us. We were certain that the bourgeoisie would attempt to provoke us. Comrade Lenin said: We need to make use of the revolutionary mood of the masses, our task is to appeal for a peaceful demonstration in order to apply pressure. . . . When members of the Central Committee come to us and talk about the counterrevolution, I maintain that it is groundless. . . . We foresaw all: not Cossacks but machine guns doing the shooting. The experience of the Moscow uprising [of December, 1905] showed that the Cossacks are nonsense. To think that the demonstration would be peaceful was infantile.

Tomsky also brought up the June 9 early evening meeting and followed with an attack on the way the eventual cancellation had been decided upon:

> Upon the initiative of Kamenev, Nogin, and Zinoviev, it was proposed that we reconsider our demonstration decision. What were the motives? The Congress was against us; this we recognized when we made our original decision. . . . We were threatened with danger, but when didn't danger threaten? We considered the question very seriously. We said: We will move out and see. If the Soviet can smash our demonstration, we will be smashed. But it is better to be smashed than to reject a fight. . . . There is always the danger of being smashed in revolution. . . . Everyone against two, the Central Committee decided that the demonstration must take place. What happened after this meeting? The Dan resolution, Tsereteli's speech—but we can't accommodate ourselves to speeches and resolutions. . . . No matter how we disguise our retreat with the words that we are wise men, that we acted wisely, the fact of our retreat remains. Our Congress delegation, which through our own fault was uninformed about our grandiose demonstration, influenced the mood of the Central Committee. Is it permissible for the delegation to pressure the party Central Committee?

In closing, Tomsky summed up his feelings regarding the conduct of the Central Committee, emphasizing the damage that had been done to its prestige. "Nobody will deny," he asserted, "that the Central Committee committed a political mistake—it was guilty of intolerable wavering. It is not important that there is widespread distrust of the Central Committee; what is important is that the faith in the [Central Committee] leadership of those of us who are [Petersburg Committee] executives has been undermined."

The next speaker was A. I. Slutsky, Executive Commission member, who concluded in a similar vein: "I agree with Lenin and Zinoviev when they appeal for careful organization, but they did everything to undermine our organization by canceling the June 10 demonstration." G. I. Boky, secretary of the Petersburg Committee, continued the almost uninterrupted barrage against the Central Committee, focusing attention on the role of the Soviet delegation in the backdown decision. "On principle," he said, "the influence of parliamentary delegations on the leading organs of the party is intolerable." Concentrating on the basic problem of the deteriorated relations between the Petersburg Committee and the Central Committee, Boky suggested that the problem was not altogether new. "We all acknowledge," he noted, "the abnormal relations between the Petersburg Committee and the Central Committee but the Petersburg Committee is at fault in that although the question of the relations between the Petersburg Committee and the Central Committee has been on the agenda of several meetings,[88] it has not been discussed because our meetings are late in getting started." Boky urged that the question be considered at once.

According to the published minutes, the only three members of the Petersburg Committee who spoke out in support of the Central Committee's handling of the demonstration were V. I. Nevsky, I. K. Naumov, and M. I. Kalinin. Nevsky suggested that the cancellation was not unwise because it had proven impossible to organize a demonstration effectively in two days. However, he blamed the Central Committee for taking so long to respond to Military Organization appeals for a demonstration. Naumov, secretary of the Bolshevik delegation in the Petrograd Soviet, criticized the party for poor planning but pointed out that the cancellation had favorable aspects. He suggested that the damage done to faith in the party leadership was not altogether a bad thing: "Let it be completely undermined," said Naumov, "it is necessary to trust only in oneself and the masses."

Kalinin, for his part, brought up the perfectly valid point that the Petersburg Committee was "judging the act of the Central Committee from a narrow Petersburg point of view at a time when its actions had national significance." Kalinin defended the influence of the party's Soviet delegation. "The Congress delegation has great significance for us and it announced: 'your demonstration will force us to leave the Soviet, that is, our organization will become illegal.' If we had been convinced," argued Kalinin, "that our demonstration would be played according to the music, we should not have canceled. But we did not have this certainty. We were not even sure whether our enemies would be still before our power, while we knew that many of our comrades would be carrying rifles and even bombs. Such a demonstration could end very tragically. In such circumstances," explained Kalinin, "one must be very audacious and irresponsible to call upon the masses for a demonstration. In this demonstration, everyone was against us—we were isolated."

One of the most significant speeches of the June 11 meeting was made by the radical M. Ia. Latsis, particularly insofar as his speech presented a clearer picture of the degree to which the conceptions of the demonstration held by many Vyborg District party members differed from the Central Committee's proposed "peaceful march." Apparently addressing Kalinin, Latsis asked: "If the cancellation was correct, when did we make a mistake?"

> The mistake was made at the time we answered the question: will the demonstration be peaceful or armed? . . . For us [i.e., the Vyborg District Bolsheviks] it was clear that the soldiers would not go out unarmed. The workers did not look at this demonstration as necessarily peaceful. . . . The workers of the Vyborg side demanded that weak elements in the demonstration

> be protected by military units. They even foresaw the necessity
> [here Latsis is referring partly to his own activity] of seizing the
> post office, arsenal, and telegraph. Every active worker took ac-
> count of what had to be done. Everyone expected a bad outcome.
> *It should have been foreseen that the demonstration could de-*
> *velop into an uprising* [*vosstanie;* italics mine]. If we were not
> ready for it, we should have approached the question of a demon-
> stration negatively from the very beginning.

The last recorded speech before the adjournment of the meeting
was by I. N. Stukov, who echoed the blunt and bitter criticism of
previous speakers and suggested that a City Party Conference be
convened at an early date in order to discuss the intra-party problems that had developed. Tomsky supported this proposal and
stated that such a conference was also favored by the Executive
Commission. Evidently in view of this proposal the meeting was
ended without having adopted a formal resolution on the question
of the cancellation.[89]

Lenin and the June 10 Movement

In his memoirs Tsereteli asserts that the Bolshevik preparations
for the June 10 demonstration left no doubt that what was intended was an armed uprising aimed at the overthrow of the Provisional Government.[90] Indeed, as we have seen, this was the major
premise upon which Tsereteli based his plea to the Soviet Congress
for decisive measures against the Bolsheviks. N. N. Sukhanov, basing his account on information purportedly received sometime
after the October revolution, alleges somewhat ambiguously that
while Lenin was not aiming directly at the seizure of power, he was
ready to seize it in favorable circumstances—which he was taking
steps to create. Sukhanov asserts that fairly elaborate plans for a
possible coup had been worked out in preparation for the June 10
demonstration, even down to such details as the precise role of
specific military regiments in the overthrow and arrest of the Pro-

visional Government.[91] Other memoirists and historians have similarly interpreted the abortive demonstration, basing their conclusions almost exclusively on Sukhanov's information.

Gaps still remaining in published materials make impossible any definite answer to the question of the full scope of Lenin's plans in regard to the demonstration. However, it should be noted that in the significant number of documents and memoirs available for study there is little concrete evidence to support some of Sukhanov's contentions. It seems quite possible that Lenin left open the question of what the proposed demonstration might ultimately become. Moreover, it is highly likely that at this time Lenin's position regarding the goals of the demonstration was unclear in the minds of rank-and-file leaders, particularly within the Military Organization. But relevant published material suggests that at the Central Committee level the possibility of a coup d'etat was not seriously considered, and that, generally speaking, the movement was viewed as a test of the "state of mind of the workers and soldiers," to use E. H. Carr's phrase,[92] and as a means of applying pressure on the Soviet Congress to take power into its own hands. At any rate, judging by the Petersburg Committee protocols, it seems clear that if Lenin had more ambitious plans at that moment, they were unknown to many of those upon whom their ultimate success was most dependent.

Sukhanov's allegations notwithstanding, there are many logical reasons for treating cautiously the hypothesis that Lenin seriously considered the June 10 movement as a direct means of seizing power. Most importantly, Bolshevik strength and support in early June, although somewhat difficult to assess, was probably far from sufficient to maintain power even if the Provisional Government could have been temporarily overthrown. On the very eve of the planned June 10 demonstration the extent of party support among workers in the capital was the subject of debate among the Petrograd Bolsheviks themselves, while even within the garrison assured strength was not nearly as great as Sukhanov's hindsight analysis suggests. Moreover, the elections to provincial Soviets, army committees, and the All-Russian Congress of Soviets laid bare Bolshevik weakness in the provinces and at the front.

As will be shown more clearly in the next chapter, Lenin and other responsible leaders in the Central Committee were aware of these realities and increasingly conscious of the potential danger of a premature uprising in the capital. As has been noted, however, there were elements within the Petersburg Committee and the Military Organization ("aiming a wee bit left") who were much less cautious—this fact manifested itself during preparations for the June 10 demonstration and became more apparent in the period of rising unrest preceding the July days.

IV

The Rise of Unrest

The Congress of Soviets' Demonstration

On the evening of June 12, during the same session at which the Bolsheviks were censured for their part in the abortive June 10 demonstration, the Congress of Soviets voted to stage an imposing march of its own on Sunday, June 18. The originators of this ill-conceived proposal, Dan, Bogdanov, and Khinchuk (all Mensheviks), viewed it as a gesture of conciliation to the embittered Bolsheviks and as a means of channeling the widespread unrest revealed in the June 10 crisis into an expression of support for the Congress.[1] With this peaceful demonstration, declared *Izvestiia* on the eve of the event, "the revolutionary democracy wants to express its desire for universal peace without annexations and indemnities, self-determination of all peoples, and the preservation of unity in the revolutionary movement of workers, peasants, and soldiers."[2]

> Above all [urged *Izvestiia* on June 18], let this day show how futile it is for the enemies of the revolution to count on internecine dissension in the revolutionary democracy. . . . This fact [a united demonstration] will show, louder than any words, that in the struggle of ideologies no single faction or group in the revolutionary democracy will ever, under any circumstances, attempt to foist its views on the majority; differences of opinion will never take the form of a fratricidal war.

All factories, worker and professional organizations, and political parties were invited to help organize and march in the grand parade, for its success was dependent upon the broadest possible participation. All garrison military units were ordered to take part without arms and even provincial Soviets were directed to organize similar demonstrations in the other major Russian cities on the same day.

The Petrograd Bolsheviks and the Organization of the June 18 Demonstration

The majority parties in the Soviet, the Mensheviks and the SR's, agreed to take part in the demonstration, while the Kadet Central Committee recommended that its followers not join the march. The Bolshevik Central Committee, still under fire from some of its own membership (both left and right), considered and approved Bolshevik participation at a meeting on June 13. In the words of the Central Committee resolution, the Bolsheviks would attempt by all possible means "to transform the demonstration, against the will of the Soviet, into an expression of support for the transfer of all power to the Soviet."[3]

Zinoviev clarified what the Central Committee had in mind to the Petersburg Committee at an emergency meeting later the same day.[4] The proposed demonstration, he explained, would provide a "political means for applying pressure on the government." "We must create," said Zinoviev, "a demonstration within a demonstration." Not only party members but trade unions and individual factories and military units should be urged to march under the June 10 slogans plus a few new ones. Petrograd, suggested Zinoviev, "should be inundated with leaflets. . . . The time is ripe for the transfer of power to the Soviets."

The Petersburg Committee's initial reaction to this proposal was mixed, with some members voicing more than a little skepticism. Tomsky for one expressed doubts as to whether the party had the technical means to turn the demonstration away from the Soviet. "If the June [10] demonstration had not been cancelled," he added not without bitterness, "the Bolsheviks would be predominant in

Petrograd and would not now be forced to follow the Soviet." Other speakers were equally unenthusiastic. Stukov, for example, argued that the best expression of opposition to the policies of the Soviet would be not to participate in the demonstration at all. I. A. Rakhia suggested that G. F. Fedorov, a Central Committee member and one of the leaders of the Bolshevik delegation in the Soviet, be censured for allowing the party to be placed in such a disadvantageous position but in the end agreed with the majority that the party "should attempt to bring about a powerful copy of the abortive June 10 demonstration." The Petersburg Committee resolved to begin immediately preparing placards, organizing mass meetings, and publishing leaflets in the name of the "Central Committee, district committees, Central Bureau of Trade Unions, Central Council of Factory Committees, non-party organizations, and individual factories and military units." A previous mistake was rectified when it was also decided to delegate two comrades from the Executive Commission to coordinate demonstration plans with the Bolshevik delegation in the Soviet. After the passage of these resolutions a Tomsky amendment was also approved. It stipulated that all party members were obligated to march under Bolshevik slogans even if the factories to which they belonged differed. These Bolshevik intentions were made public in *Pravda* the next day. A lead editorial on June 14 declared that the revolutionary proletariat would go its own way, that it would participate in the June 18 demonstration in order to fight for the goals for which it had planned to demonstrate on the tenth.

In view of the Bolsheviks' announced intention of using the Congress demonstration for their own purposes, it was proposed in the Petrograd Soviet on June 14 to allow only slogans agreed upon by the Soviet organizers in the parade. Fedorov for the Bolsheviks, and I. S. Bleikhman on behalf of the Anarchist-Communists, scoffed at the suggestion, stating that their organizations would participate only under their own banners (Fedorov emphasized that first and foremost would be the slogan, "All power to the Soviets").[5] The right of the Bolsheviks and Anarchists to do so was not challenged further. A half-hearted attempt was made at the same meeting to call off the demonstration. However, most Menshevik and SR delegates still underestimated the strength of the radical left and the instability of the prevailing situation, and the cancellation proposal was defeated.[6]

Bolsheviks vs. Anarchists

The Anarchist-Communists, in the meantime, were making some plans of their own. It appears that almost immediately after being forced to give up the idea of a demonstration on June 10 the Anarchist-Communists, through their Provisional Revolutionary Committee, began to organize an independent demonstration for June 14.[7] Anarchist-Communist leaflets invited factories and military units to send representatives to emergency organizational meetings at the Durnovo villa on June 11, 12, and 13, and though precise figures differ, it is evident that these invitations met with a ready response. Even many rank-and-file Bolsheviks, impatient with the procrastination of their own party, took part in the Anarchist-Communist gatherings.[8]

For Bolshevik leaders seeking to mobilize radical strength for an all-out show of force on the eighteenth, the activities of the Anarchist-Communists, and particularly the drain they were causing in nominally Bolshevik ranks, were a matter of serious concern. Stalin, in a *Pravda* article on June 14, condemned the activities of the Anarchist-Communists as "ruinous to the workers' revolution. Our present goal," emphasized Stalin, "is to insure that the demonstration of the eighteenth is carried out under our revolutionary slogans. And precisely because of this we must suppress all Anarchist demonstrations in order to prepare that much more vigorously for the June 18 demonstration."

The question of how to deal with the Anarchist-Communists was one of the first items on the agenda of the emergency meeting of the Petersburg Committee on June 13.[9] Rakhia opened the discussion with a report on behalf of the Executive Commission. He announced that the Commission had received calls from many factories asking advice on how to respond to the Anarchist-Communist invitations. The Executive Commission's reply to these questions, said Rakhia, was that the invitations be ignored. In spite of this, Rakhia reported that representatives of 150 factories and military units attended the Anarchist meeting on the twelfth, and that a further session of the Provisional Revolutionary Committee to discuss the forthcoming demonstration was scheduled for 7:00 that evening. According to Rakhia, the Executive Commission had decided to send two people to this meeting in order to localize the actions of the Provisional Revolutionary Committee. He urged that these preliminary measures be approved and that the full Petersburg Committee determine ways of neutralizing the Anarchists and of preventing party members and their supporters from acting as delegates at Anarchist meetings.

In revealing the care and seriousness with which the problem was approached, this and similar discussions bear witness to the fact that in the chaotic situation prevailing in Petrograd the Anarchist-Communists could not be treated lightly. "The Anarchists are dangerous," said Rakhia, "because they can bring two or three thousand people into the streets and provoke a confrontation which would undermine the revolution and incite the counterrevolution." He declared, "If two or three factories go out on the street and there is bloodshed, all Petrograd will explode." Danilevsky agreed, stating that the mood prevailing among military units was at the boiling point, and that the Pavlovsky Regiment, among others, had sent representatives to the Provisional Revolutionary Committee and would demonstrate if called upon by the latter to do so. M. Ia. Latsis, chairman of the meeting and spokesman for the Vyborg District Committee, reported that attempts had already been made by the Vyborg Committee to call its people out of the Anarchist meeting; they refused to leave, he said, but agreed not to take part in voting. V. V. Sakharov, a Military Organization leader in the First Reserve Infantry Regiment, emphasized that the soldiers, at least, were unable to distinguish between socialist and other parties.

Many soldier-Bolsheviks, he said, go to the Anarchists and are astonished because the Bolsheviks do not support the Anarchists at a time when the Anarchists seem to be standing on the side of the Bolsheviks. Tomsky, although concerned with the Anarchist threat, warned against a complete break: "By fencing ourselves off from the Anarchists, we may fence ourselves off from the masses." Sakharov commented in a similar vein and supported the suggestion that an attempt be made to act on the Anarchists "from the inside."

Upon the conclusion of this discussion the Petersburg Committee resolved to counter the Anarchists by taking all measures necessary to insure that there would be no street demonstrations before the eighteenth, by requesting all district committees to get their people out of the Provisional Revolutionary Committee, and by sending delegates to the Durnovo villa "in order to make Bolshevik attitudes known to the workers there." I. F. Kodatsky, of the Vyborg District, and Sakharov were chosen to attend the Anarchist meetings.

Implementing this position, *Pravda*, on June 14, contained an appeal which concluded: "The Petersburg Committee considers it necessary to announce decisively that all uncoordinated actions of individual units of soldiers and workers can do great harm to the revolution. Because of this all demonstrations without the summons of the Central Committee, Petersburg Committee, and Military Organization are considered absolutely intolerable."[10] Whether the *Pravda* appeal or the Bolshevik effort to influence the Anarchists "from the inside" was more effective is unknown. In any event there was no Anarchist demonstration on the appointed day.

The June 18 Demonstration[11]

It would be a mistake to assume that only the Bolsheviks attached importance to the Congress demonstration. It is true that no other party attempted to duplicate the Bolshevik "blitz" techniques and also that many moderate Soviet leaders questioned the wisdom and particularly the timeliness of the demonstration.[12] But after the march had been scheduled, a major effort was made by the Congress as a whole, as well as by the Mensheviks and SR's, to insure that it would be orderly and proceed under Congress slogans. A special demonstration committee, chaired by Bogdanov and including ranking representatives of all parties, was established to deal with organizational and administrative matters.[13] This committee worked out orders and routes of march, an elaborate ceremonial, and in the pages of *Izvestiia*, June 15-18, issued a deluge of detailed march directives. During this period much attention was devoted to the demonstration in the Menshevik *Rabochaia gazeta* and the SR *Delo naroda*, as well as in *Pravda*. The Interdistrict Committee organ, *Vpered*, supported many of the Bolshevik slogans, while Plekhanov's *Edinstvo* exhorted its followers to parade on behalf of "strong democratic government" and "support for the Provisional Government." The far right *Malenkaia gazeta* urged readers to make known their will by participating with "appropriate slogans"; only the liberal *Riech'* continued to invite its followers to boycott the demonstration.

Ironically, most of *Pravda's* front page on the seventeenth was occupied by a slightly revised version of Stalin's June 10 demonstration leaflet, the one which caused such a furor when read to the Congress by Gegechkori on June 9. This time the appeal contained all the June 10 slogans calling for the resignation of the "ten capitalist ministers" and the transfer of all power to the Soviets, as well as such timely additions as "Down with the undemocratic sections of the Declaration of Soldiers' Rights"; "Down with the break-up of revolutionary units"; and "Down with the politics of the offensive"; all of particular interest to the all-important garrison troops. "Prepare for Sunday's demonstration," exhorted another *Pravda* editorial on the eve of the march. "Exert all possible strength so that our demands will resound loudly over the whole country. We need more than a walk, we need a review of our strength. We need a demonstration which would be of practical help in realizing our demands. Take things into your own hands," continued *Pravda*, "do not rely on anyone. Adopt resolutions regarding the slogans under which your factories and units will march and make your own placards. Work! Time does not wait!"

For the June 18 demonstration the Bolsheviks conducted a skilled political campaign in a country where mass political campaigning was a relatively unknown art. Untainted by association with the coalition government, the Bolsheviks could criticize and cajole at will. Their appeal was mainly emotional. To the garrison, the Bolsheviks said, if you don't want to die at the front, if you don't want the reinstitution of Tsarist discipline, if you want better living conditions and the redistribution of land, follow us. To attract the workers, the Bolsheviks demanded, among other things, higher wages, an eight-hour working day, worker control over the factories, and an end to inflation. In front of all, Bolshevik agitators raised the ugly spectre of the counterrevolution. The message was the same as that preached by *Pravda* and *Soldatskaia pravda* ever since Lenin's arrival in April, but this time it came in a continuous five-day barrage. With the addition of nearly one hundred experienced agitators (delegates to the All-Russian Conference of Bolshevik Military Organizations which opened in Petrograd on June 16), working through cells established in almost all factories and military units, the Bolsheviks were now able to blanket the capital effectively.

Few of the workers and soldiers who initially cast their ballots for the Mensheviks and SR's had a clear notion of their respective programs, and so on the eve of the June 18 demonstration even factories of which the majority socialist parties were most confident passed resolutions endorsing Bolshevik slogans. They would on occasion vote again with the Mensheviks and SR's, but for the moment they were either apathetic or flocking to the side of the Bolsheviks.[14] "Intense preparations for the demonstration are being carried out," noted Latsis in his diary on June 15. "Today we held a meeting of factory representatives at which a decision was taken to march under slogans originally prepared for the cancelled demonstration." The next day his entry reads: "The factories are cop-

Leaders of the Bolshevik Military Organization. Seated left to right are: K. N. Orlov, K. A. Mekhonoshin, V. I. Nevsky, N. I. Podvoisky, P. V. Dashkevich, and F. F. Raskolnikov. Standing left to right are: B. I. Zanko, M. S. Kedrov, V. L. Paniushkin, and A. I. Tarasov-Rodionov. (Museum of the Revolution USSR)

Nevsky Prospect, Petrograd, June 18, 1917. (Museum of the Revolution USSR)

ing with their strength. . . . How the workers have matured!" And on the eve: "The preparations are going well—mass meetings at all factories and military units are adopting our slogans."[15]

The trend toward the left did not go unnoticed. In a prophetic report to Kerensky dated June 17, General P. A. Polovtsev, commander of the Petrograd Military District, noted that "increasingly a differentiation in the mood of the masses can be observed. Dissatisfaction is growing because of as yet unrealized demands for more organization, because of the unsatisfactory distribution of provisions, inflation, inadequate quarters, and the still unanswered questions of increases in family allowances. Consequently there is a growing dissatisfaction with the Provisional Government and an increase in support for the slogan 'All power to the Soviet of Workers' and Soldiers' Deputies!' In this situation, in spite of all the measures being taken, it is not certain that the coming grandiose demonstration will not take undesirable forms."[16]

Sunday, June 18, was a clear, windy day—ideal parade weather.[17] It was already warm in the early morning, when crowds of soldiers and workers began assembling at designated points throughout the city, and promptly at 9:00, to the strains of the *Marseillaise*, the first elements in the parade began moving down Nevsky Prospect. The Executive Committee of the Petrograd Soviet and the Presidium of the Congress marched at the head of the parade; Chkheidze was there, and Gots, Dan, Gegechkori, and Bogdanov as well. At the tomb of the heroes of the February revolution on Mars Field, the Soviet leaders and the Congress delegates who followed them left the line of march in order to review the parade from vantage points near the tomb. They watched as long columns of soldiers and workers, several abreast, filed silently by, lowering their fluttering banners in tribute to the fallen heroes, only to raise them again as they marched proudly away.

The huge demonstration (it lasted until late in the afternoon) was turned into a clear indication of the attractiveness of the Bolshevik program and the effectiveness of Bolshevik techniques. District by district, factory by factory, came the marchers, over

400,000 strong, and all published accounts agree that the sea of Bolshevik banners and placards was broken only occasionally by Congress slogans. Many of the districts, most of the factories, and almost all of the major garrison military units, among them the First Machine Gun, Pavlovsky, Grenadier, Moskovsky, Finliandsky, Izmailovsky, Egersky, 171st Reserve, First Reserve, and Sixth Engineer Regiments, marched unarmed under predominantly Bolshevik slogans. "Here and there," remembers Sukhanov, "the chain of Bolshevik flags and columns was interrupted by specifically SR and official Soviet slogans. But they were submerged in the mass; they seemed to be exceptions, intentionally confirming the rule. Again and again, like the unchanging summons of the very depths of the revolutionary capital, like fate itself, like the fatal Birnam wood—there advanced toward us: 'All power to the Soviets!' 'Down with the ten capitalist ministers!' "[18] Another memoirist, who certainly cannot be accused of having a left wing bias, made a similar observation; Paul Miliukov wrote that the June 18 demonstration "showed again that in Petrograd undoubtedly the Bolshevik slogans and mood predominated and that even in a demonstration friendly to the government to speak of support for the coalition government was simply impossible."[19]

Among factories and military units from the Petrograd side marched a contingent of Kronstadt sailors,[20] the Bolshevik Central Committee, and many of the delegates to the All-Russian Conference of Bolshevik Military Organizations. By far the largest sections of the parade, those from the Vyborg District, began passing the reviewing stands in the early afternoon. They were led by the predominantly Bolshevik Vyborg District Soviet, and marching in full force between friendly factories and military units were the Anarchist-Communists. The only demonstrators to carry arms, they sang songs, blurted out short speeches, and waved black banners with the inscriptions, "Down with government and capital!" and "To the establishment of the commune!" as they passed Mars Field. From there, the Anarchists returned to the Vyborg District to stage the only really serious incident in what was otherwise a surprisingly peaceful demonstration.

Khaustov's Escape and the Provisional
Government's Raid on the
Durnovo Villa[21]

In its planning for the June 18 demonstration, the Anarchist Provisional Revolutionary Committee decided to outdo the Bolsheviks. On June 9 the Provisional Government had arrested F. P. Khaustov, editor of the Bolshevik Military Organization frontline paper, *Okopnaia pravda*, charging him with treason for his articles against the forthcoming offensive. Like most members of the Military Organization, Khaustov, an officer in the Seventh Army, had become associated with the Bolsheviks only after the February revolution, and as F. F. Raskolnikov recalled in his memoirs, "there prevailed in him an instinctive attraction for anarchism, for rebellion."[22] On June 17 the All-Russian Conference of Bolshevik Military Organizations passed a resolution calling for his release from prison,[23] and in the course of the June 18 demonstration several delegates to the conference approached N. S. Chkheidze at the reviewing stand, demanding that Khaustov be set free by nightfall. Chkheidze agreed to look into the matter and the delegation continued on its way.[24] In the meantime, at 3:00 in the afternoon, while the demonstration was in full swing, a force of Anarchist-Communists and armed soldiers (all told, a crowd of 1,500 to 2,000 men) arrived at the Crosses, the Vyborg prison in which Khaustov was held, and obtained his release at gunpoint. Emerging from the prison, Khaustov demanded freedom for several other inmates also accused of political crimes, and in a short time these were also set free. The Anarchists then left the prison with the escapees and presumably returned to their Durnovo villa.

Word of the jail break soon reached the Provisional Government and an emergency meeting was called immediately to hear a report from the Minister of Justice, P. N. Pereverzev. After hearing his account of the situation, the Provisional Government gave Pereverzev full power, not excluding the use of force, to recapture the prisoners and to arrest those responsible for their escape.

This order was carried out early the next morning. According to the official government report, at 3:00 A.M. on June 19, elements of the Preobrazhensky and Semenovsky Regiments, a Cossack Regiment, and some armored cars, all under the command of General Polovtsev and accompanied by Pereverzev and the Chief Justice, N. S. Karinsky, surrounded the Durnovo villa. When the Provisional Government's request that the Anarchists hand over the escapees and submit to search was rejected, General Polovtsev was instructed to occupy the Anarchist headquarters. The Anarchist-Communists resisted. Some bombs were thrown but they failed to explode, and Polovtsev's forces quickly captured the villa. All sixty of the workers, soldiers, and sailors present in the villa at the time of the raid were arrested and taken to prison. Some of the recent escapees, although not Khaustov, were among those captured. Asnin, one of the Anarchist-Communist leaders, was apparently the only casualty in the unequal battle. According to the results of an official inquiry, he was accidentally shot and killed while attempting to grab a rifle from one of the attacking soldiers.

The July Offensive

The Provisional Government's attack on the Durnovo villa helped to precipitate a fresh explosion of unrest among workers and soldiers of the Vyborg District. Developments connected with the beginning of the July offensive had a similar effect, and it is to this subject that we must now turn. A detailed analysis of the background and planning of the offensive, of its relationship to the common Allied war effort, and of the complex situation at the front resulting from the almost total breakdown of discipline following the February revolution, falls outside the scope of this study. Suffice it to say that the prime movers in the promotion of the offensive, among others the War Minister Kerensky and the General Staff, viewed the offensive as a means of restoring the fighting capacity of the disorganized and demoralized troops at the front and in the garrison, of restoring the nation's shattered prestige internationally, and of unifying the divided elements of Russian society behind the

Provisional Government. Though fraught with grave risk, it was a strategy that was advocated with varying degrees of enthusiasm by the Allies, by all right-of-center elements in Russian society, as well as by the Kadets, and it was a policy supported by both the Mensheviks and SR's.

Militarily, the purpose of the advance was to force the Germans to transfer troops from the western front, thereby helping to preserve the existing stalemate until the arrival of massive quantities of fresh American troops. On June 12, against some opposition (primarily that of the Bolsheviks), Kerensky succeeded in obtaining the tacit approval of the Congress of Soviets for the resumption of military operations,[25] and thus armed, he rushed to Tarnopol, the main Russian-held town in Galicia, to deliver the order to attack personally. With a maximum of fanfare, Kerensky informed participating troops of the operation on June 16, and the word was officially announced in the capital on June 19. The day before, June 18, units of the Seventh and Eleventh Russian Armies on the Southwestern front moved forward into the attack in the direction of Austrian-held Lemberg (Lvov).

From the beginning the response to the offensive at home and at the front was mixed. In Petrograd the news was greeted by a tremendous burst of patriotism on the part of the middle and upper classes. The Provisional Government, the Soviet Congress, all of the more important parties except the Bolsheviks, and all of the major newspapers (save *Pravda*) hailed the resumption of active military operations with enthusiasm bordering on delirium. "In this decisive hour," read an official Congress proclamation, "the All-Russian Congress of Workers' and Soldiers' Deputies and the Executive Committee of the All-Russian Soviet of Peasants' Deputies appeal to the country to gather all its strength and come to the help of the army. Peasants—give bread to the army. Workmen—see to it that the army does not lack ammunition. Soldiers and officers in the rear—be ready to go to the front at the first call. Citizens—remember your duty. In these days no one dares not do his duty to the country."[26] Such appeals notwithstanding, in a large part of the garrison and among factory workers, where the peace movement and Bolshevik influence were strongest, the response was one of either apathy or outright rebellion. A number of regiments and factories immediately passed resolutions, some of them published in *Pravda* and *Soldatskaia pravda*, directly condemning the offensive and demanding that power be transferred to the Soviets.[27]

What was true of the garrison was equally true at the front. At the outset the Russian advance (due especially to the Russians' numerical superiority, the careful artillery preparation, and the low morale of the Austrian troops on the opposing front) was astonishingly successful but at the same time ominous confidential reports from division commanders told of a general lack of will to fight, mass desertions, and collective refusals to obey orders.[28] In a coded telegram to the Provisional Government on June 24, a dejected Kerensky wired:

> With a tremendous exertion of moral pressure we succeeded in moving the army into the attack and in establishing during the first days a mood of breakthrough and enthusiasm. In many cases, the breakthrough turned out to be unstable, and after the first days, sometimes even after the first hours of battle, there was a change of heart and spirits dropped. Instead of developing the initial successes units participating in the battle began drawing up resolutions with demands for immediate leave to the rear so that only with difficulty was it possible to talk them into remaining in position and there was no possibility of moving them into the attack.[29]

For the most part, this gloomy picture of the operation was kept from the Russian public; throughout the last week in June daily official published war reports continued to present a rosy view of the situation. By early July, however, several days before the launching of a massive German counterattack, even official accounts suggested that the initial thrust of the Russian advance had been halted. The July 3 evening edition of *Birzhevye vedomosti*, distributed about the time the July uprising was getting underway, brought the disquieting news that Russian forces were everywhere under attack and suffering heavy losses. But that is getting ahead of the story. For the moment we must consider developments at the All-Russian Conference of Bolshevik Military Organizations which opened in the Kshesinskaia mansion on June 16.

The All-Russian Conference of Bolshevik Military Organizations and the Rise of Unrest

As with many other important aspects of Bolshevik Party history, relatively little attention has been devoted to the proceedings of this conference. These unique meetings, however, merit close study.[30] They brought together for the first time front and garrison representatives of the Bolshevik Military Organization for the purposes of determining the All-Russian Military Organization's leadership, structure, and program and evaluating conditions within the armed forces.[31] A preliminary message to delegates stated that the conference was "to work out a unified plan of action, to agree upon the most important questions of the moment, and to forge common goals so as to be able to act in one direction upon the whole army and to prepare the army for the future expansion and deepening of the revolution."[32]

One hundred seven delegates from Petrograd and provincial garrisons, as well as from military units on the northern, western, and southwestern fronts, participated in the conference. In his report to the Sixth Party Congress Podvoisky stated that these delegates represented 26,000 party members from 43 front and 17 rear units, while another conference participant estimated that 30,000 Military Organization members were represented.[33] Most delegates were rank-and-file soldiers, though there was a smattering of officers and a few civilians. The majority of the participants had joined the Bolshevik Party in 1917.[34]

It should be remembered that the conference took place during the tense period immediately before and after the Congress demonstration, the Durnovo villa raid, and the launching of the Kerensky offensive. Actually, it opened on June 16 and closed on June 23. Conference participants played a major role in the Congress demonstration[35] and were caught up in the spirit of that victory at the very moment when the offensive which they had opposed so bitterly began. Most soldier-delegates came to conference sessions direct from teeming garrison barracks, with rifles on their backs ready for action.[36] Many of them, as well as other rank-and-file members of the Petrograd garrison Military Organization, saw in the conference the very organ and vehicle for the seizure of power.[37] "We were forced to spend half of our time calming the masses," explained Podvoisky in his report to the Sixth Congress of the Bolshevik Party in late July.[38] Only Lenin's intervention on the morning of June 20 temporarily slowed the movement toward an immediate uprising. Indeed, the history of the conference is especially pertinent precisely because the July uprising was in part an outgrowth of the impatience, anarchy, and militant spirit exhibited there.

The substantive work of the conference began with the reading of provincial Military Organization reports at an evening session on June 16. These reports and discussion of them touched on such problems as fraternization, the relationship between unit Military Organizations and regimental committees, the successes and weaknesses of Bolshevik agitation and organization at the front, the offensive, and the difficulties posed by anti-Bolshevik repression. The reports and discussions lasted all evening. The next day (June 17) the conference listened to a speech by the usually restrained Zinoviev, who, apparently infused with the spirit of the moment, concluded: "We are now faced with death either in the trenches in the name of interests that are foreign to us or on the barricades for our own cause."[39] By this time the attention of the conference had already begun to center on preparations for the next day's demonstration and on what many viewed as the beginning of the final decisive clash with the Provisional Government. The excerpts below, from an article by A. Ia. Arosev[40] in the June 17 *Biulleten'*, mirror the mood prevailing in the conference at this time:

> Our Military Conference gathers at the moment when the whole of Russian political life is making a turn. Because of this, conference delegates are continually discussing and arguing about the coming demonstration on June 18, about the transfer of power to the hands of the Soviet of Workers' and Soldiers' Deputies. . . . Almost all of the comrades here report that they left their provincial organizations at a moment of vivid and clear protest against the usurping politics of the government, against the orders of Kerensky. Everywhere are heard the voices of comrade soldiers to the effect that the time for a decisive man-to-man fight for power has come, that the repressive measures of the Provisional Government have engendered the manifest indignation of whole military units and that it is silly to speak of . . . infusing the soldiers with will for the predatory offensive. The growth of Social Democratic organizations that has been observed recently and the wave of indignation that is rising higher and higher infuse the conference participants with strength and courage, filling them with eagerness and the strong desire for the final, great, tense battle.

The publication of this and similar articles in the *Biulleten'* is significant in that it reflects the broad interest within the Military Organization in immediate decisive action.

In order that delegates might help prepare for the Congress demonstration, no conference sessions were held on the afternoon or evening of the seventeenth. Thus the next meeting was not held until the evening of June 18, shortly after the conclusion of the march. Memoir accounts of the conference at this time present a vivid picture of the triumphant and rebellious spirit which reigned there, especially as earlier unconfirmed reports on the beginning of the offensive were verified.[41] The prevailing excitement was further heightened when it became known that F. P. Khaustov, having just been released from jail by the Anarchists, would be the evening's opening speaker. Neither the conference *Biulleten'* nor *Okopnaia pravda*, both of which reported Khaustov's appearance, discussed the contents of his speech.[42]

Khaustov's comments were followed by the continuation of provincial organization reports. A conference participant, M. S. Kedrov, remembers that "these reports seemed out-of-date as the ominous news had already come that the revolutionary army, obeying Kerensky's orders, was going to die for the glory of English, French, and other capitalists. . . . All delegates found themselves under the influence of the grand demonstration and the reports from provincial organizations were listened to only very sluggishly."[43] In his memoirs N. I. Podvoisky recalls that from time to time during this stage of the conference, "delegates from the Petrograd garrison climbed to the tribune to demand that the discussion of questions on the agenda be stopped and that the conference transform itself into an operational staff for an armed uprising."[44]

Very little documentary evidence has been published on exactly how the Central Committee and the leaders of the Military Organization responded to these demands. In his memoirs, however, Podvoisky writes that at an unofficial meeting of the Central Committee two hours after the demonstration he asked Lenin what should now be done. According to his account, Podvoisky told Lenin: "We have before us a chain of events which will undoubtedly require us to take firms steps; following the demonstration of its will, the masses will demand a demonstration of strength." Podvoisky recalls that Lenin responded by urging utmost caution on the Military Organization:

> Lenin pointed out that the proletariat had gained nothing from the demonstration. "It [the proletariat] must bury the illusion of the possibility of the peaceful transfer of power to the Soviets. Power is not transferred: it is taken with guns. The chain of events will be as follows: the bourgeoisie, recognizing the strength of our organization, taking account of the tremendous speed with which the masses are being involved, will not give us the opportunity of finally possessing them and will exercise all its strength in order to provoke these masses into a demonstration that would call forth repressions, that would break and divide them. Because of this we must concern ourselves with organization in the most intensive way possible, giving them a

definite slogan—the slogan of the impossibility of gaining power by peaceful means. It is necessary to give the proletariat instructions to the effect that all organization of its strength, in the final analysis, is for an armed uprising if not in days, if not in the coming weeks, then in any event in the near future."[45]

Podvoisky writes that it was from this point of view that the problem of the preparation of the proletariat was put before the Conference of Military Organizations. Thus the conference delegates, according to Podvoisky, were told not to play into the hands of the government by staging a disorganized, premature uprising but rather to *prepare* for a decisive clash "if not in days, if not in the coming weeks, then in any event in the near future."

The next morning (June 19), despite excitement in the Vyborg District caused by the government's raid on the Durnovo villa, the conference was able to conduct some formal business. Podvoisky gave a scheduled speech on the goals of the All-Russian Military Organization. Among other things, he stated that one of the main tasks of the Military Organization was "to destroy the permanent army and to arm all the people"; he also touched on the Military Organization's responsibilities for spreading revolutionary ideas to the peasantry. "Our goal," he said, "is to charge as many heads as possible so that they, going back to the countryside, will become spawning mushrooms, that organizational beginning with which we can win influence in the countryside."[46]

Nevsky, in describing the Petrograd Military Organization's development, got in a few particularly pertinent points on the need for better organization and increased party discipline. "At the present time," he admitted, "the Petersburg organization cannot brag about its organization. . . . There are regiments in which we have great influence but there is no formal organization."[47] Probably under pressure from the Central Committee, Nevsky emphasized the need for coordination of Military Organization activities with those of the Central Committee. He pointed out that although "the Military Organization had a special character" (i.e., that it constituted a powerful fighting force) and that although "the soldiers were in special circumstances [he was probably referring to the offensive and garrison troop levies, and hence the urgency of the military's demands], the Military Organization must be a component part of the regular party organization."[48]

Inasmuch as Nevsky's speech followed on the heels of the Congress demonstration—which was a vivid expression of both strength and organization in the eyes of most rank-and-file soldier-Bolsheviks—it probably fell on deaf ears. Nonetheless, it was a timely message. The next day (June 20), as the more responsible Bolshevik leaders appealed for patience, order, and the exercise of party discipline, representatives of the First Machine Gun Regiment, among whom were many nominal Bolsheviks, were already sounding out other regiments about the possibility of an immediate uprising against the Provisional Government, with or without the authorization of the party center. The rising unrest at this time must therefore be considered before the conclusion of the Military Organization Conference can be analyzed.

Mounting Tension in the Vyborg District

The Provisional Government's raid on the Durnovo villa, the imprisonment of the Anarchists, and particularly Asnin's death stimulated a new wave of unrest, similar to that which occurred on June 7, at the very moment when order and unity at home were of such desperate importance to the war effort. On the morning of the nineteenth, workers of the Rozenkrants, Metalist, Feniks, Staryi Parviainen, and Promet factories, all situated in close proximity to the Durnovo villa, went out on strike[49]—and crowds of idle Vyborg District factory workers and their families gathered at the villa to view Asnin's ice-covered body on display in the front yard. *Izvestiia*, June 20, reported that throughout the day a procession of old ladies, their heads covered with kerchiefs, came up to the deceased, crossed themselves, and dropped donations into a nearby box.

Representatives of Vyborg factories were sent to the Executive Committee of the Petrograd Soviet to protest the attack, the damage done to the Anarchist headquarters, Asnin's "murder," and the mass arrests. In response to these demands the Executive Committee immediately appointed an investigating committee, ordered that all of the arrested not accused of specific crimes be released, and called on the workers to remain calm and return to work.[50] At about the same time Anarchist-Communists from the Rozenkrants factory sent representatives to the Vyborg District-based First Machine Gun and Moskovsky Regiments with a proposal to demonstrate against the Provisional Government. The proposals were initially rejected,[51] but the threat of a demonstration became even more serious the next day (June 20), when a new element of more immediate interest to the garrison was injected into the situation.

That element was the reception by several garrison regiments of orders for weapons and men in connection with the offensive at the front. The First Machine Gun Regiment, for one, was given seven days to furnish 500 machine guns and on June 21 was presented with a "reorganization plan," according to which approximately two-thirds of its personnel were to be shipped to the front.[52] On June 20, the unit regimental committee resolved to comply with the weapons request, but a mass meeting of the regiment later the same day disavowed the decision.[53] Offensive or no offensive, the soldiers clearly had no interest in parting with their machine guns or dying for the Provisional Government; they based their stand on the Provisional Government's promise that units participating in the February revolution would not be disarmed or removed from Petrograd. Ostensibly in order to express opposition to the actions of the Provisional Government, the soldiers voted on the twentieth to organize an immediate demonstration, a decision in which both Anarchists and unit Bolsheviks took a positive part.[54] None of the speeches at this meeting on June 20 has been published, but Soviet historian P. M. Stulov selected the statement below from the archives as typical of the agitation heard increasingly within the regiment at this time:

> The government is bourgeois and the socialist ministers have become bourgeois. By means of war [the government] wants to destroy the proletariat. . . . Up to now [the government] hasn't

done anything. It hasn't even raised family allowances. You walk around like tramps while the officers receive huge salaries. The cost of living is growing by the hour but only because the bourgeoisie is stuffing its pockets. We must transfer all power into the hands of the Soviet of Workers' and Soldiers' Deputies and hold new elections so that only Bolsheviks will be in it. Then we will have immediate peace. We will take the factories from the bourgeoisie and then we will destroy them [the bourgeoisie]. Then bread and butter will appear at once. . . . If the soldiers want to pick their own commanders, the bourgeoisie yells "anarchy" but when Kerensky gives officers the right to shoot soldiers—that isn't anarchy. Comrade machine gunners! For the bourgeoisie you are fire! They cannot digest you—step in with arms. We will force the Soviet of Workers' and Soldiers' Deputies to take power in their hands. Don't believe the officers trying to talk you out of it—the whole garrison and Kronstadt is with you. You have only to demonstrate and there will be no bourgeois ministers.[55]

The same day, June 20, representatives of the First Machine Gun Regiment were sent to other garrison units to obtain support for a mass armed demonstration. *Novaia zhizn'* reported that two of the machine gunners appeared at a hastily called meeting of the Grenadier Regiment at 5:00 in the afternoon and won its support.[56] Soldiers from the First Machine Gun Regiment were also dispatched to, among others, the Moskovsky, Preobrazhensky, and Petrogradsky Regiments.[57]

This activity on the part of the First Machine Gun Regiment was soon reported to the Executive Committee of the Petrograd Soviet. It immediately sent the following telegram to all units of the garrison:

According to information received by the Executive Committee, the First Machine Gun Regiment has sent delegates to all units with a proposal to demonstrate against the Provisional Government. The Executive Committee's Military Section absolutely condemns the machine gunners' call, which acts against the All-Russian Congress and Petrograd Soviet and is a stab in the back of the army heroically and selflessly fighting at the front for the triumph of the revolution, the establishment of universal peace, and the common good of all people. . . . The Military Section calls on all regiments to remain calm, not to listen to any appeals by individual groups or regiments and to be ready to act at the first call for the Provisional Government, in coordination with the Soviet, for the protection of freedom and against the threatening anarchy.[58]

Apparently this pressure from the Petrograd Soviet, as well as efforts by the Petrograd Bolshevik Party leadership to keep the First Machine Gunners from rushing into the streets, caused the First Machine Gun Regiment to reconsider its demonstration decision.[59] On June 21 they elected to halt their activity and limited themselves to the following resolution, rejecting in advance future Provisional Government troop levies:

(1) . . . In the future we will send commands to the front only when the war has taken on a revolutionary character; this will occur only when the capitalists have been removed from the government and the government has been transferred into the hands of the democracy represented by the All-Russian Soviet of Workers', Soldiers', and Peasants' Deputies.

(2) If the Soviet of Workers' and Soldiers' Deputies threatens this and other revolutionary regiments with forcible dissolution, in response we will likewise not stop at using armed strength to break up the Provisional Government and other organizations supporting it.[60]

Parenthetically, it should be mentioned that unrest in connection with the Durnovo villa raid was not confined to Petrograd. Since some of the arrested were sailors, there was an outbreak of protest, at least partly in response to Anarchist propaganda, in Kronstadt. At a series of mass meetings on June 20, 22, and 23, it was decided that unless the arrested sailors were released, troops from Kronstadt would be employed to free them by force; an ultimatum to this effect was presented to the Minister of Justice on June 25.[61] The sailors also threatened to hold as hostages members of the Provisional Government commission then investigating the imprisonment in Kronstadt of former Tsarist naval officers. (The commission conducted hearings during much of May, June, and

July; it released a high percentage of prisoners to the bitter displeasure of the majority of sailors who were intent on making the officers pay dearly for the suffering and injustices of the Tsarist period.)[62]

Lenin, the Military Conference, and the Question of an Immediate Uprising

It will be remembered that the first Durnovo villa crisis was welcomed by all but possibly a small minority of the Bolshevik Central Committee. This was not the case, however, with the demands of left Bolsheviks at the Military Conference, the Anarchist-fomented unrest in the Vyborg District, the activities of the First Machine Gun Regiment beginning on June 20, and the ominous threat from Kronstadt. During this period Lenin and the majority of the Central Committee were conscious of the ever increasing danger of a premature uprising. On June 19, at the same time that anti-government demonstrations threatened to break out in the Vyborg District, the Provisional Government, the Soviet, and most of the newspapers in the capital were triumphantly hailing the offensive, as crowds of marchers waving patriotic banners had their day on Nevsky Prospect. It appeared not at all unlikely that a swing away from the Bolsheviks might be taking place; indeed, such a possibility contributed to the growing impatience of the radical left. At any rate these factors were among many that had yet to be digested and to which the tactics of the party would ultimately have to adjust. All this makes one wonder whether the decision of the Central Committee, taken at this time, to convene the long proposed Sixth Party Congress as soon as possible, was wholly coincidental.

Among other things, the purpose of the congress was to assess the party's strength and the general situation prevailing in the country, to evaluate the "current moment," to revise the party program, to prepare for the Constituent Assembly, and to elect a new Central Committee.[63] In regard to strategy and tactics, the proposed congress was very important, for it would provide a forum for debate between the more conservative provinces and the revolutionary capital, between the Bolshevik Soviet delegations and the party itself, and between the Kamenev, Zinoviev, and Nogin Central Committee "right," the Leninist center majority, and the "left" position of Stalin and Smilga, the Military Organization, and the Petersburg Committee. According to an announcement in *Pravda* on June 20, the congress was to begin between July 1 and July 5, that is, approximately ten days from the initial announcement. Apparently this did not allow enough time for preparation because a second *Pravda* notice on June 24 moved the opening date back to July 20. Also on June 20 the Petersburg Committee set the date for the opening of its important Second City Conference for July 1.[64] In addition to preparing for these meetings, the Central Committee now strove to prevent the unstable situation in the capital from exploding prematurely. This, stated very briefly, was the general situation when, on June 20, Lenin came to speak before the All-Russian Conference of Bolshevik Military Organizations.

M. L. Sulimova, a participant in the conference and a dedicated party worker since 1905, remembers "that on this occasion Lenin's outward appearance was calm. To those of us who knew him, however, it was obvious that he was agitated."[65] M. S. Kedrov recalls that addressing himself to "the spirit prevailing in some party circles to the effect that there was no point in waiting, that it was now time to seize power, Lenin came out hotly and sharply against such views. For a large part of the conference his views were received with disappointment or even dissatisfaction. The delegates of this group expected that Lenin would undoubtedly approve their 'revolutionary spirit' and 'leftism.' "[66] Sulimova adds that for these "hotheads" Lenin's speech was like a "cold shower."

In his address Lenin minimized the question of preparing for an armed uprising and concentrated instead on calming his restless followers. Below is that portion of his speech directed against the growing movement toward an immediate uprising:

> We must be especially attentive and careful, so as not to be drawn into a provocation. . . . One wrong move on our part can

wreck everything. . . . If we were now able to seize power, it is naive to think that having taken it we would be able to hold it.

We have said more than once that the only possible form of revolutionary government was a Soviet of Workers', Soldiers', and Peasants' Deputies.

What is the exact weight of our fraction in the Soviet? Even in the Soviets of both capitals, not to speak now of the others, we are an insignificant minority. And what does this fact show? It cannot be brushed aside. It shows that the majority of the masses are wavering but still believe the SR's and Mensheviks.

This is a basic fact, and it determines the behavior of our party. How can we push the petty bourgeoisie to power, if this petty bourgeoisie is already able but does not want to take it?

No, in order to gain power seriously (not by Blanquist methods), the proletarian party must fight for influence inside the Soviet, patiently, unswervingly, explaining to the masses from day to day the error of their petty bourgeois illusions.

The counterrevolutionaries want to break up this policy. By all possible means they are trying to provoke us into premature, separate action, but we will not take the bait—no, we will not give them that pleasure.

And when the masses see that the conciliatory government is deceiving them because it is controlled by the Russian and allied bourgeoisie and dances to its tune—and the events of the last days [the offensive] demonstrate this deception better than anything else—they will come to the Bolsheviks, the only party that has not compromised itself.

Events should not be anticipated. Time is on our side.[67]

No specific information regarding the response to this speech was printed in the *Biulleten'*. It would appear at first glance that Lenin was successful in attracting delegates to his point of view since on the subject of the "current moment" the conference passed a relatively moderate resolution fully consistent with his thinking. Point three of this resolution called for a firm struggle against the spirit of anarchy and against attempts at partial, disorganized mass revolutionary actions, which, if premature, could only play into the hands of the bourgeoisie.[68] It would be a mistake to assume, however, that this settled the question.

On the day following Lenin's address, that is, at a time when the offensive appeared to be developing auspiciously, the Military Conference discussed the question of the policy to be pursued by the party in regard to it. During the ensuing debate a moderate and a radical position emerged. Very generally, in the prevailing situation the moderates were against continuing to encourage isolated refusals to fight, either by individuals or units, feeling that this would serve no useful purpose and would only provoke reprisals. This position was fully consistent with the view of the offensive now advocated by the Central Committee. The radicals, on the other hand, favored total rebellion at the front, and, for them, pursuit of this aim was coupled with hopes for an immediate uprising in the capital. For this reason Lenin's evaluation of the "current moment," and particularly his position on the question of an immediate uprising, arose again during an argument on the offensive. An extraordinary record of a part of this debate was published in the *Biulleten'* on June 24. In this exchange L. M. Kaganovich and N. V. Krylenko[69] defended the more moderate "Leninist" position against Vasiliev and Shemaev[70] of the radicals. Kaganovich evidently initiated the argument:

> Lenin's speech is invulnerable, regardless of the aspect from which it is approached. . . . The people who do not distinguish between the situation existing before the revolution and [the situation] now are making a great mistake. The Tsarist government aroused against itself almost all classes of the population, and we had only to make our tactics conform to the established situation. Now we are observing something different. At the present time the majority of the population is following the SRs and the Mensheviks. And if this is so, then our methods of struggle must be different from the ones we used earlier. Propaganda—that is our method of struggle; we must inculcate all who can possibly be inculcated with our point of view. Only in this way can we insure that the [proletarian] class . . . will completely adopt our point of view. This is what we must achieve. But until this has occurred, the seizure of power by us can only result in a venture disastrous to the proletariat. The consequences of it can be a civil war, not a class war, but precisely a civil war— one which does not pit class against class but one part of the population against another.

At this point Vasiliev rose to present the other side of the argument. "What is worrying the delegates from the front?" he asked. "Undoubtedly, the events of the last few days, the unrest in the regiments, among the working masses, etc. To us it appears that Lenin did not clarify sufficiently the situation of the masses at the front. He did not point to a concrete way out of the situation which has been created. It is necessary to look truth in the eye," underlined Vasiliev. "The army at the front has been placed under the control of counterrevolutionary leaders. The offensive has the approval of the government. The army cannot look at these facts with indifference. Of course, it expects concrete steps from us. It seems to us that the Central Committee is acting too slowly. Apparently it isn't aware enough of the situation of the masses at the front." Vasiliev continued:

> What shall we tell the army when we return? What should be our course in regard to the question of the offensive? For me, a worker, one thing is clear: "It is better for the workers to die here on the barricades than there at the front for goals completely foreign to the proletariat." These words of Zinoviev are the best answer to my question.
>
> We must not be passive. Taking place before our eyes are government actions aimed at dividing the worker and the soldier, the army and the rear. . . . We must respond to this in a precise way. It is time we remembered that we represent not only socialism, but it should also be added, *revolutionary socialism*. And this determines our tactics.
>
> I will speak clearly. Our soldier masses are passive, they are used to the corporal's stick. This stick is now in the hands of the bourgeoisie. We must tear this stick from its hands and take it into our hands. Believe me, the front will support us. At the front the mood is not Bolshevik; no, there the spirit is *anti-war*. And that tells all.

With these words Vasiliev ended his contribution, and Kaganovich got in the last word. "We have come to the question of seizing power," he said, "but seizing power in Petrograd does not mean seizing power in Russia. Yes, and in the final analysis, in regard to the government question, even in Petrograd itself one does not observe unanimity. The Soviet of Workers' and Soldiers' Deputies does not support our position, and until it does, all our efforts will be unsuccessful. Our task is to apply pressure on the Soviet, to obtain a new election."

N. V. Krylenko, who tended to minimize Bolshevik strength during the conference,[71] ended the discussion by stating that only the mass refusal of military units to participate in the offensive could help the situation. "Isolated movements can only bring negative results. But in order that these mass movements occur," he concluded, "we must occupy ourselves with increased agitation for our ideas. And only when the ideas of Bolshevism are shared by the broad masses of soldiers can we turn from words to deeds."[72] Clearly the question of an immediate uprising was far from settled within the Military Conference, which ended on June 23—and it was not alone.

The Petersburg Committee and Immediate Revolutionary Action

On June 20, at the time when the Anarchist-inspired movement for an armed demonstration appeared to be spreading (though before the activities of the First Machine Gun Regiment became known), the Petersburg Committee met in emergency session to evaluate and deal with the prevailing situation.[73] The reports of most district leaders expressed the view that dissatisfaction with the Provisional Government after the launching of the offensive and the attack on the Durnovo villa had reached a new high and had infected many factories and units previously apathetic to Bolshevik propaganda. There were, in addition, economic reasons cited for the increase in dissatisfaction. For example, S. M. Gessen reported that unsolved labor problems in the huge Putilov factory were resulting in a sharp increase in Bolshevik support there. It was also reported, though with less unanimity, that among some sections of the population the apparently successful offensive had stimulated a distinct rejuvenation of patriotic spirit. As usual, there were significant differences of opinion within the committee in regard to the action that should now be taken. (At one point the debate seemed so critical that a member was delegated to find some representatives of the Central Committee to participate in the proceedings.)

Discussion of this subject revealed that there was a conservative minority, which, like Lenin, warned against premature action and emphasized the need for a patient, sustained campaign for increased mass support. Kalinin was spokesman for this group. He accused more radically inclined Petersburg Committee members of being "confused" and of "exaggerating the party's strength." "We must understand," he said, "that the Mensheviks still have a majority in the streets." In the prevailing situation, stated Kalinin, the party's task was to arm the masses and "fight for control of the Soviet."

There was also a significant middle group, which, though it did not agree with Kalinin's evaluation of Bolshevik strength and did not emphasize the need to win control of the Soviet, acknowledged the untimeliness of an uprising. Tomsky and Volodarsky, who belonged to this faction, suggested that decisive action should await the inevitable breakdown of the offensive, or at any rate a precipitant other than Anarchist-inspired unrest (Volodarsky suggested that another strike at the Putilov factory might be more suitable). Latsis evidently shared this view, though he was more pessimistic than either Tomsky or Volodarsky about the possibility of holding back the masses.

The protocols of this meeting reveal that opposed to the conservative and middle groups were some much more radically inclined Petrograd Bolsheviks, who clearly were not immune to the spirit of restlessness and impatience prevailing among the masses. For example, I. K. Naumov severely criticized the party for "an absence of leadership" and urged that the Bolsheviks present the Soviet with an ultimatum: either take power or the Bolsheviks will be duty-bound to take command of the developing movement. "We will testify to our own political bankruptcy if we avoid taking political action. . . .

The temporizing policy of the Central Committee," claimed Naumov, "cannot withstand criticism."

Others, like I. N. Stukov, A. Dylle, and P. A. Zalutsky, tended to view the offensive as a turning point in the revolution. Stukov stated that with the beginning of the counterrevolutionary offensive the revolution and counterrevolution had reached the point at which a clash was inevitable. The revolution had been challenged, he said, and had to rise to meet the challenge. Since the provinces evidently did not share the revolutionary spirit of the capital, Stukov suggested "that the possibility of repeating the history of the Paris Commune of 1871 not be overlooked." Dylle disagreed with Kalinin's estimate of Bolshevik strength and urged that the party "organize itself to assume leadership of the developing movement." "We must act apart from the Congress, or the masses will act without us. . . . In revolutionary times," he explained, "we cannot act by parliamentary means." Zalutsky suggested that the time for revolutionary action might indeed be ripe but that the question could not be decided at that meeting. He added that if the soldiers were rushing into the streets, they should be encouraged to go to other regiments not yet so inclined in order to win their support.

Upon the conclusion of this discussion the Petersburg Committee, by a vote of 19 to 2, passed a resolution sponsored by Volodarsky and Tomsky authorizing the Executive Commission, in conjunction with the Military Organization and the Central Committee, to draw up an appeal calling on the proletariat not to participate in isolated revolutionary actions and to exert all efforts toward winning increased influence among other classes of the population. This was a measure fully consistent with the Central Committee's opposition to the developing movement. An amendment proposed by Latsis and carried 12 to 9 was not; it stipulated that "if it proved impossible to hold back the masses, the party should take the movement into its own hands and use it to apply pressure on the Soviet and Congress of Soviets." Ostensibly, the purpose of this amendment was to insure that the Volodarsky-

Tomsky resolution would not prevent the Petersburg Committee and particularly the Vyborg Committee from assuming control of the demonstration movement if it could not be contained. But its effect was to justify and encourage the actions of radical leaders like Latsis, Naumov, Dylle, and Stukov, and the many more rank-and-file party members at the district and unit levels who already considered an early uprising inevitable and desirable.

The Petrograd Military Organization
and the Question of an Uprising

It has already been suggested that among unit level leaders of the Petrograd Military Organization, sentiment at this time was heavily in favor of immediate direct action against the Provisional Government. It has also been noted that the decisions taken on this point by the Petersburg Committee on June 20, and by the All-Russian Military Conference on June 21, were, to say the least, indecisive. On June 22 the problems of the garrison in the prevailing situation were the focus of attention at an unofficial meeting of the Central Committee, Petersburg Committee, and Military Organization. There is evidence that this meeting was called by the Military Organization in order to assess the possibility of an armed demonstration against the Provisional Government.[74] The absence of many Central Committee and Petersburg Committee members made impossible the convening of an official meeting, but representatives of all the "Bolshevik" regiments were in attendance. (Among those present were soldiers from the First Machine Gun, Sixth Engineer, 180th Reserve Infantry, First and Third Reserve Infantry, Egersky, and Grenadier Regiments.)[75] Thus, despite its informality, the gathering is not without interest.

The only subject on the meeting's agenda was the "current moment," and in this connection the first and major problem discussed was that of the recent garrison troop levies. Two of the most influential unit level leaders, Semashko of the First Machine Gun Regiment and Sakharov of the First Reserve Infantry Regiment, voiced the apparently widely held view that the recent troop requisitions were merely thinly disguised attempts to break up the more revolutionary regiments. At any rate, both speakers emphasized that because of the Provisional Government's guarantees to regiments participating in the February revolution the orders were illegal and should by no means be fulfilled. This categorical position was supported by Beliakov, a representative of the Military Organization All-Russian Bureau, as well as by a number of other speakers.

The statements of Petrograd Military Organization unit leaders on the question of garrison levies are especially interesting because they reveal the wide gulf between their evaluation of the "current moment" and that of the Central Committee, particularly in regard to the party's weakness and the need for restraint. With but one exception, all of the speakers representing the regiments emphasized the enormous power now at the party's disposal. Semashko, *de facto* commander of over fifteen thousand machine gunners, evidently spoke for the majority when he said that the Petersburg and Central Committees lacked "a clear understanding" of the party's strength. He declared, "Almost the whole garrison is with us."[76] "In general," observed Sakharov, "the speeches of the soldiers boil down to the fact that they all demand active operations and are against limiting themselves to resolutions. The soldiers say these lead nowhere." Among Military Organization unit representatives only M. M. Lashevich, an old Bolshevik and non-commissioned officer in the First Machine Gun Regiment who was a member of the Petrograd Soviet, spoke in support of the Central Committee position. "We must now be especially careful and restrained in our tactics," he argued, "but in the speeches of the last few days this is precisely what is missing. Frequently," said Lashevich, not without sarcasm, "it is impossible to make out where the Bolshevik ends and the Anarchist begins."

Within the Military Organization such notions were not very popular. Beliakov termed Lashevich's position "surprising." For him the unrest in the regiments and the activities of soldier-Bolsheviks were no cause for alarm: "In my view the political crisis is liquidating itself in our favor. I maintain that the ferment in the regiments is only consciousness of the turning point." It should be noted that these attitudes were encouraged during the discussion by at least a few members of the Petersburg Committee, apparently unrestrained by the decision reached by the committee two days earlier. For example, Stukov again came out strongly for action, implying that a successful offensive would serve to strengthen the hand of the Provisional Government. "The policy of containing the masses," he asserted, "is no longer satisfactory." Another Petersburg Committee member, M. M. Kharitonov, explained that it was hard to tell where the Bolshevik ended and the Anarchist began because included among the party's followers were sympathizers who did not subscribe to Bolshevik theory. Kharitonov suggested that restraint was all well and good, but that concessions were impossible. Adding fuel to the fire, he stated: "We must be ready to fight even when we do not wish to."

The published protocols of this meeting break off rather abruptly. As far as they go, these minutes contain no evidence of any actual resolution on the "current moment," and it is conceivable that this unofficial gathering did not attempt to arrive at a formal consensus. According to V. I. Nevsky, however, the meeting was ultimately quite significant. In an article prepared for the fifth anniversary of the October revolution Nevsky wrote that "on June 22 we were able to convene a conference, at which it was ascertained that up to thirty thousand soldiers were organized. The organization was growing all the time but at the same time we could see that it would be impossible to restrain the soldiers from revolutionary action [*vystuplenie*]. And we took upon ourselves the working out of a plan for an armed movement: Let it be, we decided, the first attempt at an uprising [*vosstanie*]."[77]

Pravda and *Soldatskaia pravda* Diverge

The divergence between the Central Committee and the Military Organization in their estimate of the revolutionary situation and of the party's strength was reflected in their respective organs, *Pravda* and *Soldatskaia pravda*. *Pravda* was under Lenin's strict control at this time. For practical purposes, *Soldatskaia pravda*, headed by Podvoisky, Nevsky, and A. F. Ilin-Zhenevsky, enjoyed virtual autonomy. Differences between the two newspapers were some-times ones of emphasis—often what was not said was as important as what was said—but these differences were nonetheless significant. Indeed, upon close analysis *Pravda's* relatively cautious approach in the days immediately following the launching of the offensive con-trasts rather sharply with the unrestrained tone of *Soldatskaia pravda*.

Lenin's attitude toward the "current situation" in the immediate aftermath of the apparently successful July offensive and in the face of the stubborn refusal of the Soviet to take power was ex-pressed on June 21 in a lead *Pravda* editorial, "The Revolution, the Offensive, and Our Party."[78] Here Lenin repeated some of the arguments presented privately to the morning session of the Con-ference of Military Organizations a day earlier. "The faith of the majority of the masses in the petty bourgeois policies of the Men-sheviks and SR's," he explained, "determines our position and the behavior of our party." Russia, said Lenin, was passing through a stage in the revolution when the people were still under the influ-ence of "petty bourgeois illusions" propagated by the "Tseretelis and Chernovs." It was a state, he implied, that could only be over-come gradually, presumably by patient exposure of government policy. In this article Lenin specifically cautioned against "absurd" faith in uncoordinated, disorganized revolutionary action and while he did not predict how soon this period would end, in another *Pravda* editorial the next day, titled "To What State Have the So-cialist Revolutionaries Brought the Revolution?" he suggested that it might not last long. It is worth noting that Lenin's apparent lack of interest in the immediate seizure of power at this time can easily be overemphasized. Basically, Lenin's concern in this regard was undoubtedly that of timing, but precisely for this reason his imme-diate objective was to preserve the *status quo*.

From this time until the July days, *Pravda's* line was generally consistent with Lenin's position.[79] By and large, immediately in-flammatory material was toned down and kept to a minimum, and attention was focused on preparations for the Sixth Party Congress, the elections to the Constituent Assembly, and the need for a mass campaign to win control of the Petrograd Soviet. This approach was continued in the last days of June, when Lenin left the capital for a few days of rest at the summer home of V. D. Bonch-Bruevich in Finland. On June 30 and July 1, for example, lead editorials in *Pravda*, the former by Zinoviev, called for a new mass, "to-the-people" movement of Petrograd workers and soldiers to stimulate Bolshevik support among the peasantry prior to the Constituent Assembly elections. This is not to say that pressure on the Provi-sional Government and the moderate socialist parties, particularly in connection with the offensive, was not maintained, but only that on the surface at least, the emphasis was on peaceful forms of struggle.

Interestingly, *Pravda* bears witness to the fact that momentarily Lenin's tactical position now resembled that of the right wing of the party. Indeed, an attack by Kamenev on the party's left faction in the June 22 *Pravda* (it was entitled "Not So Simple, Comrades") could well have been written at this time by Lenin himself. In his article Kamenev referred to demands from soldiers and workers "new to our party" for the "immediate realization of slogans, whose complexities they are not always able to understand. To them we say, the situation is not so simple that your sympathy for our party is enough for its immediate victory. The tasks before the proletariat are many times more difficult than they may seem." Like Lenin, Kamenev emphasized the party's weakness in the prevailing situa-tion. He wrote that "the majority of the Russian democracy does not have faith in the world proletariat and the world proletarian revolution; it believes," he added, "in the diplomats, the General Staff, and 'socialist agents' of imperialist governments, and it en-trusts its hopes to them." Kamenev suggested that nobody could say how long this would last, but, like Lenin, he warned against untimely revolutionary action. "Uncoordinated demonstrations of individual regiments and companies attempting to eliminate the unavoidable petty bourgeois stage by means of sabotage are foolish and inexpedient. . . . The proletariat will prepare for the new stage in the revolution," concluded Kamenev, "not by anarchistic demonstrations and disorganized partial endeavors, but through renewed organizational work and unity."

Turning now to *Soldatskaia pravda*, it should be noted that in the stormy period immediately after the attack on the Durnovo villa and the beginning of the offensive, it, too, came out against "disorganized demonstrations." A front-page proclamation on June 21, for example, called on workers and soldiers to ignore appeals to demonstrate issued without authorization of the Military Organization. However, this announcement left the door open for a Bolshevik-led demonstration by stating that "in the event of necessity, the Military Organization would call for a demonstration in agreement with the Central and Petersburg Committees." Moreover, nowhere in either the June 21 or June 22 issue, or in any subsequent issues prior to the July days, was there the sort of emphasis contained in *Pravda* on basic Bolshevik weaknesses and on the need to overcome the phase of "petty bourgeois illusions" before proceeding to the next stage in the revolution. The closest *Soldatskaia pravda* came to this was on June 23, in an article entitled "Organization Before All," but even here major emphasis was on the inadvisability of disorganized revolutionary action and on the need for verification of appeals made on behalf of the Military Organization.

Between June 23 and the outbreak of the July days there were no articles whatever supporting the Central Committee's policy of caution. To the contrary, throughout this period *Soldatskaia pravda* continued to fan the flames of discontent, now centering anti-government propaganda on the injustices of the offensive. On June 26, when deserters from the frontline Grenadier Regiment, one of several units that had refused to advance against the Germans during the first days of the offensive,[80] arrived in the capital appealing for help and demanding the transfer of power to the Soviets,

Soldatskaia pravda pledged them full support.[81] And most important, *Soldatskaia pravda*'s implied solution to the many problems connected with the war was still direct action. Thus, on the very eve of the July days (indeed, after organization of the movement had already begun), at a time when *Pravda* was focusing attention on Zinoviev's grass roots propaganda campaign and on the campaign to win control of the Petrograd Soviet, *Soldatskaia pravda* published an inflammatory front-page article by L. Chubunov, which concluded:

> Comrades! Enough of sacrificing ourselves for the welfare of the bourgeoisie. The time has come not to sleep but to act. Comrades! Chase the bourgeoisie from power and since they cry "war to complete victory," away to the front with the whole damn lot of them. All of us are worn out by this awful war which has already taken away the lives of millions, which has made millions cripples, and which has brought with it unheard-of poverty, destruction, and hunger.
>
> Wake up, whoever is asleep. The SR's and the Mensheviks want to fool you. . . . I appeal to you to be ready at any minute to repulse the counterrevolution. It stalks Nevsky Prospect led by Plekhanov and Rodzianko. Soon the "Black Hundreds" will come out, but you, comrades, with all your strength protect the freedom that has been won. All power must pass into the hands of the workers, soldiers, and peasants. Remove from power the bourgeoisie and all its sympathizers.
>
> Hail all power to the Soviets of Workers' and Soldiers' Deputies![82]

V

The July Uprising Begins

The First Machine Gun Regiment, the Anarchist-Communists, and the Military Organization on the Eve of the July Days

The July uprising was initiated in the First Machine Gun Regiment. Pinning down the precise time when plans for the rebellion began within the regiment itself is difficult, but it appears clear that this occurred well before the July 3 cabinet crisis[1] often cited by Western and Soviet sources as one of the uprising's major precipitants.[2] As was noted in the previous chapter, the Kerensky offensive threatened many garrison units with immediate transfer to the front and only after the exertion of pressure from the Petrograd Soviet and the Bolshevik Party leadership was a soldiers' rebellion averted during the earliest days of the Russian advance. At that time members of the First Machine Gun Regiment canceled preparations for an immediate uprising, satisfying themselves with a repudiation of their Regimental Committee and a declaration of their refusal to fulfill further Provisional Government troop levies.[3]

On June 23 the All-Russian Congress of Soviets issued an urgent appeal to all garrison units to respond to orders immediately,[4] and in the succeeding few days the Petrograd Military District was able, although evidently with great difficulty,[5] to arrange for transfer of minimal numbers of soldiers and weapons from the First Machine Gun Regiment. Throughout this period, however, the heavily Anarchist-Communist and Bolshevik influenced unit remained wary of any major shipment of troops and as a result, the atmosphere within the regiment continued to be explosive. The mood was such, testified a witness at the subsequent Provisional Government hearings on the July uprising, "that it seemed an armed rebellion would take place if not today, then tomorrow, and everybody knew it." "Every day," recalled one Lieutenant Popov, "headquarters was informed that the regiment planned to go out with arms the following day."[6]

Toward the end of June the First Machine Gun Regiment again received orders for an especially large transfer of men and machine guns (there were rumors that this was a prelude to the complete dismemberment of the unit), and at about the same time (June 30) a representative of the Military Section of the Petrograd Soviet, G. B. Skalov, visited the regiment to discuss the transfers.[7] According to Soviet historian P. M. Stulov, Skalov and the SR-Menshevik controlled First Machine Gun Regimental Committee elected to move their discussion to the Taurida Palace, to the great displeasure of unit Bolsheviks and Anarchists, who eventually came to the immediate conclusion that a sell-out was in the making. At a mass regimental meeting the same day (June 30), Ia. M. Golovin, a Bolshevik and leader of the abortive June 20-21 rebellion, argued that the Regimental Committee was acting improperly in not bringing the whole regiment into the discussions with Skalov. Stulov attaches major significance to this concern over the action of the Regimental Committee, commenting that the incident was fraught with serious consequences. Rumors of a mass transfer spread quickly among the apprehensive First Machine Gunners and already on July 1 "the soldier-*aktivisti* were engaged in unyielding discussions regarding the necessity of preventing a new attempt to disarm the regiment by means of an armed movement into the streets."[8]

That plans for the July uprising were initiated as early as July 1 is supported by a number of other sources. Nevsky recalls that the All-Russian Bureau of the Military Organization first learned of the machine gunners' plans for a demonstration on July 1,[9] and at the

Sixth Party Congress in late July Podvoisky acknowledged that the Military Organization leadership knew on the second of plans for an uprising the next day.[10]

On July 2 the Military Organization appealed to the party Central Committee (minus Lenin, Nogin, and Miliutin, who were out of the city) for directives.[11] Military Organization leader A. F. Ilin-Zhenevsky recalls that in discussions at this time representatives of the First Machine Gun Regiment openly argued that because of the large quantity of machine guns at their disposal, the regiment could easily overthrow the Provisional Government by itself.[12] Nevsky adds that A. Ia. Semashko was even then insisting that the movement could not be stopped, a fact that Nevsky asserts was already evident.[13] Presumably all this was made known to the Central Committee on July 2. Its response was a categorical order to the Military Organization (and probably to the Petersburg Committee as well) not to participate in the movement and to take all possible steps to prevent an outbreak.[14]

Although this order must have put the Military Organization in an extremely difficult position, it was apparently not implemented in any but the most formal sense. It is significant that at a meeting of the Petersburg Committee on August 27, 1917, Kalinin suggested that Bolshevik agitators at this time, while appearing to be restraining the masses, were actually urging them to act.[15] Similarly, two years after the October revolution, Nevsky quoted Semashko as remarking on July 2 that far from calming the soldiers, the Military Organization leaders sent to the regiment at this time only served to confirm the soldiers' belief that it was necessary to act.[16] Moreover, in one of Nevsky's last memoirs on the revolutionary period, published in the independently inclined historical journal, *Katorga i ssylka*, in 1932, he described this episode even more candidly:

> Some comrades at the present time ask the question: who initiated the July events—the Central Committee or the Military Organization—or did the movement erupt spontaneously?
>
> To some degree this is an unimportant and doctrinaire ques-

tion. Certainly the movement ripened within the depths of the broad masses, dissatisfied with the policies of the bourgeois government and starving for peace. . . . However, there is no need now to hide the fact that we, the responsible leaders of the Military Organization, i.e., especially Podvoisky, myself, Mekhonoshin, Beliakov, and other active workers, through our agitation, propaganda, and enormous influence and authority in the military units, promoted the spirit that aroused the demonstration.

If my memory fails and I incorrectly (though not purposely) named the people above, I can say the following about myself: although I am a rank-and-file Communist and did not play a big role in the revolution, comrades will not deny that the soldier masses knew me and counted my words as the word of the Military Organization. And thus when the Military Organization, having learned [on July 1] of the machine gunners' demonstration, sent me as the more or less most popular Military Organization orator to talk the masses into not going out, I talked to them, but in such a way that only a fool could come to the conclusion that he should not demonstrate.[17]

Whether such activities as Nevsky alludes to above extended to units of the garrison other than the First Machine Gun Regiment is unclear. In a speech to the Second City Conference on July 16, 1917, Podvoisky referred to meetings of Military Organization collectives on the second.[18] Precisely what was said by Military Organization leaders to these gatherings of garrison representatives is open to speculation, but Podvoisky's contention that the subject of a possible uprising was not even raised is untenable. It seems likely that the assembled were advised to keep in close contact with the Military Organization leadership and to be cautious and circumspect until such time as the situation within the First Machine Gun Regiment and the position of the Central Committee were clarified further.

As the state of affairs within the First Machine Gun Regiment worsened, it became inevitable that the Anarchist-Communists would become involved, and the fact is that they played a significant role in starting the July uprising. According to an unpublished memoir written by A. Fedorov, a member of the Petrograd Soviet

and a major figure in the Anarchist-Communist organization, a secret meeting of the Anarchist-Communist leadership was held on
the afternoon of July 2. Among the fourteen participants in the
meeting were, in addition to Fedorov, I. Bleikhman, P. Golubushkin, D. Nazimov, and P. Pavlov. In his memoir Fedorov reports that
the gathering voted to mobilize immediately the whole Anarchist
organization and the next morning (July 3) to call the workers and
soldiers to an armed uprising. Key to the proposed rebellion was to
be the First Machine Gun Regiment, and Bleikhman, Golubushkin,
and Pavlov were designated to insure the machine gunners' participation.[19]

This same afternoon (July 2) the belligerent mood of the First
Machine Gun Regiment was publicly demonstrated. The occasion
was a Sunday afternoon concert-meeting organized as a farewell
for the "last" shipment of troops to be sent to the front. The event
in itself was not unusual as some sort of patriotic send-off was a
custom in the revolutionary period. What distinguished the First
Machine Gunners' concert-meeting was that it was sponsored by
unit Bolsheviks in order to raise money for "literature" to be sent to
the front along with the departing troops. According to a front-
page *Pravda* announcement on July 2, Zinoviev, Kamenev,
Trotsky, Lunacharsky, Dashkevich, Lashevich, and Zhilin were
scheduled to give talks and the First Machine Gun Regiment's
string orchestra and a variety of soldier-singers and poets were to
entertain. Despite the tension in the unit, the affair was held on
schedule, attended by an estimated five thousand soldiers and
workers,[20] although it is perhaps not without significance that
Zinoviev and Kamenev failed to show up. From available reports, it
appears that the event turned into a wild anti-government rally.
Apparently neither Trotsky nor Lunacharsky did anything to calm
the general mood which speakers from the regiment and a soldier
Rutkovsky, one of the returnees from the mutinous Grenadier
Regiment at the front,[21] built up to a fever pitch. "The mood of the
meeting," remembers Raskolnikov, "was such that the more harshly
individual speakers formulated their statements, the more applause

they got."[22] "The mood was exalted," recalls Trotsky. "They denounced Kerensky and swore fealty to the revolution, but nobody made any practical proposal for the future."[23] At the close of the meeting a sharply worded resolution was passed attacking the Provisional Government and Kerensky for his handling of the offensive.[24]

After this rally broke up, the First Machine Gunners, evidently with renewed vigor, pressed ahead with preparations for the next day's operation. According to Stulov, "no one could think of sleep; conversations went on all night about the impossibility of being patient any longer."[25] Detailed discussions in connection with the contemplated insurrection were probably still confined to the unit Anarchist and Bolshevik organizations—the soldier-*aktivisti*, as Stulov refers to them—although evidently some representatives of the regiment, very likely Anarchists, were already in contact with their counterparts in other garrison regiments and Vyborg District factories. According to Miliukov, these representatives carried mandates appealing for support of the machine gunners "in their decision to overthrow the Provisional Government the next day, July 3."[26]

The Military Organization was also active on the eve of the proposed coup. At that time Military Organization leaders met with several members of the Petersburg Committee "to discuss a plan of action in the event that a demonstration actually broke out the next day."[27] What relation this plan had to the scheme to handle an uprising reported by Nevsky as having been drawn up by the Military Organization after June 22, presumably with precisely this sort of eventuality in mind, is impossible to tell.[28] According to Nevsky, late on the evening of the second all garrison Military Organization collectives were placed on alert, military communications were established between all units and the Kshesinskaia mansion, and an attempt was made to conduct a strength survey.[29] Simultaneously with these preparations, deliberations somewhat removed from the problems of the garrison but of subsequent significance for the development of the July days were taking place within the Provisional Government.

The Government Crisis over the Ukraine[30]

Among the many urgent problems facing the Provisional Government when it assumed power after the February revolution was that of formulating a policy toward the non-Russian areas of the former Tsarist Empire. During its first days the young revolutionary government proclaimed the abolition of all restrictive legislation imposed on the minorities by the Tsarist regime, established full equality of all citizens regardless of religion, race, or national origin, and introduced the beginning of local self-rule by placing administration of the borderlands in the hands of local figures. Moreover, in separate decrees, Poland was promised independence and some, albeit unacceptable, concessions were made to Finnish autonomy. To the other minority peoples with national ambitions the cautious Lvov government, immediately concerned with maintaining unity and order, counseled patience. Fundamental changes would have to await convocation of the Constituent Assembly. "This attitude," comments Richard Pipes, "sound from the moral and constitutional points of view, proved fatal as political practice." The February revolution had set into motion forces which would not wait and nowhere was this more evident than in the Ukraine.

A discussion of the rapid and tangled development of the movement in behalf of Ukrainian autonomy which led to the crisis of early July falls outside the scope of this study. Suffice it to say that by early summer a number of Ukrainian national groups had coalesced around the Ukrainian Central Rada in Kiev, which now began challenging the authority of the Provisional Government by claiming to be a legitimate Ukrainian national government. This claim was flatly rejected by the Provisional Government, and so a short time later, in a ceremony on the square at Saint Sophia, the Central Rada issued the so-called First Universal, in which, addressing itself to the entire Ukrainian people, it announced that the Ukraine would henceforth decide its own fate and would take all measures necessary to maintain order and to distribute the land within its borders. In implementation of this decree a General Secretariat with the functions of a cabinet was created; in Petrograd it was rumored that the Ukrainians had gone so far as to appoint a Foreign Minister,[31] and although this was incorrect, an autonomous Ukrainian Republic had been proclaimed and the authority of the Provisional Government openly challenged.

Within the Provisional Government there was little unanimity in regard to the handling of the Ukrainian problem. Very generally, the socialist ministers (most of whom were not opposed to the principle of Ukrainian autonomy) were apprehensive of the danger of alienating thirty million Ukrainians by not making immediate concessions to the Rada. They were motivated, too, by the threat of a political crisis in the rear of the Southwestern army at the height of the offensive. The Kadet ministers, on the other hand, refused to consider the legitimacy of the Ukrainian claims. They tended to view the actions of the Rada as a conspiracy against the Provisional Government and held fast to the principle of postponing settlement of such basic political issues until the Constituent Assembly. Nonetheless, when at a cabinet meeting on June 26 it was suggested that a high-level delegation be sent to Kiev immediately, the Kadets did not object, stipulating only that the negotiators should not have the power to make final decisions binding on the government.

Cabinet ministers Kerensky, Tsereteli, and M. I. Tereshchenko were selected to make the trip to Kiev, and their negotiations with Ukrainian leaders began on June 28. These discussions lasted for three days, after which a compromise agreement representing a substantial victory for the Rada was reached. Above all it recognized by implication what the Rada had until then claimed in vain: that the Rada as an institution was authorized to speak for the Ukrainian people.[32] The accord also legitimized the General Secretariat as a regional administrative organ to be appointed by the Provisional Government in consultation with the Central Rada, and authorized the Rada to prepare its own proposals on the land question for submission to the Constituent Assembly. For its part, the Rada pledged its loyalty to revolutionary Russia, gave up demands for a separate Ukrainian army, and promised to forgo further independent action in the direction of increased autonomy until the

Constituent Assembly. Armed with this agreement, Kerensky, Tsereteli, and Tereshchenko returned to the capital on July 2 to obtain approval of it from the other members of the coalition government.

A cabinet meeting to consider the agreement was held in Prince Lvov's home the same evening. According to Tsereteli, the Kadet ministers made plain their unalterable opposition to the accord at the very outset. They based their objections on the grounds that the agreement put an end to the Provisional Government's authority in the Ukraine, that it recognized the questionably constituted Central Rada as the government of a Ukraine whose boundaries were not even specified, and that it predetermined the Ukraine's future form of government in advance of the Constituent Assembly. Tereshchenko, Tsereteli, and Kerensky, the "triumvirate," as Miliukov called them, defended their negotiations and emphasized that only approval of the agreement without changes would be binding on the Rada. The bitter debate lasted several hours. After it was over a vote was taken; the Kadets A. I. Shingarev (Minister of Finance), A. A. Manuilov (Minister of Education), V. A. Stepanov (Acting Minister of Trade and Industry), and D. I. Shakhovsky (Minister of Welfare) denied approval, and upon the instructions of their Central Committee, left the government. The remaining Kadet, N. V. Nekrasov, favored the compromise with the Rada and submitted his resignation to the Kadet Party rather than leave the government.

In a press interview on July 3 Prince Lvov emphasized that basic differences in points of view between the socialists and the bourgeoisie rather than the Ukraine problem itself were at the heart of the crisis. That the relatively conservative Kadets were increasingly out of tune with the attitudes of the majority in the government is doubtless true. Miliukov himself acknowledges that the controversy over the Ukrainian accord was not the fundamental reason for the Kadet resignations, that this was only the last of several disagreements concerning the policies of the coalition government in which the Kadets had been left in the minority and which made further cooperation with the socialist ministers impossible.[33] Be that as it may, the abrupt defection of the Kadets left the Provisional Government, now composed of six representatives of moderate socialist parties and only five "capitalists," in a disorganized and altogether vulnerable position on the eve of perhaps its greatest challenge.

The First Machine Gun Regiment's Rebellion

Monday, July 3, a warm sunny day in Petrograd, began ominously. In the early morning the city's postal workers suddenly went out on strike in support of demands for higher pay, while many thousands of disgruntled "over-forties" staged a protest demonstration on Nevsky Prospect.[34] Both incidents were indicative of prevailing instability, although neither was directly related to the scheme about to be set in motion by the First Machine Gun Regiment.

By mid-morning the plot was ready to unfold. In the words of a veteran machine gunner, "gun barrels had been cleaned, parts had been tested and oiled, and machine guns loaded."[35] Fortunately for the historian, published documents on the Provisional Government investigations into the organization of the July uprising and a large number of memoir and secondary accounts permit a fairly detailed reconstruction of this phase of the July days. At about 11:00 A.M. the First Machine Gun Regimental Committee gathered for a meeting in its headquarters in the Soldiers' Building. Since the talks between the Regimental Committee and the Military Section of the Petrograd Soviet in connection with the shipment of replacements were scheduled for resumption later in the day, it seems not unlikely that the Regimental Committee meeting was to touch upon this very sensitive question. At about the time the Regimental Committee began its meeting, some First Machine Gunners (presumably the "soldier-*aktivisti*") led by the now familiar Ia. M. Golovin assembled in another part of the same building, elected

Golovin as their chairman, and began discussing the activities of the Regimental Committee and the impending discussions with the Soviet. The audience at this second meeting multiplied very rapidly. Many soldiers responded after being called to participate in the name of the Bolshevik Military Organization,[36] with the result that by midday the attendance already numbered a few thousand.[37]

Upon his election as Chairman, Golovin set the tone for the meeting by ridiculing the unit Regimental Committee for its conduct of the discussions with Skalov. He argued adamantly against the sending of reinforcement companies and machine guns to the front because, in his words, "the offensive had been launched against the will of the people and the sending of help to the army could lead only to a prolongation of the war."[38]

I. Bleikhman, acting in accordance with the plans formulated at the Anarchist-Communist meeting the preceding afternoon, was the second speaker. He was under no obligation to be circumspect, and his fanatic appeal was simple and direct: "Overthrow the Provisional Government immediately, not in order to turn power over to the 'bourgeois' Soviet, but to take it into your own hands!"[39] Trotsky, who must have heard Bleikhman speak frequently, provides us with this picture:

> There appeared at this meeting the anarchist Bleichman, a small but colorful figure on the background of 1917, with a very modest equipment of ideas but a certain feeling for the masses—sincere in his limited and ever inflammable intelligence—his shirt open at the breast and curly hair flying out on all sides. . . . The soldiers smiled delightedly at his speeches, nudging each other with their elbows and egging the orator on with pithy comments. They plainly liked his eccentric looks, his unreasoning decisiveness, and his Jewish-American accent sharp as vinegar. By the end of June, Bleichman was swimming in all these impromptu meetings like a fish in a river. His opinion he had always with him: It is necessary to come out with arms in our hands. Organization? "The street will organize us." The task? "To overthrow the Provisional Government just as it overthrew the tsar although no party was then demanding it."[40]

Bleikhman's speech had the desired effect. Upon its conclusion Golovin was able to limit discussion to the sole question of an immediate movement of the regiment into the streets for the purpose of overthrowing the Provisional Government.[41]

According to the testimony of several witnesses, in addition to Bleikhman, P. Golubushkin and P. Pavlov (both Anarchist-Communists) and the soldiers Ia. M. Golovin, I. Kazakov, K. N. Romanov, and I. Ilinsky (all members of the Bolshevik Military Organization collective) spoke out in favor of an immediate coup d'etat. Ilinsky promised that as a member of the Military Organization he would take upon himself responsibility for the mobilization of the rest of the garrison. According to the findings of the Provisional Government investigation, the speakers differed only on the question of timing, some calling for a postponement of the operation until the next day in order to facilitate better organization.[42]

For the battle-hungry First Machine Gunners, evidently even one day's delay was too much. A resolution proposed by Golovin authorizing a demonstration was passed "unanimously" with the proviso that the operation begin at 5:00 the same afternoon. A second part of this resolution created an *ad hoc* Provisional Revolutionary Committee to lead the regiment and authorized the selection of emissaries to be sent immediately to other regiments, factories, and the Kronstadt naval base to obtain their support. Upon the recommendation of Ilinsky, A. Ia. Semashko was elected head of the Provisional Revolutionary Committee, which also included Bleikhman and Military Organization members I. Ilinsky, K. Romanov, G. Maslov, A. Poliakov, A. Zhilin, and Golovin.[43] The selection of this committee and of emissaries was completed by early afternoon. Then, under Semashko's direction,[44] the Provisional Revolutionary Committee set about mobilizing all companies of the First Machine Gun Regiment, sent out patrols and posted guards, authorized the immediate confiscation and arming of civilian and military vehicles, and drew up operational plans.

First Machine Gunners carrying mandates signed by Golovin and in many cases by members of the unit's Military Organization fanned out across the city and its environs.[45] As nearly as can be determined, delegations were sent to, among others, the Moskovsky, Grenadier, First Infantry, 180th Infantry, Pavlovsky, Izmailovsky, Finliandsky, and Petrogradsky Reserve Regiments and to the Sixth Engineer Battalion and the Armored Car Division, to such Vyborg District factories as Novyi Parviainen, Novyi Lessner, Russkii Reno, Erikson, and Baranovsky, and to the Putilov works in the Narva District. Additional delegations were sent to the military installations in Kronstadt, Oranienbaum, Strelna, and Peterhof. The machine gunners generally arrived in trucks mounted with machine guns between 3:00 and 5:00 P.M. and hurriedly organized mass meetings either on their own or through regimental and factory committees. The testimony of G. I. Torsky of the First Infantry Reserve Regiment typifies descriptions of the First Machine Gunners' arrival:

> On July 3 at about 5:00 P.M. soldiers who called themselves a delegation from the First Machine Gun Regiment came to see me as the chairman of the Regimental Committee. . . . The delegation declared that it was sent by the Machine Gun Regiment to demand that we should immediately demonstrate, arms in hand, in the streets of Petrograd for the purpose of overthrowing the capitalist ministers and of transferring all power into the hands of the Soviet of Workers', Soldiers', and Peasants' Deputies. The soldiers of the Machine Gun Regiment and the workers who came with them declared that the whole Petrograd garrison and all the workers of the city had already decided to go into the streets with arms at five o'clock in order to express their protest and therefore they asked us to do the same.[46]

A meeting of the First Infantry Reserve Regiment was arranged, and ultimately the unit participated in the uprising armed and in close to full strength.

At a few regiments the First Machine Gunners' appeals never got past local committees and were flatly rejected. Among military units in this category were the Litovsky, Volynsky, and Preobrazhensky Regiments, all three of which had played key roles in the February revolution. Some other units responded with a pledge of what Znamensky calls "benevolent neutrality." This was the case, for instance, in the Petrogradsky Regiment, whose Regimental Committee resolved "not to oppose a demonstration of machine gunners as long as it was peaceful."[47] On the other hand, the proposal of the First Machine Gunners attracted sizable support in a significant number of garrison military units and in many factories. By mid-evening the Moskovsky, 180th Reserve Infantry, Finlandsky, Grenadier, and Pavlovsky Regiments as well as the Sixth Engineer Battalion could probably be counted as having joined the insurrection.[48] On the Vyborg side factories stopped operating as soon as trucks bearing the machine gunners appeared,[49] and workers in many of them scurried for their weapons almost immediately. Something like ten thousand armed sailors in Kronstadt and thirty thousand workers in the Putilov factory were soon to follow suit so that already on July 3 the insurrection assumed ominous proportions. Although materials available for study are inexplicit, perhaps a few tentative observations can safely be made on at least some important aspects of this lightning expansion.

First, it should be noted that study of pertinent newspapers, memoirs, and published documents seems to place in somewhat altered perspective some of the widely accepted reasons for the outbreak of the July uprising. For example, it appears that the resignation of the Kadet ministers had a rather secondary importance. There was nothing in the July 3 morning papers about the cabinet crisis,[50] and although rumors in connection with it were probably already rife by midafternoon, they did not figure at all in the appeals emanating from the First Machine Gun Regiment. Several memoirs indicate that word of the Kadet defections reached many demonstrators only upon their arrival at the Taurida Palace in late evening. After the news became more widely known, however, its effect was undoubtedly of importance in subverting the remaining vestiges of the Provisional Government's prestige. Similarly, it is interesting that the slowing down and impending collapse of the offensive does not seem to have figured prominently in the early stages of the rebellion except insofar as the obvious absence of any notable victories finished snuffing out the patriotic spirit of the city's war-weary masses, rekindled briefly during the promising early days of the advance.[51]

What then were the key factors provoking expansion of the insurrection? It is significant that alongside the general sources of mass instability described in earlier chapters, most of the major rebelling elements had particular, often very immediate, grievances. Provisional Government documents and memoirs indicate, for example, that for the First Infantry Reserve Regiment (as for the First Machine Gun Regiment) the primary reason for the insurrection was to head off transfer to the front.[52] The fundamental spur to Kronstadt's participation seems to have been the conviction that such activities as the Provisional Government's attack on the Durnovo villa, the launching of the offensive, and the continuing liberation of former tsarist naval officers from the Kronstadt prison foreshadowed a reversion to the unbearable injustices of the sailor's life in the Imperial fleet. Bitterness at the General Staff's treatment of the Grenadiers at the front was the single most important source of discontent in the garrison Grenadier Regiment,[53] while in the 180th Infantry Reserve Regiment one major disrupting factor was widespread bitterness at the Military District's unyielding prohibition of all leaves.

At the Putilov metal works, where labor unrest had helped to spark the 1905 and February revolutions, a basic cause of tension was the growing conviction that a long-postponed increase in the minimum wage, if left in the hands of the "capitalist controlled" Provisional Government, would never be effected. Another disrupting factor among Putilov workers was opposition to the imminent shipment to the front of part of the Turutinsky Regiment, left to work in the Putilov factory when the bulk of the unit moved to the front after the revolution.[54] Among undisciplined workers in the Vyborg section, a seemingly trivial incident was a barometer of the anarchy prevailing in that quarter. This was the public clamor on July 2 over a case of suspected meat speculation in the main produce store; workers plastered the director with his own rotten meat and dragged him through the streets.[55] The entry in Latsis' diary for July 2 reads: "All day spent at the conference [the Bolshevik Second City Conference]. There is uneasiness in the [Vyborg] District—a meat speculator was caught and the mob was ready to take care of him on its own. The surge is coming to the surface. It is beginning . . . ."[56]

One important point that should be made in regard to expansion of the rebellion on July 3 is that analysis of pertinent materials does not bear out the notion encouraged by most Soviet sources that in response to Central Committee directives, an honest effort was made by Bolshevik cadres to restrain the masses. Turning aside the question of the Military Organization's complicity in fomenting the insurrection in the first place, the fact of the matter appears to be, as the Soviet historian K. Shelavin acknowledged, "that rank-and-file Bolsheviks everywhere turned out not to be steadfast and quickly joined the movement."[57] A major figure in the Petersburg Committee, M. I. Kalinin, had about the same thing to say in 1920, in an article commemorating the July days. "We must admit," he wrote, "that the majority of Communists in the districts took upon themselves an active role [in the uprising] even though there was still no firm decision in the center."[58] In his article Shelavin suggests that the problem grew out of the fact that from February to July the Petersburg organization increased by more than thirty thousand members and the absorption of all these new people proved not to be an easy matter.

This was undoubtedly part of the trouble. Another factor was that the role of "fireman" (as the Central Committee's policy of late June was sarcastically labelled) was distasteful to rank-and-file Bolsheviks generally. "Again we must be firehoses," wrote Latsis at this time; "how long will this last?"[59] Krupskaia singled out this same factor in a speech touching on the July days delivered in 1934: "You know," she said, "when it is necessary to agitate in favor of action, that's easy. . . . But when people want to act and it's necessary to say: 'No comrades, the barricades must come down. . . .

You will have to wait with your uprising,' that's very difficult. And for Bolsheviks it was very hard to do this."[60]

To a degree, the difficulty at the local level probably also stemmed from the ambiguous position adopted by the Petersburg Committee on June 20 (i.e., that the party should not abdicate leadership if holding back the masses proved impossible). At any rate, on the afternoon and early evening of July 3 things were so hopelessly confused that Bolsheviks obeying the directives of the Central Committee and agitating in favor of postponing an uprising found themselves in conflict with party people urging support for one. Such a situation developed during a stormy meeting in the Putilov factory. There Bolshevik Sergei Bogdatiev, secretary of the Putilov factory committee, appealed for immediate action, after which Bolsheviks Anton Vasiliev and Sergei Ordzhonikidze called for restraint. One worker published this recollection of Bogdatiev's action after a soldier from the garrison finished making an emotional bid for Putilov's support:

> Following him, Comrade Bogdatiev spoke out also calling on us to go out into the streets (not knowing the position of the party, he was then acting on his own).
> His appeal: "Down with the Provisional Government! Into the streets! Move out!" was fraternally echoed by the huge crowd.[61]

A similar situation occurred at a meeting of nearly ten thousand sailors and workers in Kronstadt not long after the arrival of the machine gunners.[62] The Anarchist-Communist leader Iarchuk recalls that "at the same time Roshal [Kronstadt Bolshevik S. G. Roshal] was talking in terms of an immediate armed uprising under the slogan 'All power to the Soviets,' some other members of the Bolshevik Party in company with Raskolnikov held back. . . . In answer to Raskolnikov's question to Roshal, 'and what if the party does not act?' the latter replied: 'Don't worry, we will compel them to do so from here.' "[63] An early Soviet account of the same incident explains that "Raskolnikov had already received news from

Petrograd. Kamenev had told him that the First Machine Gun Regiment had gone out on its own without the sanction of the party and it was necessary to restrain Kronstadt. But how? Who can stop an alpine avalanche? Roshal spoke next. But soon that spontaneous figure surrendered to the mood of the masses and instead of 'stay back' cried 'forward.' "[64] In the Provisional Government documents dealing with Kronstadt's role in the July days, another Kronstadt Bolshevik, F. V. Gromov, is quoted as appealing for an immediate departure for Petrograd with arms and "in all available boats lest the Kronstadt sailors be taken for traitors and erased from the ranks of revolutionary units." A short time later Gromov and Roshal brought the question of participation to a vote; the shouts of the assembled settled the issue in the affirmative.[65] While the sailors repaired to their quarters to prepare for battle, a committee selected by the Kronstadt Soviet Executive Committee departed for the capital to assess the situation.

Soviet historians present the July "demonstrations" as a peaceful protest movement, the last event in the "peaceful period" of the struggle for transfer of power to the Soviets. Significantly, however, source materials on the mass meetings of July 3 indicate that the ostensible objective of the July movement as it was formulated by the Anarchist-Communists and the First Machine Gun Regiment was the overthrow of the Provisional Government by armed force. What remains hazy is precisely how the conspirators expected to achieve this objective and whether it was planned for power to be transferred to the Soviet, the Bolsheviks, or some *ad hoc* organization. Actually, in studying the beginnings of the July insurrection one has the feeling that the anarchists and semi-anarchists who launched it, particularly those within the garrison, may not have been very clear in their own minds about the answers to these questions. Moreover, they seemed to have viewed revolution as a relatively simple matter not requiring much organization or planning. It was a spirit perhaps best typified by Bleikhman's solution to the organization of the overthrow: "The street will organize us!" This spirit was strong within the Military Organization and among the Kronstadt sailors. Nevsky recalls a June meeting during which Lenin asked for precise information on party strength in the garrison. "Then," writes Nevsky, "this seemed insignificant to me. . . . We will start a demonstration and that will be enough."[66] In regard to Kronstadt, Flerovsky comments: "Despite all their revolutionary virtues . . . the Kronstadt sailors had one serious weakness; they naively believed that the pressure of their enthusiasm would be enough for the power of the Soviets to be established in all Russia."[67] The mood was probably an outgrowth of such factors as the relative ease with which Nicholas II had been overthrown, the apparent absence of governmental authority, and the large stores of arms and ammunition in the hands of the workers, soldiers, and sailors. The existence of this mood and the chaos in Bolshevik ranks help to explain some of the confusion and apparent lack of direction of the July days.

The Soviet Executive Committees and the Beginning of the July Uprising

The political crisis over the Ukraine compromise presented the majority socialist leaders in the Soviet with a very difficult dilemma. At the recent All-Russian Congress of Soviets, Bolshevik opposition had been turned aside in order to buttress the Provisional Government preparatory to the resumption of active operations against the Central Powers. The Congress-sponsored demonstration of June 18 had shown how unpopular this decision was in the capital. Now the abrupt departure of the Kadets appeared to render futile hopes for a socialist-liberal united revolutionary front and inevitably reopened the question of whether or not the Soviet should take power into its own hands. To be sure, another meeting of Soviet delegates drawn from all parts of the country would probably again support an attempt to form a coalition government pending the convocation of the Constituent Assembly. But what of the elementally explosive workers and soldiers of Petrograd, more susceptible than ever to influence by the Anarchists and Bolsheviks? What would they say? And, in the meantime, what was to become of the crumbling offensive?

It was against this altogether dismal background that on the afternoon of July 3, members of the All-Russian Central Executive Committee of the Soviet of Workers' and Soldiers' Deputies and the All-Russian Executive Committee of the Soviet of Peasants' Deputies gathered for a joint meeting in the Taurida Palace. Tsereteli, reportedly looking tired and worn, opened discussion with the proposal that the present Provisional Government, minus the Kadet ministers, remain in power until a plenum of the Central Executive Committee (i.e., a meeting to include representatives from provincial Soviets[68]) could be convened to determine the composition of a future government. It was a practical stop-gap measure (unanimously supported in advance by the Menshevik-SR leadership)[69] aimed at insuring that all of Russia, not just turbulent Petrograd, would have a voice in the government question.

But Tsereteli barely had time to sit down when discussion of his proposal was interrupted by initial reports of the ominous preparations among city workers and soldiers for a march on the Provisional Government in support of the intransigent First Machine Gun Regiment. This occurred at precisely 4:00 in the afternoon, at which time the obvious need for immediate precautions resulted in the suspension of debate on the government crisis.[70] While a special committee headed by Woytinsky tried frantically to arrange for defense of the Taurida Palace in the event of attack, telegrams were dispatched to all garrison troop units and to the Kronstadt naval base reaffirming the ban on demonstrations of any kind.[71] In addition, a proclamation was prepared (it was already being distributed among workers and soldiers at 7:00 P.M.) condemning the movement as traitorous and emphasizing that "all available means" would be employed to combat it.[72] This done, the joint Executive Committee meeting was adjourned until late evening so that representatives of the Soviet could be sent to known trouble spots in the hope of nipping the rebellion in the bud.[73]

The Second City Conference,[74] the Central Committee, and the Movement in the Streets

At about the time Menshevik-SR leaders in the Taurida Palace first became aware of the immediate danger of an armed uprising, delegates to the Bolshevik Petrograd Second City Conference, which opened on July 1 in the Kshesinskaia mansion, were engaged in debate on the sensitive question of whether or not the Petersburg Committee should override Lenin's opposition and begin publication of a separate newspaper. The issue had arisen because a majority of the Petersburg Committee insisted that *Pravda* was not meeting the agitation and organizational requirements of the city party organization. In addition, many members apparently viewed the establishment of a separate organ as a means of enhancing the power and flexibility of the Petersburg Committee at the expense of the more conservative Central Committee. But from late May, when the question first arose, Lenin had adamantly opposed creation of a city party newspaper precisely because he viewed it as a reflection of the Petersburg Committee's tendencies toward separatism.[75] The debate was evidently long and heated. Upon its conclusion 51 City Conference delegates, a sizable majority of those present, voted in favor of establishing a Petrograd newspaper with 19 opposed and 16 abstentions.[76] The decision was an undeniable expression of the Petersburg Committee's spirit of independence—but it was pushed into the background almost immediately by the sudden intrusion of two members of the Military Organization collective in the First Machine Gun Regiment. One of them, I. N. Ilinsky, immediately took the floor to announce that in order to avert liquidation, the regiment had decided to march on the Provisional Government at once and had already enlisted the support of other military units and factories.[77]

The effect of this declaration among conference delegates was that of an exploding bomb. Volodarsky is reported to have told the newcomers that the party was against such a march and that party members were obliged to abide by that decision.[78] Undaunted, the machine gunners left in a huff declaring "that leaving the party was preferable to opposing a decision of their regiment."[79] In the published City Conference protocols reference to this episode is fragmentary, merely a one-line entry referring to an out-of-order announcement by the First Machine Gun Regiment of growing unrest among units of the garrison.[80] There is no mention of any formal expression by the Conference of its attitude toward the movement in the streets, but a footnote refers the reader to the memoirs of E. N. Egorova, secretary of the Vyborg District party organization, and V. I. Egorov, both first published side by side in *Leningradskaia pravda* in 1926. Egorov's brief reminiscences suggest that at this point the conference in effect reaffirmed its policy of June 20, that is (in Egorov's words), "it voted by an absolute majority to entrust leadership of the demonstration into the hands of the party if this proved necessary."[81] The meeting was apparently adjourned shortly after this. In her memoir Egorova writes that at the conclusion of the meeting she and her colleagues dashed for home, but she implies (as do several other memoirists) that by the time she reached there the movement was in full swing and it was already too late to restrain the masses.[82]

News of the Provisional Government crisis and the activities of the First Machine Gun Regiment caught many members of the Bolshevik Central Committee in the Taurida Palace, where they were making plans for an evening meeting of the Workers' Section of the Petrograd Soviet.[83] Kamenev immediately called Raskolnikov in Kronstadt to warn him against taking part in the movement and at around 4:00 in the afternoon the Bolshevik leadership formally discussed the position of the party in regard to the latest developments. Unfortunately, no protocol of this crucial meeting has been published. At the Sixth Party Congress Stalin referred to the position adopted at this meeting, declaring that the Central Committee was still primarily concerned with avoiding a decisive clash until the offensive had collapsed completely so that blame for the latter could not be shifted to the Bolsheviks. In the aftermath of that inevitable debacle, implied Stalin, opportunities for a new revolution presumably would be more propitious.[84]

It is doubtful that this cautious strategy was supported unanimously. Under the circumstances Smilga, for one, would certainly have demurred.[85] At any rate the Central Committee, for the second time in two days, voted against participating in a demonstration, with Trotsky of the Interdistrict Committee evidently supporting this position. In implementation of the decision, Kamenev and Zinoviev prepared an appeal designed to restrain the masses for insertion in the next day's *Pravda*.[86] Supporting directives were sent to the Presidium of the Second City Conference, and party members from the Petrograd Soviet were delegated to try to restrain the First Machine Gunners.[87] Evidently, an explanatory message was also immediately telephoned to Nogin who was then in Moscow.[88] Following this, members of the Central Committee looked in on the joint Soviet Executive Committee meeting, where Stalin had the party's official position read into the record.[89] Not surprisingly, the Soviet majority leaders greeted Stalin's words with considerable skepticism. And at the Second City Conference, where the Presidium laid upon Tomsky the task of announcing the Central Committee's stand, it was not implemented in any but the most formal sense.

Interestingly, the early evening speech in which Tomsky made his announcement seems to represent a temporary compromise (evidently worked out earlier within the Presidium) between the eagerness for action of Petersburg Committee radicals like Latsis, on the one hand, and the active policy of restraint advocated by the Central Committee, on the other. The record of Tomsky's speech is significant enough to be quoted at length:

> At the behest of the conference Presidium Comrade Tomsky informs the conference . . . that four Kadets are leaving the cabinet as a result of disagreements over government policy toward the Ukraine. The Bureau of the Central Executive Committee of the Soviet of Workers' and Soldiers' Deputies has decided to issue an appeal against a street demonstration. . . . Armored cars

have been ordered to the Taurida Palace. They want to arrest the heads of the movement. The chairman of the Peasants' Congress declared that 'it is necessary to shoot all traitors!' . . . There are reports that in the suburbs artillery has opened fire on demonstrating units. The Executive Committee is seeking a compromise with the Kadets and will probably find one. . . .

Our Central Committee invites party members and sympathizers to restrain the masses from further demonstrations. [It suggests] telling them that the Central Committee and the Petersburg Committee, having found a street demonstration necessary on June 10, did not make that decision independently but brought in representatives from the factories and regiments; that the regiments presently going into the streets acted in an uncomradely way by not inviting the committees of our party to discussions regarding a demonstration; [and that] because of this our party cannot assume responsibility for the demonstration. The Central Committee proposes that the conference (1) issue an appeal restraining the masses; (2) prepare an appeal to the Central Executive Committee to take power.

It is impossible to speak now of a demonstration without wanting another revolution. [But at this time] we cannot determine all the "ifs" of the prevailing situation. To take the initiative in our own hands would be risky. We will see how the movement develops. We must obey the decision of the Central Committee but we need not rush to the factories to put out the fire since we did not light it and we cannot put fires out for everybody.[90]

After Tomsky's speech reports were made by, among others, E. N. Egorova, V. M. Molotov, and G. D. Veinberg, all of whom were just returning from the workers' districts. Their reports suggested that the movement begun by the machine gunners was snowballing very rapidly although some factories and regiments were holding back and waiting for an official go-ahead from the party. Longtime Bolshevik M. A. Saveliev commented that the situation at the Putilov works was very tense, and Nevsky pointed out that one could sense dissatisfaction with the Central Committee on the Petersburg side. G. F. Kolomin of the Moscow District "proposed that in view of the latest developments, the party should im-

Members of the First Machine Gun Regiment appeal for support
during the July uprising. (State Museum of the Great October Socialist Revolution)

July 4, 1917, in Kronstadt: a military regiment assembles for the journey to Petrograd. (Museum of the Revolution USSR)

mediately take the leadership of the movement into its own hands."[91] B. K. Slutskaia, apparently supporting him, argued that the Central Committee was not aware of the latest developments when it made its decision to oppose the movement into the streets. She asked what the conference's attitude was to the fact of the demonstration, but there is no evidence that she received a formal reply.

Rakhia commented impatiently that the conference looked like the Paris Commune that talked even while being surrounded by hostile troops. He suggested that the Petersburg Committee, while abiding by the directives of the Central Committee, arrange an immediate meeting of factory and military representatives with the Central Committee, presumably better to assess the developing situation and to apply pressure on the Central Committee. This proposal was adopted with the proviso that, among others, representatives of the Interdistrict Committee and the Menshevik-Internationalists also be invited. Toward the end of the meeting a formal resolution by Kaktyn, Ogretsa, and Salna to support the rebelling regiments was defeated. Rather it was agreed to send a delegation to the Central Executive Committee with the ultimatum: take power now or face an armed uprising. And the conference was again adjourned.[92]

The First Machine Gun Regiment Takes the Lead

It was now a little after 7:00 in the evening and Petrograd had by this time taken on the appearance of a battlefield. Machine gunners had already occupied the Finland station and machine guns had been positioned along the tracks at nearby stations. Soldiers and machine guns were posted on the approaches to the Troitsky and Liteiny bridges leading to the center of the city, while on Nevsky Prospect trucks bristling with machine guns rushed about on orders from the Revolutionary Committee.[93] At about 7:45 one of these trucks appeared at the Baltic station, and its occupants announced that they had come to arrest Kerensky. They left upon learning that Kerensky had departed for the front two hours earlier.[94]

In the Vyborg District at this time the First Machine Gun Regiment's First, Second, and Fourth Battalions, in full battle dress, began to fall out on Samsonievsky Prospect, which was already jammed with civilian demonstrators. Promptly at 8:00, their preparations completed, Semashko, Bleikhman, Golovin, and the other members of the Provisional Revolutionary Committee climbed into the trucks and the order to march was given.[95] A Vyborg District Bolshevik proudly recalled that on this occasion "under the red banners marched only workers and soldiers; the cockades of the officials, the shiny buttons of students, the hats of 'lady sympathizers' were not to be seen. All that belonged to four months ago, to February."[96]

According to plan, the First Machine Gun battalions, followed by columns of workers, were to march along separate routes through the Vyborg District picking up other rebelling regiments and factories along the way. Thus, the Fourth Battalion proceeded along Samsonievsky Prospect and soon appeared at the Moskovsky Regiment, where Semashko allayed some last-minute indecision within that unit. Meanwhile, the First Battalion marched down Nystadt Street and made a scheduled stop at the Mikhailovskoe Artillery Academy. There Semashko demanded some artillery pieces and when this was refused, four pieces with shells were seized by force.[97] A short time later the First Battalion and the Moskovsky Regiment, the artillery pieces in tow, crossed the Liteiny bridge, met the Sixth Engineer Battalion and headed for the Taurida Palace. The description below is by Stulov:

> The appearance of the demonstration was undoubtedly impressive: the artillery, the Moskovsky Regiment's orchestra, the placards with the slogans: "Down with the ten capitalist ministers," "All power to the Soviet of Workers', Soldiers', and Peasants' Deputies," "Remember, capitalism, machine guns, and steel will

smash you," "Down with Kerensky and with him the offensive," and finally the trucks mounted with machine guns accompanying the procession—all this produced a significant effect on the frightened inhabitants and the bourgeoisie.[98]

In the meantime the First Machine Gun Regiment's Second, and later Fourth, Battalions made contact with the Grenadier Regiment in the Petrograd District and started for the headquarters of the Bolshevik Party only a short distance away.

In the Kshesinskaia Mansion

Judging by the memoir literature, Bolshevik headquarters was still in a state of chaos and confusion even as columns of armed workers and soldiers neared the Kshesinskaia mansion. In an upstairs master bedroom members of the Military Organization's All-Russian Bureau and the Petersburg Committee's Executive Commission (Stalin and Sverdlov of the Central Committee were evidently also present) considered the rapidly narrowing courses of action open to the party,[99] while in the halls outside, agitated party workers from factories and military regiments awaited directives. Only Podvoisky made frequent appearances from inside the bedroom; he received late reports from new arrivals and then disappeared behind the closed door. A fragment from the memoirs of A. Tarasov-Rodionov of the Military Organization's collective in the Infantry Officers' Academy at Oranienbaum captures the prevailing mood:

> The Military Organization's headquarters is noisy, but no one knows anything for sure. . . .
>
> An elderly soldier dressed in a torn overcoat, sweating and waving his arms, tries to convince everyone that there is no point in holding [the masses] back any longer. . . . "Let them demonstrate and attest to the fact that we are still alive. . . ."
>
> More and more contacts between the garrison and factories and the Military Organization and Petersburg Committee rush in. Their faces are tired and burning. They shake their heads and stubbornly declare:

"The Vyborg District can't be stopped! They don't even want
to listen!"

"The Putilov workers are already forming. . . . It was necessary
to agree with them and approve their actions!"

"Without the sanction of the Central Committee?"

"Without the sanction of the Central Committee! . . . The
masses can no longer be restrained and there is no reason to [re-
strain them]."[100]

Inside the bedroom the Petrograd party leadership was faced
with the fact that several regiments were already in the streets and
that Bolsheviks everywhere were taking an active part in the demonstration. In his early memoir Kalinin points out that now the
question was not whether the Bolsheviks would join the movement,
but rather whether they should lead the demonstration and give it a
definite direction or merely be passive participants. Kalinin writes
that the large majority of the party leaders in attendance favored "a
most energetic role."[101]

This meeting was evidently still in session as the two battalions of
the First Machine Gun Regiment, soon followed by the Grenadier
Regiment, a band, and thousands of workers, filled the grounds below the now famous Kshesinskaia balcony to receive the party's
decision. Podvoisky and Stalin later testified that, among others,
Podvoisky, Sverdlov, Ilinsky, Lashevich, and Nevsky were sent out
on the balcony to harangue the soldiers and workers into returning
to the Vyborg District.[102] One cannot but wonder about the
genuineness of these appeals. At any rate, after they were vocifer-
ously rejected, it was announced that the Military Organization
was prepared to support and lead the movement.[103] Blessing was
given for an immediate march to the Taurida Palace so that the
demonstrators might present their demands, and (according to
Podvoisky) at the same time members of the Military Organization
left the Kshesinskaia mansion to coordinate negotiations with the
Soviet.[104]

At the first session of the Second City Conference after the July
days Stalin justified this eleventh-hour decision to take an active
part in the demonstration on the grounds that the Bolsheviks did

not have the right to wash their hands of a proletarian demonstration; that once it had begun, the party of the proletariat was duty-bound to interfere and give the movement a peaceful and organized character.[105] In all fairness it should be said that for the Petrograd Bolshevik leaders to leave the demonstrators (and their own hard-won rank-and-file) to their own devices on the evening of July 3 would have been extremely difficult. The movement on the streets was, after all, a response to Bolshevik propaganda and a genuine reflection of the increasing "bolshevization" of the masses. However, in evaluating the unofficial decision by members of the Bureau of the Military Organization and the Executive Commission of the Petersburg Committee, account must also be taken of the fact that within the upper echelons of these organizations the policy of immediate direct action had previously found strong support.

In any event, having decided to take charge of the street movement, the Petrograd Bolshevik leadership was suddenly faced with the crucial question of what it was and what it would become. In Kalinin's words, "was this to be merely a demonstration or something more? Was it perhaps the beginning of the proletarian revolution, the start of the seizure of power?"[106] There is no evidence that the Military Organization-Executive Commission meeting resolved this question, and it is quite possible that no attempt to do so was made since responsibility for major policy decisions rested first of all with the Central Committee, many of whose members were then in the Taurida Palace.

It is notable, however, that the problem of defining the movement in the streets received attention during a gathering of Second City Conference delegates with garrison and factory representatives at 10:00 P.M. in the Kshesinskaia mansion. In his earliest published memoirs Ilin-Zhenevsky recalled this episode: "Spent a short time at the city conference. . . . The majority of district delegates were extremely excited, part of them insisting on an armed uprising. 'How can this be a peaceful demonstration?' cried a tall, frantically gesticulating delegate; 'there is shooting in the streets. This is a new revolution!' "[107]

This consultative meeting lasted until after 11:00. During its

course a recommendation that the street demonstrations be continued the next day under Bolshevik auspices was adopted.[108] Focus
of the mass protest was to be shifted from the injustices of garrison
troop levies to the bankruptcy of the government as reflected in
the resignation of the Kadets. Nothing was said about an armed
uprising, and it seems doubtful that any such possibility was formally voted upon. According to one anonymous report, the conference leadership "emphasized that the demonstrators should not
seize any governmental institutions independently."[109] Thus, it
would appear that the question of an organized effort was left open
(this is also suggested by other sources). There are numerous references in literature on the July days to the fact that it was understood that the demonstrations would be armed, although this was
not formally specified. In this connection Latsis' diary contains the
following entry: "Machine guns are chattering on Nevsky, and
here [in the conference] there is talk of a peaceful demonstration.
I speak out in favor of an armed demonstration but in the end it is
decided not to say anything about peaceful or armed, but merely to
say demonstration. Perhaps this is necessary for external appearances, but for party members such vagueness is dangerous."[110] The
official resolution as adopted by the conference declared:

> The current government crisis will not be decided in the inter-
> ests of the people if the revolutionary proletariat and the garrison
> do not immediately declare forcefully and resolutely that they
> are in favor of the transfer of power to the Soviet of Workers',
> Soldiers', and Peasants' Deputies.
> With this objective in mind, it is recommended that the work-
> ers and soldiers go into the streets immediately to demonstrate
> their will.[111]

The Bolshevik Military Organization
Assumes Command

Although the Bolshevik Central Committee did not reverse its
former official position opposing street demonstrations until the
early morning hours of July 4, for practical purposes the positive

decision taken by the Executive Commission of the Petersburg Committee and the All-Russian Bureau of the Military Organization and the resolution adopted at the consultative Second City Conference session marked a major turning point in the July movement. From this point on, the First Machine Gun Regiment's Provisional Revolutionary Committee seemed to vanish, its functions taken over entirely by a special operational staff created by the Military Organization and headed by N. I. Podvoisky, V. I. Nevsky, and K. A. Mekhonoshin.

Simultaneously with the party's initial positive declaration, this operational staff assumed control of the demonstration and began mobilizing the most formidable and broadest possible military support, including reinforcements from regiments in the suburbs. Thus Military Organization member E. I. Spets, telephoning Oranienbaum from the Kshesinskaia mansion, ordered the First Machine Gun Regiment's Third Battalion quartered there to prepare for departure for Petrograd at 8:00 the next morning, "with all available machine guns and rifles and as much ammunition as possible."[112] Similarly, Tarasov-Rodionov of the Infantry Officers' Academy left the Kshesinskaia mansion for Oranienbaum upon the conclusion of the Military Organization-Executive Commission meeting in a commandeered automobile belonging to Tsereteli. Arriving late in the evening, he directed the mobilization of the Oranienbaum garrison for an early morning departure for Petrograd with all available arms and then took part in a short-lived seizure of power in Oranienbaum.[113]

Representatives of Military Organization collectives waiting for instructions in the Kshesinskaia mansion now received verbal orders to join the regiments already in the streets with all possible haste while the following administrative instructions, bearing the Military Organization stamp, were rushed to party members in all units of the garrison:

> 1) Organize a committee made up of members of our organization to lead the battalion.
>
> 2) Select leaders for each company.

3) Organize company meetings at which our instructions shall be read.

4) Establish communications with the Military Organization designating two comrades to be sent us for this purpose.

5) Maintain contact with neighboring units.

6) Check on who sends out detachments and where they are sent; detachments should be given our instructions.

7) Be prepared but do not leave the garrison without a summons from the Military Organization.[114]

During this initial flurry of activity armed cars from the Reserve Armored Car Division were dispatched for duty at the Kshesinskaia mansion, the Nikolaevsky station, key bridges, and Liteiny Prospect. The Sixteenth Company of the First Machine Gun Regiment was ordered to maintain security around the Kshesinskaia mansion and to occupy the historic Fortress of Peter and Paul.[115] At the same time announcements regarding the Bolshevik decision were sent to such key points as the Fortress of Peter and Paul and the Armory. The dispatch below, dated July 3, was evidently sent to the Fortress of Peter and Paul before the arrival of the First Machine Gun company:

3 July No. 215

RSDLP MILITARY ORGANIZATION UNDER
THE CENTRAL COMMITTEE

The Fortress of Peter and Paul:

The Military Organization informs the garrison of the Fortress of Peter and Paul that today's demonstration was spontaneous; that it was not called by our party. After ascertaining the impossibility of restraining the demonstration, and in the interest of preventing the counterrevolution from crushing the soldiers who have come out, we have proposed to all comrade soldiers that they support the revolutionary military units in the streets.

At this time we call on the garrison of Peter and Paul not to go anywhere without a call from the Military Organization and to inform us of all orders from the government.

For the chairman of the Military Organization,
V. NEVSKY
Secretary, MEKHONOSHIN[116]

"Victory" in the Workers' Section
of the Petrograd Soviet

We must now backtrack a bit and shift our attention to the Taurida Palace, destined to be the center of activity throughout the
July days. Here, late on the evening of July 3 and all day July 4, the
Soviet Executive Committees grappled with the government crisis
and the chaotic situation in the streets, and it was to this point that
factory upon factory and regiment upon regiment came to present
their demands. Even the Bolshevik Central Committee now shifted
its command post to the Taurida Palace quarters of the Bolshevik
delegation in the Petrograd Soviet.[117]

Beginning in the early evening one of the halls of the Taurida
Palace was the scene of an emergency meeting of the Workers'
Section of the Petrograd Soviet (along with the Soldiers' Section a
major subcommittee of the Soviet), in which, for the first time, the
Bolsheviks were able to win a majority. Subsequently, the meeting
passed a resolution supporting the street demonstrations and demanding that all power be transferred to the Soviets. Indeed, a
special commission was created for the dual purpose of insuring that
the demonstration would be peaceful and exerting pressure on the
Soviet to take power. In view of this, the question arises as to
whether the Bolshevik victory in the Workers' Section had any
direct connection with the movement in the streets. An answer is
suggested by the proceedings of the meeting and its immediate
background.

It will be remembered that one of the main Bolshevik objectives
suggested by Lenin after the cancellation of the June 10 demonstration was winning control of the Soviets and the organs of the Petrograd Soviet (the Workers' Section among them) first of all. At the
factory level this campaign was pursued with the Bolsheviks' usual
thoroughness. New elections to the Workers' Section could be
called at the discretion of each factory's employees. In the latter
part of June Bolsheviks in a number of factories were able to take

advantage of labor unrest and dissatisfaction with the offensive, at first to pass anti-government resolutions and subsequently to arrange for replacement of SR and Menshevik deputies, naturally unwilling to support these resolutions, with people who would.[118] The campaign appeared to be going so well, in fact, that by late June the Bolsheviks were ready for a test of strength in the Workers' Section.

On June 23 *Pravda* reported that the Bolshevik delegation in the Petrograd Soviet was exerting pressure on the Petrograd Soviet Executive Committee to call an emergency meeting of the Workers' Section for the purpose of considering methods for dealing with the counterrevolution. This initial announcement contained the draft of a ten-point Bolshevik resolution to be presented for adoption at the proposed meeting. Among other things, this resolution called for the preservation of the agreement between the Soviet and the Provisional Government in regard to the maintenance of the revolutionary nucleus of the garrison in Petrograd, complete freedom for agitation among military units in the garrison and at the front, immediate investigation of all organizations conducting undercover and open counterrevolutionary agitation, and the division of paper reserves, quarters, printing presses, etc., so that the needs of worker, soldier, and peasant newspapers would be filled first.

On June 30 *Pravda* announced that a meeting of the Workers' Section was scheduled for the next evening and that attendance was absolutely mandatory for all eligible party members. The Executive Committee of the Petrograd Soviet subsequently postponed this meeting until July 3, and so on July 2 *Pravda* repeated its appeal of June 30. Moreover, at the close of the Second City Conference morning session of July 3, delegates were reminded of the utmost importance of being present for the "decisive struggle" planned for the Petrograd Soviet that evening.[119] The point to be made out of all this is that the campaign in the Workers' Section, originally scheduled to take place on July 1, had no direct connection with the movement in the streets on July 3. To the contrary, like the campaign for strength in the Constituent Assembly, it was one of the alternatives to immediate direct action advocated at this time by Lenin and the majority of the Bolshevik Central Committee.

At 7:00 P.M. on July 3, the meeting of the Workers' Section was convened. It began with a clash over the adoption of an agenda. The major importance of this clash was that it was won by the Bolsheviks; what is most interesting about the agenda itself was that it followed the plans laid out by *Pravda* on June 23 and thus contained no mention whatever of either the government or the activities of the First Machine Gun Regiment.[120] Judging by what was to come, this suggests that at the time the meeting started, Kamenev, Zinoviev, and Trotsky, who formulated tactics for this meeting and who were also the leaders of the "moderate" Bolshevik-Interdistrict Committee elements, firmly opposed to the armed demonstration, were not yet convinced that the movement begun by the machine gunners could not be stopped.[121]

Thus, the first half of the July 3 meeting was taken up with debate on the Bolshevik proposal for dealing with the counterrevolution. Only sometime after 9:00, when word was received that the movement would not be restrained, indeed that elements of the First Machine Gun and Moskovsky Regiments would begin arriving at the Taurida Palace momentarily, was this debate suspended. By this time Kamenev and Zinoviev were informed of the crucial decisions taken in the Kshesinskaia mansion in their absence.[122] Knowing this, the Bolsheviks, with Trotsky's support, now sought to commit the Workers' Section to a similar policy. Thus, Chkheidze's suggestion that the meeting be adjourned immediately so that its participants might try to restrain factories and regiments not yet involved was countered by Kamenev, who proposed that with the masses already in the streets it was necessary to create a special commission (including Mensheviks and SR's) charged with the task of insuring that the demonstration would be peaceful. In the course of a very bitter argument over this proposal the Mensheviks and SR's walked out of the meeting, and a short time later the following resolution was approved:

> In view of the government crisis, the Workers' Section considers it necessary to insist on the All-Russian Congress of the Soviet of Workers', Soldiers', and Peasants' Deputies taking power into its hands. The Workers' Section pledges to promote this objective with all its strength and hopes to obtain support for this policy from the Soldiers' Section. The Workers' Section selects a commission which is charged with acting in the name of the Workers' Section in contact with the Petrograd and All-Russian Soviet Executive Committees. All other participants in this meeting will go to the districts to inform the workers and soldiers of this decision and, remaining in constant contact with this commission, will try to give the movement a peaceful and organized character.[123]

It is important to note that the commission created by this resolution appears to have had little subsequent importance, aside from giving the July movement less of an exclusively Bolshevik appearance, perhaps partly because effective control of the street movement was already firmly in the unremitting hands of the Military Organization. But Kamenev's proposal is significant in that it may well have been an honest attempt by Bolshevik moderates to transfer responsibility for control of the demonstrations from exclusively party organs.

The March on the Taurida Palace

Nevsky Prospect between the Admiralty to the west and Znamenskaia Square to the east was the main thoroughfare and commercial center of Petrograd, as much the citadel of the hated bourgeoisie as the Vyborg District was the haven for the factory workers. Beginning on the afternoon of July 3, the uneasy tranquility of this area was shattered first by trucks of the First Machine Gun Regiment, mounting as many as three, five, and six machine guns, and then by columns of demonstrating workers and soldiers.

As might be expected, it was precisely here that senseless clashes, between the excitable and heavily armed demonstrators, many of them obviously bent on shooting up the bourgeoisie, and individuals intent on provoking or disrupting the processions, occurred most frequently during the chaotic first night of the July days. At the time the question of who fired first seemed vitally important. Fifty years later, study of a confusing array of newspaper accounts, documents, and memoirs leaves one with the feeling that in all probability trigger-happy demonstrators, *provocateurs*, right-wing elements, and quite often sheer confusion and panic were equally to blame.[124]

On the evening of July 3 one of the most serious of these clashes occurred when the 180th Reserve Infantry and Grenadier Regiments passed the Gostiny Dvor, a block-square shopping arcade on Nevsky Prospect, and the Public Library in the course of a roundabout journey from the Kshesinskaia mansion to the Taurida Palace. "At around 11:00," recounts a participant, "we reached Gostiny Dvor. . . . Our path was blocked and it was dark. . . . Suddenly we heard a bomb go off in front of us, someone threw a hand grenade, and the blast seemed to be a signal. Several machine guns began chattering immediately. For an instant the crowd froze, then it backed its way faster and faster into the courtyard of the Armenian church and the arcade of the Gostiny Dvor. Some of the soldiers crouching down on the pavement . . . returned the fire while others retreated with the rest of the crowd. . . . The machine guns chattered for several minutes, the whistle of bullets and crackle of rifle fire drowning out the moans of the wounded."[125]

By midnight, in spite of such delays, elements of most of the "Bolshevik" regiments, i.e., the First Machine Gun, Moskovsky, Finliandsky, First Infantry, Pavlovsky, Grenadier, and 180th Infantry Regiments as well as the Sixth Engineer Battalion, the four artillery pieces, and thousands of Vyborg District factory workers were massed in the streets surrounding the Taurida Palace.[126] At about 2:00 A.M. they were joined by 30,000 Putilov workers, some of them accompanied by wives and children. Thus, by this time the number of demonstrators was probably in the neighborhood of sixty to seventy thousand. Opposed to this, the force defending the Taurida Palace was negligible. "The best we could get," remembers Woytinsky, "were some promises from a few garrison regiments that they would send a detachment [for duty at the Taurida Palace] if detachments were sent from other regiments. The situation was abominable. An armed group of say two hundred could easily have seized the Taurida Palace, dispersed the Central Executive Committee and arrested its members."[127]

Fortunately for the majority socialist leaders, the First Machine Gun Regiment and Anarchist-Communists were no longer in control of the workers and soldiers and the Bolsheviks had yet to agree among themselves about whether they were witnessing a demonstration or a revolution. The Putilov workers, for their part, vowed to remain at the Taurida Palace until the Central Executive Committee announced its willingness to take power and to arrest the "ten capitalist ministers." The imposing mob presented its demands and waved red banners with the slogan "All power to the Soviets." It cursed the Provisional Government and listened with obvious distrust to speeches by Chkheidze and Woytinsky, who begged the soldiers and workers to go home and promised that their wishes would be taken into consideration. It responded enthusiastically to speeches by Trotsky and Zinoviev, who agreed that the time had come for the transfer of power to the Soviets.[128] But the artillery, machine guns, and rifles remained silent, and the demonstrators stood or wandered about aimlessly, probably wondering at the stubbornness of the majority socialists and the indecisiveness of their own leadership. Toward dawn, frustrated, tired, and hungry, but in the understanding that they would return later in the day, the soldiers and workers drifted back to their districts.

Meanwhile, inside the Taurida Palace's grand White Hall a frantic joint meeting of the Soviet Executive Committees was drawing to a close. It had begun at midnight with the adoption of a controversial proposal stipulating that resolutions supported by a majority would be binding on all participants in the meeting. This was an oblique invitation for the Bolsheviks to leave the hall (evidently no Bolsheviks were present, but members of the Interdistrict Committee walked out in protest) and the prelude to a long condemnation of the demonstrations and the Bolsheviks, which lasted for several hours. Tsereteli voiced the indignation of the majority when he condemned the demonstrations as counterrevolutionary and stated that "the decisions of the revolutionary democracy could not be dictated by bayonets." The Menshevik leader R. A. Abramovich sternly attacked the Bolsheviks and demanded that "they come out and say directly: this is our work." The meeting ended at 5:00 A.M. (so that delegates could go to the factories and regiments to explain the majority socialist position) with the adoption of the following statement:

> *Comrade workers and soldiers!*
> ... [Yesterday] certain military units came out on the streets ... attempting to gain control of the city, seizing automobiles, arbitrarily arresting individuals, and acting threateningly and violently. Appearing at the Taurida Palace with arms in hand, they demanded that the Executive Committees take full power. . . . The All-Russian executive organs of the Soviets of Workers' and Peasants' Deputies indignantly oppose all attempts to influence their will by force. It is outrageous that a part of the garrison in one city should attempt to force its will on the whole of Russia by means of armed demonstrations. . . .
> The All-Russian organs of the Soviets of Workers' and Peasants' Deputies protest against these ominous signs of disintegration which undermine all popular government. . . . The All-Russian executive organs of the Soviets of Workers', Soldiers', and Peasants' Deputies demand that such demonstrations, which bring shame to revolutionary Petrograd, be ended once and for all. The Executive Committees of the All-Russian Soviets of Workers', Soldiers', and Peasants' Deputies call on all those who defend the revolution and its conquests to wait for the decision of the lawful organs of democracy on the government crisis. All those to whom the cause of freedom is dear must accept this decision, which will be an expression of the voice of all revolutionary Russia.[129]

The Central Committee
Sends for Lenin

Not long after the Executive Committees began their joint meeting (that is, at about 1:00 A.M.), the Bolshevik Central Committee, its membership together for the first time in several hours, met with representatives of the Petersburg Committee and Military Organization in the Taurida Palace. Soon they were joined by Trotsky and other Interdistrict Committee leaders who had just departed under protest from the Joint Executive Committee meeting. Judging by memoir accounts, of all the important Bolshevik meetings during the revolutionary period for which there are no published protocols, this one was undoubtedly among the most interesting. The major topic of discussion was, of course, the City Conference's recommendations for prolonging the street demonstrations. Apparently even at this late date Kamenev and Zinoviev tried vainly to save the party from the serious defeat which they were certain would result from a massive armed confrontation with the Soviet. Countering the majority of participants in the meeting, who implied that the point of no return in regard to the demonstrations had already been passed, Kamenev stubbornly proposed that an attempt be made to organize district rallies instead.[130] Trotsky claims that he supported Kamenev's position until he became convinced that there was absolutely no hope of preventing the masses from returning to the streets the next day.[131] Zinoviev affirms that only after the arrival at the Taurida Palace of thirty thousand Putilov workers and the receipt of a phone call from Raskolnikov in Kronstadt, who stated categorically that nothing and nobody could stop the sailors from departing for Petrograd in the morning, was it finally decided that the Central Committee would authorize and lead a "peaceful though armed" demonstration of workers and soldiers the next day.[132] And now, in view of the critical position in which the party found itself, the Central Committee also decided to send for Lenin immediately.[133]

Sometime in the early morning hours of July 4, while a Central

Committee messenger hurried to Lenin in Finland, the appeal restraining the masses drafted earlier by Kamenev and Zinoviev was
removed from the matrix of the day's *Pravda*. It was apparently
decided not to hold up the edition for a new proclamation, and so
on July 4 the party's indecision was reflected by a large blank
space on page one. By 4:00 A.M. a leaflet drafted by Stalin and
signed by, among others, the Central Committee, Petersburg Committee, and Military Organization was being distributed in the
streets. It read in part:

> *Fellow workers and soldiers of Petrograd!*
>   . . . The coalition government has collapsed—it fell to pieces be-
> cause it was unable to carry out the tasks for which it was cre-
> ated. The revolution is faced with most tremendous and difficult
> problems. A new power is needed which, united with the revo-
> lutionary proletariat, revolutionary army, and revolutionary
> peasants, will decisively take up the task of consolidating and
> extending the victories already gained by the people. This power
> can be only the power of the Soviets of Workers', Soldiers', and
> Peasants' Deputies.
>   Yesterday the revolutionary garrison and workers of Petro-
> grad demonstrated and proclaimed this slogan: All power to the
> Soviets! We call upon this movement that arose in the regiments
> and factories to become a peaceful, organized expression of the
> will of the workers, soldiers, and peasants of Petrograd.[134]

Thus the Bolshevik Central Committee, against the better judg-
ment of several of its members, now stood at the brink of a decisive
clash with the Soviet and the Provisional Government. In one of his
early memoirs V. I. Nevsky wrote that if it had been possible to
defeat the bourgeoisie in July, not a single Bolshevik would have
refused to make use of the opportunity provided by the demonstrations.[135] Raskolnikov suggests the same in a *Pravda* memoir on the
July days entitled "Armed Uprising or Armed Demonstration?"
"Did we renounce the possibility of seizing power?" he recalls.
"Certainly not. In the mind of each of us [Bolsheviks] was the
thought of seizing power. All that was needed was a suitable
moment."[136]

"Was this to be merely a street demonstration or . . . the start of the seizure of power?" Stated another way, would the party risk everything in the hope of overthrowing the Provisional Government immediately or would it limit its commitment in the hope of preserving as much strength as possible for the future?[137] This was the difficult choice which Lenin would face the next day upon his return from Finland.

VI

The July Uprising: Culmination and Collapse

Petrograd on the Morning of July 4

By dawn of what was to be a warm but drizzly day, the workers' sections of Petrograd were already alive with preparations for a renewal of the previous evening's street demonstrations. In the commercial district insurgent armed trucks and armored cars were once again careening about, pausing infrequently to direct hails of bullets at real and imagined enemies. Most banks and shops opened for business, then quickly closed when it became apparent that the demonstrations would continue. City industrial life remained at a standstill; most workers elected either to join the street marches or go home, and by 10:00 A.M. even the street cars had stopped running.[1] Only the city's hospitals, already overburdened with casualties, were busy as they prepared for a fresh influx of wounded. Doctors were placed on alert, medical aid stations were set up in private homes on Nevsky and Liteiny Prospects, and ambulances were ordered to cruise the streets.[2]

In the Kshesinskaia mansion the Military Organization's operational staff had labored through the night drawing up demonstration plans and instructions.[3] Although there is very little material on this aspect of the July movement, it appears that in its planning the Military Organization did not ignore the possibility of overthrowing the Provisional Government.[4] In the morning a steady stream of factory and garrison representatives in armed trucks and automobiles arrived for briefings. The focal point of the demonstration was again to be the Taurida Palace, and delegates were to be elected from each factory and military unit to present to the Executive Committees the demand for transfer of "All power to the Soviets."

While district party workers flocked to the Kshesinskaia mansion for instructions, Bolshevik agitators in factories and barracks all over the city and its suburbs competed with Menshevik and SR representatives of the Soviet for the support of workers and soldiers. The response to the Bolshevik appeal to demonstrate was mixed. While, on the one hand, the spirit prevailing in the factories was still rebellious, and the participation of, among others, the 176th and 171st Infantry Reserve Regiments from Krasnoe Selo, the Third Infantry Reserve Regiment from Peterhof, the Third Battalion of the First Machine Gun Regiment from Oranienbaum, and the sailors from Kronstadt seemed assured, reports reaching the Military Organization on the precise situation in the Petrograd garrison itself were not as promising.[5] Apparently, among less revolutionary regiments the excesses, bloodshed, and frustrations of the previous evening had had something of a sobering effect, and some of the units which had demonstrated the day before had second thoughts about coming out again.[6] Moreover, those garrison regiments which had not responded to the appeals of the First Machine Gun Regiment on July 3 remained adamantly unwilling to participate in the rebellion. Thus, already on the morning of July 4 there were definite signs that the revolutionary wave was nearing its crest. But this was probably small consolation to the majority party leaders in the Soviet because all told an enormous number of workers, sailors, and soldiers (contemporary estimates of the number of demonstrators on July 4 ran as high as half a million) were ready to follow the Bolsheviks. And equally important, among troops of the garrison a readiness to support the Soviet (not to speak of the Provisional Government) continued to be virtually nonexistent.

In his memoirs Woytinsky describes the Central Executive Committee's totally fruitless efforts to enlist detachments from the garrison for the defense of the Taurida Palace and the restoration of order. He concludes that "there really was nothing with which to defend the palace. . . . With difficulty it proved possible to maintain the outside guard and some patrols which kept us informed of developments in nearby districts."[7] Requests for troops were sent to the Preobrazhensky, Semenovsky, and Izmailovsky Guards Regiments, among others. According to Miliukov, all responded with declarations of neutrality.[8]

Yet if the position of the Soviet was bad, that of the Provisional Government was infinitely worse. Its significance was in fact almost completely discounted. Even some regiments and factories pledging to obey the Executive Committee's ban on demonstrations nonetheless adopted resolutions calling for the transfer of power to the Soviet. In this regard Woytinsky writes that the neutrality declared by such units as the Semenovsky, Preobrazhensky, and Izmailovsky Regiments was between the Central Executive Committee and its Bolshevik opposition. "The Provisional Government was, in fact, forgotten or more accurately," he comments, "the Provisional Government was regarded as no longer in existence and the argument centered on the government that would replace it."[9] During the peak moments of the July crisis non-socialist government ministers were huddled with General Polovtsev in the General Staff headquarters off the Palace Square, but, with perhaps the exception of the Minister of Justice, P. N. Pereverzev,[10] they were helpless to influence the course of events.

On the evening of July 3 and the following morning the Petrograd Military District attempted, with no success, to bring non-demonstrating garrison regiments into action against insurgent troops. And so on the morning of July 4 the sum total of the forces at General Polovtsev's disposal were a few detachments of Cossacks, who were ordered to conduct roving patrols, and some war wounded, who were deployed to guard the Winter Palace and the headquarters of the General Staff. Relatively meager reinforcements were expected from the suburbs, but these would not arrive before evening.[11] Thus, for practical purposes Polovtsev's order to the garrison to arrest and disarm insurgent workers and soldiers,[12] issued on the afternoon of July 4 and published on July 5, was to remain for the time being a dead letter.

It should be noted that at the time negotiations were in progress between the Executive Committees and the Petrograd Military District, on the one hand, and garrison regiments, on the other, both the Provisional Government and the Soviet were also in contact with Fifth Army headquarters in Dvinsk on the Northern front.[13] Already late on the third A. A. Vilenkin, chairman of the Fifth Army Committee, and General Danilov, commander of the Fifth Army, began organizing a powerful composite field force for shipment to the capital in the event of a request for troops from the Soviet.[14] On the morning of July 4, B. V. Stankevich, newly appointed commissar of the Northern front, also took part in these preparations.[15] But despite the seriousness of the moment, probably because of hesitancy to take a step which might weaken the front and partly, too, for reasons of pride, the majority socialist leaders balked at issuing the orders which would start loyal troops from the front to the capital.[16]

This, very briefly, was the hopeless position of the Provisional Government and the unenviable situation of the Soviet when word reached the Taurida Palace at 10:20 A.M. that a flotilla of boats and barges from Kronstadt had been sighted at Peterhof on its way to Petrograd. But before turning to this and the demonstrations of July 4, a few words should be said about Lenin's reappearance in the capital.

Lenin's Return

At about 6:00 A.M. on July 4, M. A. Saveliev, the party comrade sent by the Central Committee to fetch Lenin, reached the latter at V. Bonch-Bruevich's villa near the Finnish village of Neivola. Thoroughly alarmed by Saveliev's report of the uprising in Petrograd, Lenin made hurried preparations to depart for the capital. "Is this the beginning of decisive operations?" asked Saveliev. Lenin is reported to have replied that "this would be quite inopportune."[17]

In any event there was no time for delay, and accompanied by his sister Maria Ilinichna, Saveliev, and Bonch-Bruevich, Lenin caught the 6:45 train for Petrograd.[18] Hunching behind the morning papers so as not to be recognized, he devoured initial reports on the bloody street demonstrations of the previous evening. At this point, recalled Bonch-Bruevich, Lenin seemed much more concerned with the animosity toward the Bolsheviks reflected in all of the morning papers than with the fact that the masses had come into the streets.[19] Saveliev reports that during the tense journey Lenin was buried in his own thoughts and spoke very little.[20] At about 11:00 the train pulled into the Finland station, near which crowds of armed Vyborg District factory workers were already gathering for another march on the Taurida Palace. The distance from the Finland station to the Kshesinskaia mansion was not great, so that despite the columns of workers and soldiers who swelled the streets, Lenin was soon safe in the turbulent but friendly confines of his own command post.

Kronstadt Arrives in Petrograd

An entry in the Executive Committee's records reads: "10:30—the machine gunners from Oranienbaum have arrived bringing their machine guns with them. . . . We have also been informed that the Kronstadt sailors have been sighted passing Peterhof aboard eight tugboats, two barges, three trawlers, three gun boats, and a torpedo boat. We are told that all [of the sailors] are armed."[21] Although the unnamed informant from Peterhof evidently missed a number of passenger ferries, the gist of the message was correct. What must have been one of the most motley flotillas in history (ironically, it was commanded by the future "Red Admiral of the Fleet," F. F. Raskolnikov) was necessitated by the fact that there was only one broken-down military vessel of any importance in the whole of the port of Kronstadt on the morning of July 4, and it was incapable of moving from its mooring.[22] Thus for their long-awaited massive assault on Petrograd the ten thousand or so sailors and workers[23] were crammed aboard every military and civilian boat capable of holding even a few passengers. The Kronstadters, almost without exception, were armed and brought with them at least sixty thousand rounds of rifle ammunition, five hundred revolver shells, a medical team with stretchers, and a marching band.[24]

Near the mouth of the Neva the flotilla from Kronstadt was met by a representative of the Executive Committee of the Petrograd Soviet aboard a tugboat. In vain he explained that no one had called the sailors and urged them to return home. The boats from Kronstadt steamed by without slowing down and soon were tying up along the Nikolaevsky and University quays near the Nikolaevsky bridge. There the sailors were greeted by cheering crowds of workers on their way to the Taurida Palace from factories on Vasilievsky Island. As the disembarkation proceeded, agitators (the indefatigable Bleikhman among them) exhorted the sailors to overthrow the Provisional Government, and some workers, evidently remembering the sniping of the previous evening, shouted to gawking students and professors in the university to shut their windows. "Did all the regiments of the garrison join the previous evening's demonstration?" asked an arriving sailor. In response to queries as to why they had come, other Kronstadters declared: "We have been called and have come to restore order because the bourgeoisie has gotten too far out of line here."[25]

The tying up and unloading of the boats took over an hour, and before this was finished a light rain had begun to fall. During this time Raskolnikov and Roshal were briefed by Liubovich and Flerovsky.[26] Instead of heading directly for the Taurida Palace, the sailors were now to go to the Kshesinskaia mansion in order to make contact with other military forces,[27] and presumably to see Lenin. One suspects that this was also to allow Lenin to have a look at the sailors. In any event, this change caused no little friction between the Bolshevik and non-Bolshevik leaders of the march, especially a short time later when Raskolnikov ignored a request to allow the Left SR leader, Maria Spiridonova, to address the sailors.[28] Meanwhile the Soviet Executive Committee had rushed some more deputies to the quays, but their appeals had no effect,[29] and leaving them and Maria Spiridonova behind, the huge procession moved forward.

Along the University quay, across the Stock Exchange bridge to the Petrograd side, then through the Alexandrovsky park to the Kshesinskaia mansion—this was the route of march taken by the sailors. Flerovsky remembers that were were not many banners and the band played very little. "The lighthearted boisterousness that usually accompanied our demonstrations was missing," he writes. "Seriousness was written on the faces of the black columns of sailors. . . . To force the compromisers to submit to the will of the people [was the goal], but nobody quite knew how this was to be achieved and the uncertainty created an air of uneasiness."[30]

The procession halted at the Kshesinskaia mansion, around which crowds of workers, a scattering of soldiers (though no whole regiments), and some armored cars were already gathered. Standing on the second floor balcony were some women holding up Central Committee, Petersburg Committee, and Military Organization banners, and Nevsky, Sverdlov, and Lunacharsky, who shouted instructions to the arriving march elements.[31] While Sverdlov and then Lunacharsky addressed the sea of armored workers, soldiers, and sailors, Raskolnikov and Flerovsky went inside to ask Lenin to make an appearance. At this point some of the Kronstadt Left SR's under G. Smoliansky and the Anarcho-Syndicalist-Communists led by Iarchuk protested these protracted, purely Bolshevik ceremonies and departed, with Iarchuk remarking that "they hadn't come to Petrograd for meetings."[32]

According to Flerovsky and Podvoisky, Lenin initially refused to address the crowd. "I asked him to speak and a Kronstadt delegation did the same," writes Podvoisky in his memoirs, "but Lenin said no, explaining that his refusal would show that he was against the demonstration."[33] In the end, however, Lenin yielded, stepped out on the balcony, and was greeted by what even impartial observers called a thunderous ovation.[34] It should be noted that while

Lenin's annoyance at having to appear before the demonstrators was very likely genuine, his first refusal should probably not be taken to imply at this point he was ready to halt the demonstrations (indeed, new agitation and mobilization efforts were initiated well after Lenin's return) or that he precluded the possibility of using the demonstrations to overthrow the Provisional Government. To the contrary, Kalinin recalls that Lenin's answer to the question of whether the movement on the streets was the beginning of the seizure of power was "we shall see—right now it is impossible to say!" Kalinin adds that this by no means excluded the possibility of throwing the regiments into battle in favorable circumstances, or, on the other hand, of ultimately retreating with as few losses as possible.[35]

This would be Lenin's last public speech until after the October revolution, but his message was not what the sailors had expected to hear and many of them were evidently disappointed. Lenin voiced a few words of greeting and expressed the certainty that the slogan "All power to the Soviets" would win out in the end. He concluded by appealing to the sailors for self-restraint, determination, and vigilance.[36] A Kronstadt Bolshevik recalls that for many of the sailors, Lenin's emphasis on the necessity of a peaceful demonstration at this time was unexpected. He writes that "not only the Anarchists but some of the Bolsheviks could not see how a column of armed men, craving to rush into battle, could limit itself to an armed demonstration."[37]

Following Lenin's appearance, Sverdlov told the workers, soldiers, and sailors to "demand that the capitalist ministers be thrown out of the government. . . . If the Soviets refuse to take power, the situation will become clear. . . . In this event you should wait for further instructions."[38] At this point some of the sailors were drafted for continued mobilization efforts in factories and garrison regiments not yet involved in the demonstrations. At the same time the main body of Kronstadt sailors, the Vasilievsky Island workers, and armored cars, joined by Nevsky and Podvoisky, began to cross the Neva.

The demonstrations in Petrograd on July 4, 1917. (Museum of the Revolution USSR)

Shooting on Nevsky Prospect, July 4, 1917. (Museum of the Revolution USSR)

The Demonstration on July 4[39]

The crossing of the Troitsky bridge leading to the center of Petrograd by the Vasilievsky Island factory workers and Kronstadt sailors coincided with ominous reports received by the Soviet of demonstrators gathering or already on the move throughout the city.[40] At around 1:00 P.M. columns of armed Vyborg District factory workers, accompanied by women and children protected by armed trucks, and flanked by the First Machine Gun Regiment (still commanded by Semashko), crossed the Liteiny bridge and were soon reported nearing the Taurida Palace. A short time later the Putilov workers and part of the Second Machine Gun Regiment made contact with other Narva District factories assembled at the Narva Arch, and with an armed light truck bearing S. Bogdatiev and M. Voitsekhovsky, the commanders of the Putilov Red Guard, in the lead, they again started for the Taurida Palace. When at mid-afternoon this estimated sixty thousand-man procession passed a church on the corner of Sadovaia and Apraksina streets, again as if by signal, this time from the church bell, a hail of bullets descended on the marchers from upper windows and roof tops. Later Bogdatiev proudly testified to the Provisional Government Investigating Commission that the Putilovites made short work of the snipers.[41] A Soviet deputy who witnessed the exchange reported seeing five demonstrators killed and twenty-seven wounded.[42] Such reports began to reach the Soviet at 12:15 P.M., and from then on they were received throughout the day, almost without interruption.[43]

One of the most serious of these street clashes on July 4 occurred at about 3:00 P.M., when lead elements of the Kronstadt procession were not far from the Taurida Palace. At that time the main body of sailors was stretched out along Nevsky and Liteiny Prospects, along which buildings and shop windows were freshly decorated with banners supporting the Provisional Government and the Russian offensive. Raskolnikov, who was in the first row of marchers, recalls that "at the appearance of the sailors windows opened wide and whole families of the rich and well-bred came out on the balconies of their luxurious apartments."[44] Flerovsky remembers that because the relatively narrow street was unbelievably crowded, conditions for panic were ideal. "The sounds of the band in the rear could barely be heard," he continues. "The sun peeked out from behind the clouds . . . and suddenly there was the sound of gunfire behind us."[45] According to Iarchuk, one of the first to be felled was a standard bearer carrying the black flag of the Anarchists.[46]

As on the previous evening, the columns of marchers panicked almost as soon as the firing began. The more trigger-happy sailors began to shoot in all directions, while others hit the ground and crawled into nearby doorways for cover. Casualties were many, largely because of the confusion. After the firing had died down, the buildings from which the shooting appeared to have started were cordoned off, and a short time later a Military Organization armored car forced its way into the street and sprayed these buildings with machine gun fire.[47] Some sailors were sent inside to search upper story apartments, and the newspapers later reported that they turned up some machine guns, rifles, and a considerable amount of ammunition and that several persons suspected of having taken part in the shooting were lynched. While this was going on, the bulk of the sailors and workers, now in almost complete disorder, made their way to the Taurida Palace where they were greeted by the enthusiastic cheers of the First Machine Gun Regiment.[48]

What the mood of the thousands of Kronstadt sailors would have been had they not just experienced what they believed was an ambush by the despised bourgeoisie is perhaps uncertain. But all participants' memoirs agree that now, as the sailors joined crowds of Vyborg District factory workers and the First Machine Gun Regiment besieging the still relatively unprotected meeting place of the Soviet, they were more than ever bent on a final reckoning with the Provisional Government. "When we reached the Taurida Palace," reported Iarchuk to the Kronstadt Soviet a few days later, "everybody was so stirred up that I expected the sailors to storm the palace."[49] In a similar vein Flerovsky recalls that the mood of the

Kronstadters was such "that they would undoubtedly have gotten pleasure out of strangling all of the 'compromising' [i.e., the liberal and majority socialist] leaders."[50]

Yet if in this respect the threatening attitudes of the Kronstadt masses were general and well defined, it should be pointed out that there was no such unanimity among their chiefs.[51] Thus, while the Left SR and non-party Kronstadt leaders viewed the street movement solely as a means of applying pressure on the Soviet to take power and were inclined to pack up and go home if it did not,[52] the influential Anarcho-Syndicalist-Communists under Iarchuk looked at the armed demonstrations as the start of an uprising which was to culminate in the complete destruction of the government.[53] Finally, wavering indecisively in the middle were the usually effective Kronstadt Bolshevik leaders. They were as impatient as the Anarchists to do away with the Provisional Government and undoubtedly helped promote the notion that this was the purpose of the movement, but were as hamstrung by the indecision of the party Central Committee as the garrison Military Organization leaders had been the night before.[54] In these circumstances the Kronstadt sailors lacked effective leadership and were more like a mob than an army.

But to return to developments at the Taurida Palace—while Raskolnikov led a delegation of sailors into the building, the bulk of the Kronstadters took part in one of the July uprising's more sensational events—the seizure of the SR Minister of Agriculture, Victor Chernov. This episode began when some of the more aroused and impatient sailors demanded to see the Minister of Justice, P. N. Pereverzev, for an explanation of why a certain Anatoli Zhelezniakov, one of the sailor-anarchists arrested in the government raid on the Durnovo villa, had not yet been released from prison. And when it became known that Pereverzev could not be found, these sailors began to break down the Taurida Palace doors, demanding an accounting from another of the government ministers.[55]

The Soviet leaders, evidently confident of Chernov's persuasive powers, sent him out to calm the workers, soldiers, and sailors. In his official statement to the Investigating Commission, Chernov later recalled that as soon as he stepped outdoors, someone cried: "Here is one of those who shoots at the people."[56] Some sailors rushed up to search him, and there were demands from all sides for his arrest. Chernov climbed on a barrel and tried with no success to explain the Soviet position on the government question. He attacked the Kadets, but the mob's response was even more menacing, its exasperation classically formulated in the cry of a fist-shaking worker: "Take power, you son-of-a-bitch, when it's given to you!"[57]

Questioned by a Bolshevik Petersburg Committee member as to why nothing had yet been done about the land question, the Minister of Agriculture replied that this problem was just then under consideration. Turning to go back into the palace, Chernov found himself surrounded by a group of unruly hecklers. One witness later identified them as sailors from the radical, Bolshevik controlled Kronstadt Machine School,[58] while another spectator indicated that the group also included civilians, many of whom displayed the black standards of the Anarchists.[59] In any event they declared that Chernov was under arrest; he was hauled down and thrust into a waiting car.

The news that Chernov was being torn apart by the mob brought pandemonium to a joint session of the Executive Committees, which only a few minutes earlier had decided to proceed with its regular business regardless of the havoc outside. Chkheidze hurriedly proposed that Kamenev, Martov, Steklov, and Woytinsky see what could be done about freeing Chernov. However, Trotsky, accompanied by Raskolnikov, was evidently the first to reach the car in which Chernov was being held.[60] Spying Raskolnikov, the sailors holding Chernov offered to entrust their prisoner to him, but Raskolnikov declared that the arrest was not permissible.[61] Sukhanov, who was close by, captures the spirit of what now took place:

> The mob was in turmoil as far as the eye could reach. . . . All Kronstadt knew Trotsky and, one would have thought, trusted him. But he began to speak and the crowd did not subside. If a shot had been fired nearby at that moment by way of provoca-

tion, a tremendous slaughter might have occurred and all of us, including perhaps Trotsky, might have been torn to shreds. Trotsky, excited and not finding words in this savage atmosphere, could barely make the nearest rows listen to him. . . . When he tried to pass on to Chernov himself, the ranks around the car began raging. "You've come to declare your will and show the Soviet that the working class no longer wants to see the bourgeoisie in power [declared Trotsky]. But why hurt your own cause by petty acts of violence against casual individuals? . . . Every one of you has demonstrated his devotion to the revolution. Every one of you is ready to lay down his life for it. I know that. Give me your hand, Comrade! Your hand, brother!"

Trotsky stretched his hand down to a sailor who was protesting with especial violence. But the latter firmly refused to respond . . . It seemed to me that the sailor, who must have heard Trotsky in Kronstadt more than once, now had a real feeling that he was a traitor: he remembered his previous speeches and was confused. . . . Not knowing what to do, the Kronstadters released Chernov.[62]

Humiliated and severely shaken, probably as much by shock at the fickleness of the Petrograd masses as by fright, Chernov returned to the palace. Recovering by evening, he composed eight scorching editorials against Bolshevism for *Delo naroda*, although the editors on duty ultimately decided that four would be enough for one issue.[63]

The continuing street riots, the menacing actions of the Kronstadt sailors, the reappearance a short time later of armed columns of Putilov workers, the imminent arrival at the Taurida Palace of insurgent regiments from the suburbs, and most important, the continued hesitation on the part of nominally loyal garrison regiments to provide for the defense of either the Provisional Government or the Soviet—all these factors combined to arouse the majority socialist Soviet leaders into considering more drastic measures, in the closest cooperation with the Petrograd Military District, aimed at bringing a quick end to the ever more threatening demonstrations. Among the important decisions now adopted was that authorizing the immediate dispatch of front line troops to the capital, a step which Kerensky had proclaimed unthinkable at the time of the June 10 crisis.[64] Tsereteli informed A. A. Vilenkin, chairman of the Fifth Army Committee, of this decision in the early evening of July 4, and the latter responded with a promise that loyal troops would be dispatched from the Northern front at once and could be expected in Petrograd no later than July 6.[65]

The response to a similar request for help to the Baltic fleet was not as encouraging. At this time the Naval Ministry, with the Soviet Executive Committees' authorization, suddenly issued an urgently worded telegram to the headquarters of the Baltic fleet requesting the immediate dispatch into the Neva of four destroyers, both as a show of force and for possible use against the rebelling units from Kronstadt. A telegram to this effect from the Assistant to the Naval Minister, B. P. Dudorov, was sent to D. N. Verderevsky, commander of the Baltic fleet, at 7:15 P.M. on July 4. But Helsingfors was not the front, and fifteen minutes later, Dudorov, evidently fearful lest his first order act as a spur to forces sympathetic to the rebellion, telegraphed Verderevsky that "any ships attempting to depart for Kronstadt without specific orders were to be sunk by the submarine fleet."[66]

Dudorov's apprehension was not unfounded. Indeed, the unreliability of the Baltic fleet at this time is reflected by the fact that the strongly Bolshevik-influenced Baltic fleet Central Committee (Tsentrobalt) monitored Dudorov's top-secret coded telegrams and forced Verderevsky to reject the orders. Pledging support to the rebelling workers and soldiers of Petrograd, Tsentrobalt resolved to send a representative delegation to the capital to ascertain the situation there and to arrest the "counterrevolutionary" Dudorov.[67] Soon Verderevsky's telegraphed reply was received by the worried government leaders: "Cannot carry out your orders. If you insist, please advise to whom I should turn over command of the fleet."[68] In a later telegram Verderevsky added: "According to the accepted procedure, I am personally responsible only for operational activities. At the present time the dispatch of destroyers into the Neva is a political act . . . [one which] can be taken only in agreement with the Central Committee. . . . The request for the sending of destroyers into the Neva would effect a split in the fleet and greatly weaken its fighting strength. . . . Because of this, the Central Committee is against such action, a position with which I am in agreement."[69]

Further evidence of the spirit of urgency reigning in the Taurida Palace at this time was a frantic appeal sent to Polovtsev for some of the troops from the suburbs then finally beginning to arrive at the headquarters of the General Staff. "Now," remembers Polovtsev with obvious relish, "I was free to assume the role of savior of the Soviet."[70] It appears that there was another aspirant to that title. On the afternoon of July 4, Minister of Justice P. N. Pereverzev began taking steps to reverse the Bolshevik tide by circulating information suggesting that the Bolsheviks had deliberately provoked the July uprising on instructions from the German General Staff.

The German Agent Question

The charge that Lenin was working for the German General Staff, which became a significant factor during the July days, was first made well before then; the right-wing Petrograd press had initiated the accusations not long after Lenin's return to Russia. But apart from the facts that Lenin had been allowed safe passage through Germany and that his avowed aim of subverting the Provisional Government and the Russian war effort coincided with that of the Germans, there was no evidence to substantiate the allegations. The Petrograd masses were much more receptive to Bolshevik propaganda on behalf of immediate peace and revolutionary progress than they were to the dirt slung by rejuvenated monarchists in such reactionary papers as *Malenkaia gazeta* and *Zhivoe slovo*, and as a result the German-agent accusations did not gain wide credence.

The Provisional Government first took an interest in the allegations against Lenin around the middle of May. At that time Kerensky was informed that a former Tsarist police agent, Lieutenant

Ermolenko, captured by the Germans early in the war and then drafted for pro-German agitational work in Russia, had turned himself in to the Russian General Staff. During the course of his interrogation Ermolenko alleged that two German General Staff officers had told him that Lenin was one among many German agents then operating in Russia. Ermolenko supplied no proof of this charge, and by no stretch of the imagination could he be characterized as a reliable source of information. At the time of the July crisis the Provisional Government's investigation of the matter, directed in secret by Lvov, Kerensky, Nekrasov, and Tereshchenko, was far from complete. Indeed, as nearly as one can tell, the proof then in the hands of the government consisted of Ermolenko's testimony, a statement from one Z. Burstein alleging that there was a German espionage ring in Stockholm headed by the German Social Democrat Parvus which supplied money to Lenin through the Bolsheviks Ganetsky and M. Iu. Kozlovsky,[71] and twenty-nine telegrams which did no more than suggest the possibility that the Bolsheviks were the recipients of funds supplied by the German government.[72]

Be that as it may, on July 4 Pereverzev, evidently convinced that any delay might be fatal, decided to let the neutral garrison regiments still balking at providing support for the Provisional Government have a look at the evidence already compiled against Lenin. "I felt that releasing this information would generate a mood in the garrison which would make continued neutrality impossible," wrote Pereverzev in his own defense a short time later. "I had a choice between a proposed definitive elucidation of the whole of this grand crime's roots and threads by some unspecified date and the immediate putting down of a rebellion which threatened to overturn the government."[73] Pereverzev first tested the effect of the material in his possession on representatives of the Preobrazhensky Regiment called to the headquarters of the General Staff precisely for this purpose. According to witnesses, the impact of Pereverzev's disclosures upon them was so profound that the information was immediately passed on to representatives of other equally promising regiments. Subsequently a portion of this data (consisting of the General Staff's summary of Ermolenko's testimony and an endorsement by the former Bolshevik Duma deputy, G. Alexinsky, and a journalist, V. Pankratov) was released to the press for publication the next day. All this was done on the afternoon and early evening of July 4 without the sanction of the harried Soviet Executive Committees then deliberating on the crisis in the besieged Taurida Palace.

The Soviet Executive Committees
and the Turn of the Tide

The joint meeting of the Soviet Executive Committees which convened at 6:00 P.M. on July 4 was one of the most tense and crucial sessions of the February to October period. Upon its outcome hinged the fate of the crippled Provisional Government. According to Woytinsky's actual count, at its beginning the force protecting the Soviet from the threat of dispersion and seizure by raging mobs consisted of fourteen Pavlovsky Regiment soldiers and eighteen men of the Armored Car Division—a puny force which was literally swept away at about 9:00 P.M., when crowds of demonstrators stampeded into the palace, more in panic than with intent to do harm.[74] A semblance of order was somehow preserved throughout this frantic time, though the urgently worded speeches of the Soviet leaders were constantly interrupted by shouts and jeers from the galleries, by the roar of the crowds and the staccato of small-arms fire outside, and by reverberations from bombs and artillery shells exploding in the distance. Many hours later, when the meeting finally broke up, troops loudly proclaiming their solidarity with the aims of the Soviet had replaced the insurgents on the Taurida Palace Square, Lenin and other top leaders were preoccupied with preparations to go into hiding, and a serious, perhaps decisive defeat for the Bolsheviks seemed assured.

It will be recalled that early on the morning of July 4, at the instigation of the Bolsheviks, delegates from Petrograd factories and military units were selected to present to the Executive Committees of the Soviet the demand for transfer of all power to the Soviet. In the late afternoon of July 4 ninety such delegates purporting to represent some fifty-four Petrograd factories and military regiments gathered in one of the smaller halls of the Taurida Palace to organize their presentation.[75] Initially, the majority socialist leaders refused to consider receiving the worker representatives, but later it was agreed that five of them would be allowed to give very brief speeches at the beginning of the Executive Committees' formal deliberations. The fragmentary published protocol of this meeting does not identify the delegates ultimately appearing before the Soviet, but from other sources it can be determined that among them were M. Ia. Latsis and G. D. Veinberg of the Bolshevik Vyborg District Committee and a representative of the Putilov workers, quite likely Sergei Bogdatiev. Typical of their brief but emotional statements, delivered with rifles in hand, were these by the second and fourth speakers:

> Second factory delegate: "You see what is written on our placards. Such is the decision passed by the workers. In the factories we are menaced by hunger. We demand the departure of the ten capitalist ministers. We trust the Soviet, but not those whom the Soviet trusts. The socialist ministers have entered into agreements with the capitalists—but these capitalists are our mortal enemies. We demand that the land be seized immediately and that [worker] control over industry be established at once, and we insist on a struggle against the starvation threatening us!"
>
> Fourth factory delegate: " . . . The masses sense that the situation in the country is serious. What you see before you is not a mutiny, but a fully organized demonstration. We demand that the land be turned over to the peasants and that orders directed against the revolutionary army be rescinded. We demand the adoption of all possible methods of struggle against sabotage and lockouts by the industrialists and capitalists. It is necessary to establish control over industry. As long as the policy of compromise with the bourgeoisie continues, there can be no calm in the country. Enough of warming this foul creature in our bosoms. Now that the Kadets have proclaimed their refusal to work with us, we ask you: who else will you barter with?"[76]

It does not appear that these appeals made any significant impression on the majority socialist leaders in the Soviet, most of whom clung to the notion that the aspirations of the workers and soldiers in the capital did not represent the will of the country as a whole and that to yield to mob pressure and to attempt to form a government without the participation of non-socialists would be disastrous. This was the view voiced by Tsereteli, speaking on behalf of the entire SR-Menshevik majority bloc:

> The present situation in Petrograd makes it impossible to make new decisions of any kind. . . . If we changed the government which was sanctioned by the Congress to that demanded by part of the garrison and some of the workers of Petrograd, the whole country would not take it as an expression of the will of the democracy, but as a concession to minority pressure. The only way out for the democracy is . . . to recognize the Provisional Government as it now stands as the lawful holder of revolutionary power and to convene an emergency Congress in two weeks' time, in a place where it can work unhindered, preferably in Moscow, for the purpose of making a final decision on the Provisional Government question.[77]

At this point the mob outside, perhaps sensing the futility of its position, became particularly menacing. Some Putilov workers interrupted Tsereteli to declare that unless he appeared outside at once they would carry him out. Chkheidze explained that Tsereteli was busy giving a speech. For the moment this evidently satisfied the Putilovites, and the debate on the government question continued.

Among others, Steklov, Martov, Grinevich, B. D. Kamkov, and Spiridonova of the left opposition rose to speak against the majority socialist position as formulated by Tsereteli. The often wavering Iu. M. Steklov, one of a number of non-party Social Democrats associated with Gorky's newspaper, *Novaia zhizn'*, now declared that Tsereteli was wrong in thinking a decision on the government question could be postponed. "Nine-tenths of the population," he asserted, "would greet a socialist ministry with enthusiasm perhaps greater than that displayed at the overthrow of the Romanovs." Martov, always to the left of the majority socialists in spirit, chose this occasion for a sharp break with them on the government question. Like Steklov, he rejected the possibility of postponing a decision for two weeks, arguing that this might be fatal and that history demanded that the Soviet take power into its own hands. "It has been said here," stated Martov, "that the demonstrators are a minority in the country. But this is a very active minority. It supports us while the majority is passive." Rejecting the idea of convening a congress in Moscow, Martov emphasized the necessity of forming a socialist government "capable of moving the revolution forward."[78]

Actually, even many people who sided with Tsereteli on the question of continuing to support the Provisional Government found the idea of moving the deliberations of the Soviet to Moscow unpalatable. Woytinsky was apparently one of them. He wrote in his memoirs, "It was not difficult to foresee that having shifted its meeting from Petrograd to Moscow, the directing organs [of the Soviet] would reconsider the wisdom of remaining in Petrograd at all and whether it was possible to hold the Constituent Assembly there. For us," he continued, "the convening of a plenum in Moscow was an extreme measure, a tragic necessity, and an unfortunate defeat."[79] At the joint Executive Committee meeting, Grinevich, a Menshevik-Internationalist, put the matter in a similar way. He called the suggestion to hold an emergency meeting outside Petrograd "blindness" and expressed the opinion that the transfer of decision-making to Moscow would recreate the Commune of 1871 and make Moscow a new Versailles.[80] This argument was evidently effective, for there was no mention of a plenum in any place other than Petrograd in the resolution ultimately adopted by the Executive Committees.

B. D. Kamkov and Maria Spiridonova, both left SR's, also spoke out in favor of the immediate transfer of all power to the Soviets, while in the upstairs galleries factory and garrison representatives waited and watched. Eventually three resolutions were placed before the floor: one by Gots pledging support to the existing Provisional Government until the convocation of an Executive Committee plenum but ostensibly leaving the door open to a possible transfer of power to the Soviets; a second by Martov calling for a new Provisional Government of which at least a majority would be made up of Soviet representatives; and a third by Lunacharsky severely condemning the Provisional Government and calling for the transfer of power directly into the hands of the Soviets.

It was now close to midnight, and in the hours since the joint Executive Committee meeting had begun the Putilov workers had replaced the Kronstadt sailors on the square outside the Taurida Palace. After demonstrating for a short time, they in turn were supplanted by the 176th and 171st Infantry Reserve Regiments arriving from Krasnoe Selo on foot, the Third Infantry Reserve Regiment from Peterhof, the Third Battalion of the First Machine Gun Regiment from Oranienbaum, and the garrison First Infantry Reserve Regiment with Sakharov at its head. Gradually even these elements returned to their barracks, the thunder of artillery fire and a sudden downpour scattered the last diehards, and now parked outside the meeting place of the Soviet were only a few armored cars, their large angular silhouettes faintly visible through the falling rain.

There was an uneasy quiet in other parts of the city. The ships of the Kronstadt flotilla rocked gently at their moorings near the Nikolaevsky bridge; most of the sailors (evidently by agreement with the Bolshevik Military Organization, the Kronstadt Bolsheviks, and the Anarcho-Syndicalist-Communists) retired to various barracks of the garrison, the Fortress of Peter and Paul, or the Kshesinskaia mansion to dry off and to get food and rest.[81] Even the area near the Liteiny bridge, which earlier had been the scene of a pitched mid-evening battle between the First Reserve Infantry Regiment returning from the Taurida Palace and a detachment of Polovtsev's Cossacks and some artillery on their way there, was now still. On Nevsky and Liteiny Prospects, near the center of town, there was some looting of shops, and fights broke out here and there between straggling insurgent workers, soldiers, and sailors and Cossacks or townspeople. The situation in the streets, recalls Podvoisky, "soon degenerated into uncoordinated actions with no definite aims."[82]

Along the approaches to the Vyborg District soldiers of the First

Machine Gun Regiment manned hastily erected barricades. About midnight they watched as the main Neva bridges were opened. Although this divided Petrograd in half, leaving the Neva's right bank for practical purposes in rebel hands, it also restricted the movement of insurgent workers and soldiers to the heart of the city, where an abandoned artillery piece, the litter of shattered shop windows and spent cartridges, and the corpses of dead horses on the wet pavement were all that remained as witness to the day's bitter struggles.

Still the debate in the Taurida Palace dragged on, its outcome never seriously in doubt. One by one, the Menshevik Theodore Dan, a representative of the peasant intelligentsia, Kondratenko, the leader of the Trudoviks, L. M. Bramson, the SR Sako Saakian, and N. V. Chaikovsky of the minor People's Socialist Party spoke out in support of the Gots resolution. Their speeches were countered in turn by Lunacharsky and Zinoviev. Tsereteli rebutted the arguments of those who demanded transfer of power to the Soviet with the claim that the mood in the provinces was completely different from that in Petrograd. Although the mood of the provinces was changing rapidly, it would take a few more months and a Bolshevik victory before this would be clear. Tsereteli was still on the rostrum at around 1:00 A.M., when the Soviet delegates were again frightened by the ominous tramp of approaching soldiers. What followed is described by Sukhanov:

> Suddenly a noise was heard in the distance. It came nearer and nearer. The measured tramping of thousands of feet was already clearly audible in the surrounding halls. . . . The hall again grew agitated. Faces looked anxious, deputies leaped from their seats. What was it? Where was this new danger to the revolution coming from?
>
> But Dan appeared on the platform as though out of the ground. He was so filled with glee that he tried without success to conceal it. . . .
>
> "Comrades!" he called out, "be calm! There is no danger. Regiments loyal to the revolution have arrived to defend the Central Executive Committee!"

Just then in the Catherine Hall a powerful *Marseillaise* thun-
dered forth. Enthusiasm in the hall—the faces of the Mamelukes
lit up. Squinting triumphantly at the Left, they took hands in an
outburst of emotion and standing with bared heads ecstatically
chanted the *Marseillaise*.[83]

The first unit to report for duty at the Taurida Palace was the
Izmailovsky Guards Regiment. It was followed in short order by
the Preobrazhensky and Semenovsky Regiments, all in full battle
dress and with accompanying marching bands. According to news
reports, the appearance of each new unit evoked fresh outbursts of
emotion on the part of the Soviet leaders and tired but nonetheless
lusty renditions of the *Marseillaise*. For the Menshevik-SR leaders
in the Executive Committees, there was justification for grateful
relief. The indignities and impossibly high tension which they had
been forced to endure by the rebelling Petrograd masses since the
previous afternoon were now over.

The cause of this sudden transformation in the mood of previously neutral regiments late on the night of July 4 is subject to
dispute. Some writers emphasize the importance of Pereverzev's
disclosures to representatives of the garrison. Thus, the SR, N.
Arsky, writes in his memoirs that "the news that the Bolshevik uprising served German interests circulated quickly through the garrison and made a tremendous impression everywhere. Regiments
which earlier had remained neutral now pledged to join in putting
down the rebellion."[84] Though all of the units reporting to the
Taurida Palace had been shown the now famous German-agent
documents before their appearance, other memoirists, Woytinsky
and Tsereteli among them, ignore this fact, emphasizing that the
documents were not published until the next day. For many of
these writers, the key factor provoking active support for the Soviet was the information, also widely disseminated on the evening
of July 4, that a powerful composite force loyal to the Soviet was
on its way from the Northern front to restore order in the capital.

Study of pertinent materials suggests that both of these factors—
the Pereverzev documents and the news that loyal troops had been

dispatched to the capital—were of importance. The profound effect of the German-agent documents upon representatives of the Preo-brazhensky Regiment has already been mentioned. It seems that theirs was a typical reaction, and after *Zhivoe slovo* published the materials early on the morning of July 5, under the screaming head-line, "Lenin, Ganetsky, and Kozlovsky German Spies," animosity toward the Bolsheviks became general. As regards the significance of the information regarding the shipment of forces from the front, it was now clear that the Northern front supported the Soviet; that the Executive Committees were determined to crush the rebellion at any cost; and that they would soon possess a force powerful enough to do so. Tsereteli claims that members of garrison regi-mental committees later told him that when this became known, the soldiers themselves began coming out in favor of immediate departure for the Taurida Palace.[85]

Yet another factor, the increasingly disorganized and ugly char-acter of the demonstrations (estimates of total numbers of dead and wounded in the two days of rioting ran to four hundred), probably also contributed to the changing mood. At any rate, in the early morning of July 5 the Executive Committees of the Soviet and the officials of the Petrograd Military District suddenly found them-selves with an armed force which alone was probably substantial enough to reassert control in the capital, particularly since the mood within many of the demonstrating factories and military regiments had by now become thoroughly demoralized. In these circum-stances the Executive Committees did not delay passage of Gots' majority resolution on the government question. This resolution, adopted at about 4:00 A.M. on July 5, stated in part:

> Having discussed the crisis created by the departure of three Kadet ministers from the government, a joint meeting of the Executive Committees . . . considers that although the departure of the Kadets can in no way be thought of as reason for depriving the government of the revolutionary democracy's support, the democracy has at the same time cause for reconsidering its atti-tude toward the government. . . .

In view of this the meeting resolves to convene a full meeting of the Executive Committee of Workers', Peasants', and Soldiers' Deputies with local representatives in two weeks to decide the question of organizing a new government. . . .

At the same time . . . the meeting confirms that until such time as the full Executive Committees make their decision, all power must remain in the hands of the present government which must act in accordance with the decisions of the All-Russian Congress of Workers' and Soldiers' Deputies and the All-Russian Soviet of Peasants' Deputies.

And in the event that the revolutionary democracy acknowledges the necessity of transferring all power into the hands of the Soviet, only a full meeting of the Executive Committees has the right to decide this question.[86]

Lenin and the Collapse of the July Uprising

In one of the most controversial passages in his history of the Russian revolution, Sukhanov describes a post-July days conversation with A. V. Lunacharsky, in which the latter recounted to him some of Lenin's plans in connection with the July uprising. Specifically, Sukhanov quotes Lunacharsky as having told him on July 7 that on the night of July 3 Lenin was definitely planning a coup d'etat, indeed, that Lenin, Trotsky, and Lunacharsky had already been selected for ministerial posts in a prospective Bolshevik government. Upon assuming power the latter was immediately to issue decrees about peace and land in order to win the support of the masses. According to Sukhanov's version of his conversation with Lunacharsky, all this was agreed upon among Lenin, Trotsky, and Lunacharsky while the Kronstadt sailors were on their way from the Kshesinskaia mansion to the Taurida Palace. The coup failed, Lunacharsky is alleged to have stated, only because the key unit in the planned overthrow—the 176th Reserve Infantry Regiment—was intercepted en route to the Taurida Palace, while for some unexplained reason, Lenin himself was late in arriving on the scene to proclaim the new government. In his memoirs Sukhanov emphasizes that his account of the conversation with Lunacharsky has been recorded precisely as he remembers it. He acknowledges that some of Lunacharsky's statements do not ring true (for example, he concedes that the principal force in a Bolshevik coup on July 4 would logically have been the Kronstadt sailors and that it was Trotsky himself who scotched their efforts to arrest Chernov). Sukhanov concedes that he, or more likely Lunacharsky, may have gotten things mixed up, and leaves the whole matter "for industrious historians to sort out."[87]

Since relevant archives are closed and few of the necessary documents have been published, this is at the present time an impossibility for Western scholars, no matter how industrious. For their part, official Soviet interpretations reject the possibility that Lenin even thought about seizing power during the "peaceful period" of the revolution, which in their scheme ended only after the July days, and point out that on the night of July 3 Lenin was not only not planning a coup but was not even in Petrograd. "This story of intent to seize power and of the creation of a Bolshevik ministry," sums up O. A. Lidak, "is the fruit of Sukhanov's idle fantasy."[88]

Granting that factual errors and implausibilities cast doubt on the reliability of Sukhanov's recollections and that there is no other evidence to support the contention that Lenin stood at the head of an unsuccessful coup on July 4, there appears to be little reason for doubting Kalinin's assertion that after his return to Petrograd Lenin left open the question of whether or not the movement in the streets was the beginning of the seizure of power. As this study has suggested, Lenin appears to have rejected the value of political demonstration as a consequence of the June 10 experience rather than of the July days. Thus, his concern with regard to the seizure of power in late June and early July was very likely already one of proper preparation and timing. However, on July 4 the alternatives open to the party had suddenly significantly narrowed. Any hope that the Soviet would extricate the Bolsheviks from their exposed position by yielding to mass pressure and taking power was extinguished by the Executive Committees' determined response to the demonstrations. Practically speaking, the party's choice was limited either to bringing the demonstrations to a quick end in the hope of salvaging as much as possible out of the wreckage or continuing them in the hope that conditions favorable to the seizure of power might be developed. Neither course was attractive, for, on the one hand, the party's involvement in the rebellion had already gone so far that the Provisional Government, if it were allowed to survive, was bound to take drastic measures against the Bolsheviks as soon as it was able to do so. On the other hand, while the chances of seizing power in the capital may have appeared bright on the afternoon of July 4, the likelihood that such a move would be opposed by the less radically inclined provinces and, more important, by loyal government troops from the front (the same factors that made Lenin back away from the brink on June 10) could not be ignored.[89]

We have already seen that after returning to Petrograd late on the morning of July 4, Lenin apparently made no attempt to halt the street demonstrations. Yet if this means that he was contemplating the second course, as seems most likely, then the news which began reaching him late on the afternoon of July 4 could hardly have been encouraging. First, reports began to arrive in regard to Pereverzev's disclosures. N. S. Karinsky, an official in the Ministry of Justice, leaked this news to Bonch-Bruevich sometime on the afternoon of July 4. The latter immediately relayed the information to Lenin, who, according to Bonch-Bruevich, was already aware of it.[90] The seriousness with which Lenin received word of the semi-official campaign launched against him suggests that he correctly sensed its probable effect in the prevailing atmosphere.

Moreover, at about this time there came definite word of the dispatch of military forces from the front. According to Tsereteli, when rumors to this effect first began circulating, Zinoviev tried to find out whether troops from battle zones were actually on their way to the capital. Verification of these rumors was passed on to Zinoviev by the Menshevik V. A. Anisimov as soon as the Soviet leadership had agreed upon such action.[91]

By the late evening the effect of these factors on the demonstrators and on the mood of previously passive units of the garrison was already becoming apparent. The hour of decision was fast approaching, but it had come so rapidly that there was no time to gauge the response of the provinces to the demonstrations in the capital. Around two or three o'clock in the morning, undoubtedly before *Zhivoe slovo* appeared on the streets but probably after the arrival of the Izmailovsky Regiment at the Taurida Palace, a gathering of Central Committee members resolved to call upon the soldiers to return to their barracks and to terminate the street demonstrations.[92] The decision was made public in an unobtrusive back page notice in the July 5 *Pravda*, the final make-up of which was personally supervised by Lenin. The notice declared that it had been decided to end the demonstrations "because their goal of presenting the slogans of the leading elements of the working class and the army had been achieved."

Unfortunately, no protocol of the Central Committee meeting which adopted this cancellation decision has been published. K. Mekhonoshin, who represented the Military Organization during the deliberations, provides us with this interesting, albeit fragmentary description:

> The July events of 1917 had already unfolded. . . . The Provisional Government was preparing to destroy the revolutionary organizations. The city looked like an armed camp of two opposing sides. We had the preponderance of strength in Petrograd. The turning point had arrived. It was necessary to decide whether to go further or to secure the positions we had already occupied.
>
> On that day I had to represent the Military Organization at the meeting of the Central Committee. Vladimir Ilich [Lenin] addressed us:
>
> "Give me an exact count of your strength. Name the units which will definitely follow us. Which ones are wavering? Who is against us? Where are the storehouses of rifles and other military supplies? What can the enemy rely on in the areas neighboring Petrograd? Where are the food supplies concentrated and are there sufficient quantities? Has the security of the Neva bridges

been provided for? Has the rear been prepared for retreat in the event of failure? etc." These are the important questions which Comrade Lenin asked and which immediately sobered us. Frankly speaking, we had made no such estimates with a possible decisive clash in mind, having limited ourselves to a general estimate of the situation.[93]

Whether Mekhonoshin argued against the Central Committee's decision to halt the demonstrations is uncertain, although there was at least one sign that even at this point the Military Organization preserved its leftism. On July 5 *Soldatskaia pravda* contained no mention whatever of the Central Commitee's decision to halt the street demonstrations. Instead the issue's lead editorial, entitled "What is Taking Place in the Streets," concluded with a statement implying that the party of the proletariat had accepted leadership of the street movement and would continue the battle for transfer of power to the Soviets until it had been won. Yet if the Military Organization was slower than the Central Committee in sensing the need for retreat, its weakness in the prevailing situation would become clear even to its most radical leaders during the period of reaction which was to follow.

VII

The July Uprising: Retreat and Reaction

Capitulation of the Petrograd Bolsheviks

The shift in the power position of the Soviet and Provisional Government which occurred late on the evening of July 4 and in the early morning of July 5 was felt in the streets with lightning speed. By midday of July 5 troops loyal to the government were in full control of all but the worker districts of the capital, and feeling against the Bolsheviks was so high that much of the city was literally unsafe for them. Actually, not only the Bolsheviks were alarmed by the intensity of the reaction which followed the turbulent events of July 3 and 4. The left Menshevik Woytinsky remembers July 5, when the streets of Petrograd became the scene of a "counterrevolutionary orgy" and "the debauchery of the Black Hundreds threatened to destroy the victory over the insurgents," as one of the saddest days of his life.[1]

To a degree the quick emergence of the reaction was an outgrowth of the enormous amount of animosity against the Bolshevik Party stored up in the pre-July period, not only in conservative circles but by men of liberal-democratic and moderate socialist persuasion as well. Then, too, a host of rightist organizations appears to have been waiting in the wings for just such an opportunity to reassert their influence as the aftermath of the July uprising provided. For his part, the reactionary General Polovtsev had been chafing at the bit to get at the Bolsheviks for the better part of June and was not inclined to temporize now that his resolve was shared by the Provisional Government and a good many Soviet leaders. On July 4 the Provisional Government, with the concurrence of the Soviet Executive Committees, authorized Polovtsev to rid Petrograd of armed mobs, to disarm the First Machine Gun Regiment, and to occupy the Kshesinskaia mansion.[2] Late in the evening of the same day Polovtsev made concrete plans to implement this directive, and by the morning of the fifth the armed force at his disposal was fully strong enough to begin operations.

The government's offensive against the Bolsheviks was launched at dawn on July 5, when General Polovtsev dispatched a detachment of soldiers to *Pravda's* publishing plant; the unit arrived at its destination only a little too late to catch Lenin, who had just left the premises for the first of his pre-October hide-outs. The government detachment searched the *Pravda* plant, wrecked it, arrested the workers and soldiers on duty there, and returned to the headquarters of the General Staff.[3] Meanwhile, in the city districts patrols of officers, soldiers, and Cossacks began mopping-up operations. All through the day they confiscated armed trucks and disarmed and arrested suspicious looking workers, soldiers, and especially sailors, who were prevented from escaping behind barricades in the worker districts because the bridges over the Neva either remained open or were under heavy guard.

Attempting to reconstruct the activities of the Bolshevik Central Committee, Petersburg Committee, and Military Organization during this last confused phase of the July uprising is very difficult. This is partly because the party's leadership was now scattered and disorganized. Then, too, communications between higher and lower organizations were disrupted, and as a result the party's activities were now perhaps even less coordinated than they had been on July 3. Moreover, published documents, similar to those few which contribute immeasurably to the study of intra-party activity in the organization of the July uprising, are largely missing for its concluding phases, and the historian is forced to rely heavily on a confusing array of often contradictory memoirs.

The focus of attention for the events taking place on July 5 and 6 was the Kshesinskaia mansion, still the Military Organization's staff headquarters. Here, early on July 5, the Military Organization leadership responded to the destruction of the *Pravda* printing plant and initial rumors of Polovtsev's impending attack with preparations to fight.[4] It is difficult to say with any degree of certainty whether resistance was authorized by the Central Committee, although the fact that the latter agreed to allow the Kronstadt sailors to prolong their stay in the capital suggests that its position was at least indefinite. In any case, since the sailors constituted the bulk of the force at the disposal of the Military Organization, Raskolnikov was now appointed overall commander. He supervised the positioning of machine guns and the distribution of ammunition and issued firing instructions to soldiers and sailors in the mansion's outer garden who would have to act independently.

Hurried requests on Military Organization stationery, signed by Raskolnikov, were now sent to Kronstadt for four artillery pieces and a supply of shells and hand grenades,[5] to the Naval Ordnance Depot for three 47-millimeter cannon and some machine guns, and to Helsingfors for some ships of the fleet.[6] At the same time, judging by a Military Organization message to I. V. Kudelko and M. Ter-Arutuniants of the 180th Reserve Infantry Regiment some attempts were made to keep garrison units in a state of readiness. The message, also sent to other Military Organization collectives, declared that the Central Committee, the Executive Commission of the Petersburg Committee, and the Military Organization were meeting in connection with the *Pravda* plant's destruction, and appealed to the soldiers to maintain a state of readiness but not to leave their barracks until a course of action had been decided upon.[7]

In his memoirs Raskolnikov characterizes these measures as purely defensive but claims that at the time he was convinced that "the sending of one good warship into the Neva" would make the Pro-

visional Government significantly less decisive.[8] In this connection
O. A. Lidak makes an interesting observation which runs counter
to official Soviet interpretations. He writes that "when on July 5
the Military Organization took a whole series of military measures,
it undoubtedly had considerations other than self-defense in mind.
We are inclined to think," he continues, "that at the time the Military Organization had not yet oriented itself to the changed political situation and believed that it was still possible to preserve the
correlation of forces which had existed prior to July 3."[9] Trotsky
makes a somewhat similar point: "We may rather assume that . . .
the leaders of the Military Organization, including Raskolnikov,
had not yet estimated the extent of the changes in the situation,
and . . . when the armed demonstration was compelled to beat a
hasty retreat in order not to turn into an armed insurrection imposed by the enemy, some of the military leaders made certain acci-
dental and not well thought-out steps forward."[10]

In any event, it appears that the Bolshevik Military Organization's determination to fight was not very widely shared by the
masses of now deflated workers and soldiers. There were significant
exceptions. Latsis recorded that the Bolshevik Vyborg District
Committee "instinctively" put factory committees and the Red
Guard on the alert and formulated plans which included the opening of the bridges over the Nevka separating the Vyborg District
from the Petrograd side, and the construction of defensive forti-
fications at the Liteiny bridge.[11] In his reminiscences Metelev recalls that at about this time young Vyborg District workers stuffed
bombs into their pockets, boots, and coats, and crossed the Nevka
to aid the Sixteenth Company of the First Machine Gun Regiment
and the Kronstadt sailors in the defense of the Fortress of Peter and
Paul.[12] Moreover, other elements of the First Machine Gun Regiment were apparently equally bent on battle. According to Stulov,
on the morning of July 5 Military Organization members K.
Romanov and A. Poliakov affirmed the necessity of another demonstration against the Provisional Government and called on their
respective companies to ready their weapons and prepare to

march.[13] In the main, however, it appears that soon after the tide began to shift in favor of the Soviet and the Provisional Government, the Military Organization's effective strength dwindled rapidly as regiments in which Bolshevik influence had been strongest passed resolutions expressing support for the Soviet and regret for past misdeeds. Such was the case in the Grenadier Regiment where, according to a report in *Birzhevye vedomosti*, on July 5 Roshal tried unsuccessfully to interest the soldiers in further action against the Provisional Government.[14] And for their part, most workers, albeit with reluctance, prepared to return to the factories.

Parenthetically, there is almost no information on the activities of the Anarchist-Communists at this time, although it seems reasonable to assume that they were involved in some of the preparations for resistance. *Novaia zhizn'* reported that on the morning of July 5 the Anarchists were distributing proclamations declaring that the previous day's armed action had shown the strength of the Russian revolution but had achieved no practical results. The leaflet concluded that the workers and soldiers would have to come out again in order to win power decisively.[15]

It should be noted that while military commanders on both sides were making preparations for battle, members of the Bolshevik Central Committee and the Executive Committee of the Soviet were taking part in efforts to avert a serious military engagement. It appears that Lenin, for one, responded to the government's attack on the *Pravda* plant with characteristic realism. Convinced that Bolshevik losses could be cut only by retreat without delay, he directed the Military Organization, via Zinoviev, to surrender the Fortress of Peter and Paul immediately.[16]

In the early afternoon of July 5, when members of the Bolshevik Central Committee gathered with leaders of the Military Organization and those few Petersburg Committee representatives who were able to get from their districts to the Kshesinskaia mansion, Lenin's position on the futility of resistance was undoubtedly presented by Zinoviev. At this time it was probably known that front line troops were nearing the capital and that very little support for the demonstrations had been registered in the provinces. In this connection it should be noted that late on July 4 and on July 5 echoes of the Petrograd manifestations were hurriedly organized in a number of the larger provincial cities, but none of them was very encouraging. The situation in Moscow was typical. On the afternoon of July 4 the Moscow Bolshevik Party Committee, having learned of the situation in the capital a few hours earlier, met to formulate a plan of action. Rejecting demands by party radicals to seize the post office, telegraph, and telephone stations immediately (in effect to organize an armed uprising), a majority of Moscow Bolshevik leaders agreed to call a mass armed march for 8:00 the same evening. However, a short time later the Moscow Soviet placed a ban on demonstrations, and the majority of workers and soldiers did not respond to the Bolshevik summons.[17]

It appears that at this time, that is, on the early afternoon of July 5, some unit-level Military Organization people may have held out the hope that some of the regiments arriving from the front might be persuaded to join the rebels, as had happened during the February days.[18] But perhaps with the lone exception of Smilga, it is unlikely that any Central Committee members could have been guided by such thinking. In these circumstances the Central Committee voted "not to reverse the decision to end the demonstrations,"[19] and a pertinent appeal was again prepared for immediate distribution to the masses. It called on the workers and soldiers not to succumb to the provocations of the "mobilizing reaction" and to avoid demonstrations and confrontations of any kind. For the future the appeal called for patience and discipline and a renewal of the campaign to attract "backward" elements of the urban population and the provinces.[20]

Having reaffirmed its decision to call off the demonstration, the Central Committee now sent a representative to the Taurida Palace for clarification of the Soviet position in regard to the Bolshevik Party. A short time later, evidently at the invitation of Kamenev and Zinoviev, a delegation from the All-Russian Executive Committee of the Soviet arrived at the Kshesinskaia mansion, and as a result of negotiations between the Bolsheviks, represented by Kamenev, Mekhonoshin, and Boky, and the Executive Committee, represented by M. I. Liber, an agreement aimed at preventing further bloodshed was reached.[21] By this agreement, as understood by the Bolsheviks, the Soviet guaranteed that no further repressive measures would be taken against the party and promised that all demonstrators not accused of specific criminal acts would be released. In exchange, the Bolsheviks obligated themselves to call in their armored cars, to send all the sailors back to Kronstadt, and to surrender the Fortress of Peter and Paul.[22] At this point, to use Nevsky's words, "the [July] uprising was declared by the Central Committee to have been an unsuccessful demonstration."[23]

Not long afterward the armored cars still under the Military Organization's control were returned to the service shops of the Reserve Armored Car Division,[24] and by evening most of those Kronstadt sailors who had been quartered in garrison barracks had made their way along back streets to their boats, leaving behind only a few hundred sailors in the Kshesinskaia mansion and the Fortress of Peter and Paul.[25] It was just as well, for in the late evening the All-Russian Executive Committee of the Soviet, meeting in the Taurida Palace, presented a Kronstadt delegation headed by Raskolnikov, Roshal, and Iarchuk with an ultimatum. Previously offered guarantees of no reprisals against the Bolsheviks and the release of the arrested were now forgotten and the sailors were given until morning to choose between turning in their weapons and banners and leaving the capital without them or being forcibly disarmed. The Kronstadt delegation, evidently unaware that the majority of sailors had already managed to leave the capital, was engaged in discussing this ultimatum, when the delegation was suddenly informed that an answer would have to be given at once. In reply to Raskolnikov's query as to the reason behind this sudden change, Liber remarked vaguely that "iron necessity demanded it."[26] Sometime later he explained that the Soviet stiffened its position when it was informed that the Petrograd Military District was already in the preliminary phase of an assault on the Kshesinskaia mansion, although to warn the Kronstadters of this fact seemed improper.[27] Be that as it may, by Kronstadt standards it was humiliating enough to depart with the capital more than ever in the hands of the counterrevolution, but to be disarmed in the process was infinitely worse. Raskolnikov refused Liber's ultimatum on the grounds that it was impossible to accept such terms without first consulting his sailors and with this the Kronstadt delegation departed for the night.[28]

In the meantime the finishing touches on the Petrograd Military District's plans for capturing the Kshesinskaia mansion and the Fortress of Peter and Paul were completed and final orders were distributed. Information on the degree to which Bolshevik strength had deteriorated and the fact that the party's leadership was not inclined to resist government forces either failed to reach General Polovstev or were consciously ignored by him. There appears to be no other explanation for the scope of the military operation which he launched against the Bolsheviks at 3:00 A.M. on July 6. Among other elements, the attack force included the Petrogradsky Regiment, eight armored cars, one company each from the Preobrazhensky, Semenovsky, and Volynsky Guards Regiments, a detachment of sailors from the Black Sea fleet, some cadet detachments, the Aviation Academy, and a front-line bicycle brigade supported by heavy artillery.[29]

At dawn these forces, commanded by A. A. Kuzmin, assembled on the Palace Square to hear send-off speeches by Soviet leaders A. R. Gots and N. D. Avksentiev and then crossed the Neva to the Petrograd side. Quickly they isolated the Fortress of Peter and Paul and the Kshesinskaia mansion, while from a third floor window of the Marble Palace, located across the Neva from the fortress, Kuzmin surveyed the field of battle through a pair of fine field glasses lent to him by the former Prince Ivan Konstantinovich, still the Marble Palace's royal tenant. At 7:00 A.M. the Petrograd Military District ordered telephone service to the garrison "Bolshevik" regiments disrupted, and at the same time, the preliminaries completed, Kuzmin phoned the Kshesinskaia mansion and in the name of the Military District and the All-Russian Executive Committee of the Soviet demanded the Bolsheviks' immediate unconditional surrender. The Bolsheviks requested and were granted an hour to discuss the demand, upon which the phones in the Kshesinskaia mansion were also disconnected. In his reminiscences Podvoisky, who took Kuzmin's call, writes that the sailors and soldiers then still in the mansion (three hundred Kronstadters and two hundred soldiers from the First Machine Gun and Grenadier Regiments) responded to the surrender demand with renewed defensive preparations.[30] According to newspaper accounts, they even took a few random shots at government scouts.

Because the Kshesinskaia mansion was vulnerable to artillery bombardment, the Military Organization ultimately decided that staying in the Bolshevik headquarters made no sense, and the insurgent forces made a successful dash to the Fortress of Peter and Paul only a few hundred yards away.[31] A short time later Kuzmin gave his troops the order to attack, and the artillery prepared to fire on Kuzmin's command. The massive attack force, led by the armored cars and infantry, met no resistance, however; the artillery remained silent, and within a few minutes the Kshesinskaia mansion was secured. Inside the invaders seized a substantial quantity of arms and arrested seven Bolsheviks who were frantically trying to complete the evacuation of party files. Podvoisky, who was still in the mansion, managed to escape. Meanwhile, the insurgents in the Fortress of Peter and Paul, now under the command of the Military Organization's Ilin-Zhenevsky and Maltsev, checked and loaded cannon and machine guns mounted on the fortress' ramparts, watched the government troops as they advanced through Alexandrovsky park, and awaited the attack. At the same time on the street outside, a few Vyborg District Bolsheviks, Metelev among them, took up positions close to the attacking bicycle brigade and prepared to begin throwing bombs as soon as the shooting started.[32]

Meanwhile cooler heads were still trying to insure that there would be no clash. Among others, representatives of the Soviet and the Bolshevik Central Committee urged the sailors and soldiers to surrender. Negotiations between Ilin-Zhenevsky and Iarchuk, representing the insurgents, and government representatives B. O. Bogdanov and Ensign Mazurenko, overall commander of the troops arriving from the front, dragged on until midday. The government negotiators were adamant on the necessity of the rebels relinquishing their weapons and in the end Ilin-Zhenevsky turned to Stalin, who was close by, and asked whether to give in. "There is nothing else left," was Stalin's sad reply.[33] A vote was taken among the insurgent sailors and machine gunners, and a majority voted against sacrificing themselves for the revolution. Within a short time they were disarmed, the names of all the insurgents were taken down, and the sailors were led away to their boats and an ignominious return to Kronstadt. (The fate of the Anarchist-Communists was similar. Government forces dispatched to occupy the Durnovo villa on the afternoon of July 6 met little resistance and the Anarchist headquarters was quickly taken.)

Shortly after the insurgents' surrender several members of the Executive Commission of the Petersburg Committee met in the relatively safe District Duma building on the Vyborg side. At this point most members of that usually militant group were glumly resigned to the crushing defeat sustained by the party, but a few, bitterly dissatisfied with the policy of retreat pressed on them by the Central Committee, were not.[34] One of this group, M. Ia. Latsis, speaking on behalf of the Vyborg District Committee, advocated that the party rejuvenate the uprising by means of a general strike. Although a discussion of this proposal ended with only two of the five Executive Commission members in attendance favoring the idea, it was decided at least to discuss the matter with Lenin.

Later the same afternoon the Executive Commission members met again, this time in the watchman's shanty of the Reno factory, where Lenin had momentarily taken refuge. According to Latsis, Lenin was vehement in his opposition to the declaration of a general strike. Treating the Executive Commission like a group of ill-behaved school boys, he wrote the following categorical back-to-work appeal in its name:

> The Executive Commission of the Petersburg Committee RSDLP, in compliance with Central Committee's decision published in the July 6 *Listok pravdy* (a decision also signed by the Petersburg Committee), calls on workers to resume work beginning tomorrow, that is, beginning on the morning of July 7.[35]

With the conclusion of this one last feeble episode, the capitulation of the Petrograd Bolsheviks was complete.

The Petrograd Bolsheviks and the Reaction

On the evening of July 6, in a small apartment on the Vyborg side, Lenin gathered with a few members of the Bolshevik Central Committee. Zinoviev, Kamenev, and Stalin were there, and N. I. Podvoisky represented the Military Organization. Most of the meeting was evidently devoted to Lenin's analysis of the "current moment" and his predictions on the future course of the revolution. Podvoisky's memoirs contain the only detailed contemporary account of Lenin's presentation on this occasion,[36] but it appears to have been very similar to his formulations in the article, "The Political Situation," written on July 10, and the more substantial pamphlet, "On Slogans," prepared a few days later.[37]

According to Podvoisky, Lenin made no attempt to minimize the seriousness of the defeat being sustained by the party, although he was confident of its ultimate ability to survive. While predicting that during the prevailing period of reaction "all the previous work of the party would be temporarily destroyed," he emphasized some positive results of the July events. The SR's and the Mensheviks had irrevocably committed themselves to an alliance with the military counterrevolution, in whose hands actual power resided, and the proletariat would now have to shed its illusions of receiving power from the bourgeoisie peacefully. Indeed, the proletariat now had a choice, said Lenin, between the seizure of power and death. In view of this, he termed the slogan, "All power to the Soviets," outdated and called for its replacement by the new clarion call, "All power to the working class led by its revolutionary party—the Bolshevik-Communists." In effect, this may have been Lenin's first open affirmation of the absolute necessity of a direct seizure of power by the Bolsheviks, to be executed at the first suitable moment in the not-too-distant future.[38]

Podvoisky's account does not contain any information as to whether Lenin's analysis, and particularly his interest in an armed uprising and his rejection of the Soviets, were voted upon or discussed at this meeting. As far as is known, the key points in the new theses were first seriously considered at an important expanded Central Committee meeting of July 13-14, where they were rejected.[39] At the July 30-31 sessions of the Sixth Bolshevik Party Congress, they were adopted only after long debate and significant modification.[40] The Central Committee meeting of July 6, however, adopted two less momentous measures of ultimate importance. The first resolution stipulated that party organizations would attempt to weather the repressions above ground so that legal activities would not be interrupted; the second reaffirmed the decision (evidently first taken the day before) that for the time being Lenin and Zinoviev would not turn themselves in for trial.

Meanwhile the outwardly strong policy of the Provisional Government, buttressed by the arrival of massive contingents of troops from the front, upstaged the Soviet. At a late night meeting of cabinet ministers on July 6 it was formally resolved that "all organizers and leaders of the armed movement against the government and also all those making appeals and instigations in support of the demonstrations should be arrested and brought to trial as traitors to their nation and the revolution."[41] This decree was followed by orders for the arrest of such leading Bolsheviks as Lenin, Zinoviev, and Kamenev and the heads of the Interdistrict Committee, Lunacharsky and Trotsky. On July 7, upon Kerensky's recommendation, the Provisional Government decreed that all military units having taken part in the rebellion should be disarmed and dissolved, with their personnel to be transferred at the discretion of the Ministers of the War and Navy.[42]

On the same day Kerensky issued a scathing denunciation of the situation prevailing in Kronstadt and Helsingfors and on behalf of the Provisional Government ordered the arrest of the sixty-seven man Tsentrobalt delegation (as well as the apparently unreliable Verderevsky). He also demanded that "counterrevolutionary instigators" in all naval institutions and vessels of the Baltic fleet be arrested within twenty-four hours.[43] At yet another meeting of the Provisional Government two days later, after Kerensky had replaced Prince Lvov as Prime Minister (Lvov resigned on July 8 because of fundamental policy differences with socialist cabinet ministers), a special high-level Investigating Commission with extraordinary legal powers was created to conduct a thorough investigation into all aspects of the July revolt and to bring indictments against the guilty.[44] At the same time the government attempted to enforce a temporary ban on street assemblies and on the possession of firearms by private citizens.

In the days that followed, Kamenev, Trotsky, Lunacharsky, Kharitonov, Khaustov, Bogdatiev, and Rakhia, among others, were arrested and jailed; *Pravda*, *Soldatskaia pravda*, and *Golos pravdy* were ordered closed (for the moment it was almost impossible to find a press willing to publish Bolshevik materials); and several of the party's district and factory committee offices were raided, searched, and wrecked. In short, the Petrograd Bolsheviks learned the dangers inherent in "operating on the mood of the masses." Contributing to the popular revulsion against them during these days was the news, initially received late on the night of July 6, that the Eleventh Army on the Southwestern front was in headlong retreat in the face of a massive counterattack by the Austro-German armies. An open letter from Lenin and Zinoviev answering the government's charges, published in the July 11 *Novaia zhizn'*, did little to turn back the prevailing "counterrevolutionary" tide, particularly since for many individuals previously unconvinced by the published evidence, Lenin's failure to submit to trial served as an acknowledgment of his guilt. Soviet memoirs of this phase of the July events are replete with bitter recollections of the animosity and indignities which party cadres were now forced to endure at the hands of the hated middle and upper classes. And though the effect upon the masses of the July disillusionment, the rout of the army, and the personal attack on the Bolshevik leadership is largely ignored in Soviet literature, it seems apparent that the party's popularity among workers and particularly soldiers decreased sharply for a short period of time.

For once, Bolshevik mass propaganda techniques were effectively employed by the opposition. To be sure, there could be detected no mass exodus from the party, and even during the height of the reaction individual factories, principally in the Vyborg and Narva Districts, continued to pass Bolshevik resolutions. But at the same time the influx of new recruits was slowed and the mood among workers in all districts was deflated.[45] In addition, significant numbers of politically ignorant workers and soldiers appear to have been easily swayed by anti-Bolshevik propaganda as they had been earlier by the promise of an immediate victory over the bourgeoisie. Judging by a report presented by the representative from the Nevsky District at the Petersburg Committee meeting on July 10, this was evidently the case there. He complained that the majority of workers in his area subsisted on rumors and the "boulevard press," while a delegate from the Kolpinsky District declared that from the moment the demonstrations were liquidated, "the mood of the workers turned against us." At the same meeting the Porokhovsky District representative (he was one of six Bolsheviks thrown out of his factory in the aftermath of the July days) complained of "slander" against the Bolsheviks and of their being "watched," and characterized the workers of his district as a "stagnant swamp."[46]

It should be noted that very probably not a few rank-and-file Bolsheviks were themselves momentarily confused and shaken by the sudden decline in their party's fortunes. There exists no better testimony to this than a resolution passed in the aftermath of the

July days by the Executive Committee of the Bolshevik organization in the huge Vyborg District Metalist factory. This resolution pledged full support to the Soviet and placed the local party organization under its control. It demanded that the Bolshevik Central and Petersburg Committees divest themselves of authority and turn themselves in to the courts in order to demonstrate that "one hundred thousand Bolshevik workers are not German agents." Finally, the measure pronounced the factory committee independent of higher party organizations until a conference could be convened to elect new Central and Petersburg Committees. This resolution, it should be pointed out, passed by a vote of 16 to 4 with 4 abstentions.[47]

While government repressions and popular reaction led to a temporary overall decrease in Bolshevik strength, probably the most seriously affected was the Military Organization.[48] Indeed, it was now deprived of most of its leaders, part of its army, its soldiers' club, and its newspapers. The list of army and navy personnel investigated, arrested, and jailed as a result of the Provisional Government's hearings reads like a "Who's Who" of the Bolshevik Military Organization, and thus the investigation documents are an invaluable source for study of the organization in the June-July period. The two chiefs of the Military Organization, Podvoisky and Nevsky, and the First Machine Gun Regiment's A. Ia. Semashko escaped arrest, the latter successfully evading a massive search. But among many other Military Organization members imprisoned by the Provisional Government in the aftermath of the July uprising were A. Ia. Poliakov, I. N. Ilinsky, P. A. Koshelev, Ia. M. Golovin, K. N. Romanov, and E. I. Spets of the First Machine Gun Regiment; I. V. Kudelko, N. P. Vishnevetsky, V. M. Kotsubinsky, and M. K. Ter-Arutuniants of the 180th Reserve Infantry Regiment; V. V. Sakharov, I. Osipov, and G. Osipov of the First Reserve Infantry Regiment; P. V. Dashkevich and A. Tolkachev of the Third Reserve Infantry Regiment; A. Tarasov-Rodionov of the Infantry Officers' Academy; K. Mekhonoshin and S. Gan of the Grenadier Regiment; and F. F. Raskolnikov, S. G. Roshal, L. A.

Bregman, F. V. Gromov, and A. I. Remnev from Kronstadt. On the basis of available published materials it appears that a large percentage of the approximately two hundred individuals indicted by the Provisional Government for complicity in the organization of the July uprising were, or can now be, identified as members of the Bolshevik Military Organization. Of these, a few successfully evaded arrest, some were restricted to their units pending completion of the investigations, and the remainder were imprisoned. Of the last, some were released or simply walked out of jail during the Kornilov rebellion, while the rest were incarcerated until the very eve of the October revolution. None was ever brought to trial.[49]

Turning now to the fate of individual military regiments participating in the July uprising, one will remember that all such units were to be disarmed and their personnel transferred. Quite properly, the initial unit stripped of weapons was the First Machine Gun Regiment. According to Stulov, it was still in a rebellious mood on July 8 when it was marched to the Palace Square under heavy guard, disarmed, and moved to Solianoy Gorodok, a district outside the center of Petrograd; from here the regiment was broken up and its personnel sent to the front.[50] The next day the soldiers of the Grenadier Regiment and the 180th Reserve Infantry Regiment had their weapons taken away.[51]

In regard to the disbanding of unreliable units, according to a supplementary plan drawn up by General G. D. Romanovsky and approved by Kerensky on July 11 (with the pencilled notation, "agreed, but I demand that this be forcefully carried out without deviation"), regiments of the Petrograd garrison were divided into three categories depending on the extent of their involvement in the July movement. To the first category were assigned units participating in the demonstrations in full or close to full strength. Included in this group were the Grenadier Regiment, the First, Third, 176th, and 180th Reserve Infantry Regiments, and the First Machine Gun Regiment, together constituting the core of Military Organization strength in the garrison. These units were to be completely and permanently disbanded, their personnel (with the exception of those in jail) to be transferred to duty at the front. To the second category were assigned units in which only individual companies took part in the demonstration. The Moskovsky, Pavlovsky, Third Rifle, and Second Machine Gun Regiments and the Sixth Engineer Battalion were assigned to this group. Only guilty elements in these units were scheduled to be dissolved. Finally, the third category was composed of units not taking an active part in the demonstrations but containing guilty individuals. This group, which was ordered to conduct a thorough housecleaning of subversive elements, included all of the remaining regiments in the garrison. By this plan Romanovsky proposed to reduce the garrison by one hundred thousand of its most unreliable elements.[52] On the other hand, it appears that no ambitious program of this type was contemplated for individual Kronstadt units, probably because the lack of Provisional Government authority there precluded such action.[53]

Limitations of the Reaction

Although a detailed analysis of the reasons for the Provisional Government's failure to deal effectively with the spread of Bolshevism and to insure the reliability of the Petrograd garrison is beyond the scope of this study, it should be noted that the spirit of indignation toward the Bolsheviks on the part of Petrograd workers and soldiers did not last long. In the first place, the new Kerensky government proved no more able than its predecessors to cope with the basic social, economic, and political causes of mass unrest and to reestablish a minimum of public order. Moreover, the new Prime Minister's frequent declarations of the need for a strong central administration notwithstanding, every one of the short-run measures projected by the government under the immediate impetus of the July uprising and aimed at preventing the recurrence of armed manifestations was carried out only very half-heartedly and failed to achieve the desired results.

There were undoubtedly good reasons for the government's inability to implement these measures, and there is no intent to sug-

gest that the course of the revolution would have been altered had
they been carried out. But for the record it should be noted that the
policy of dissolving unreliable regiments was apparently limited to
the transfer to the front of reinforcement companies presumably
composed of the most subversive elements. This seems to have been
at least partly because allocating one hundred thousand particularly unruly soldiers was more easily said than done—quite naturally
most field commanders were not at all interested in receiving such
replacements. In any event troops belonging to the Grenadier Regiment and the First and 180th Reserve Infantry Regiments, classed as
"category one," were still in the capital at the time of the October
revolution. Similarly, except for the First Machine Gun Regiment,
the 180th Reserve Infantry Regiment, and the Grenadier Regiment,
it appears that the proposed disarmament of insurgent troops was
never carried out. Moreover, no significant punitive measures were
taken against either participating Kronstadt units or the vessels of
the Baltic fleet.

Also unfulfilled were the government's plans for disarming civilians. Most factories evidently followed a suggestion of the Bolshevik Central Committee issued on July 7 and hid their weapons instead of turning them over to government troops. In addition, some
stores of arms passed into the hands of the workers from garrison
regiments threatened with disarmament. And when the Kornilov
rebellion posed the immediate threat of a successful military coup
from the right, the Petrograd Soviet was itself forced to take a hand
in the arming of city factory workers.

Finally, most ineffectual of all were government attempts to suppress the Bolshevik Party. It appears that the attacks on Bolshevik
central and local organizations and the imprisonment of individual
party members, with the possible exception of the Military Organization, turned out to be little more than a temporary hindrance and
inflicted no serious damage on the party apparatus either at the top
or bottom. In most cases, party committees successfully weathered
the initial storm and were back on a firm footing very quickly. And
in a matter of weeks even the Military Organization, a bit wiser

and more cautious perhaps, was busily engaged in reconstituting itself in the garrison. The repressed party press made a similar comeback. After a post-July days interruption of relatively short duration, the Petrograd Bolsheviks resumed the publication of daily newspapers with slightly altered titles, but fully as hostile to the regime as before.

It should also be noted that the ambitious and many-sided investigations of the Provisional Government's special Investigating Commission, which might have significantly compromised the Bolsheviks (and particularly the Military Organization), were never completed. The Commission's official inquiry, involving a variety of subcommittees, dragged on through the summer. Delayed by the Kornilov rebellion, the proceedings were evidently nearing conclusion when the Bolshevik victory in October brought them to an abrupt halt.

The Bolshevik Central Committee vs. the Military Organization in the Aftermath of the July Uprising

As we have seen, the July uprising and the collapse of the Kerensky offensive stimulated increased antagonism toward the Bolsheviks on the part of all Russian political circles. Not surprisingly, within the Bolshevik Party itself the July defeat produced significant reactions, directed notably against the Military Organization. Ia. M. Sverdlov, in a post-July days conversation with V. I. Nevsky, alluded to members of the Central Committee who believed that the Military Organization and especially Nevsky, Mekhonoshin, Podvoisky, and Kedrov, inspired the demonstrations and were to blame for the party's defeat.[54] A rank-and-file Military Organization member, A. Minchev, recalls that after the July defeat the Military Organization was "regarded with disfavor, not only by comrades at the head of the party but also by some district committees."[55] Similarly, one of the foremost Soviet historians of the Bolshevik campaign for control of the army, S. Rabinovich, refers to 1906, when the party military organization then in existence was officially censured for its blatantly autonomous policies, and writes that "in connection with the spontaneous soldier demonstrations in the July days new accusations of separatism, of disengagement from common party organizational work, of unwillingness to abide by Central Committee directives, etc., were heaped upon the Military Organization." Because of this, Rabinovich continues, "Comrade Podvoisky was forced to speak out in the Military Organization's defense at the Sixth Party Congress."[56]

The Sixth Bolshevik Party Congress met semi-conspiratorially in Petrograd from July 26 to August 3, 1917, and there is evidence to indicate that here the campaign against the Military Organization by its detractors within the party went further than mere verbal criticism. At the Congress the Military Organization's future was discussed by a special Military Section, whose protocols have never been published. B. E. Shumiatsky, a delegate from the Mid-Siberian Bureau of the party and evidently a member of the section, writes that at the Sixth Congress Trotsky, Kamenev, and Bukharin insisted on the necessity of dissolving the Military Organization's All-Russian Bureau and the Military Organization as a whole on the grounds that it duplicated the work of regular party organizations. According to Shumiatsky, a majority of the Military Section rejected this position, acknowledging the necessity of maintaining a special Military Organization under the Central Committee.[57] In the published materials on the Sixth Congress the debate and decision concerning the Military Organization's future are reflected in the Military Section's final communiqué which, among other things, announced the adoption of the following resolution by a vote of 8 to 4:

> Because of a whole series of peculiarities in living conditions and professional and organizational matters [pertaining to] the existence and work of party members in the armed forces, the section sanctions the existence below the Central Committee, under its constant and direct supervision, of a special central Military Organization to direct the everyday work of the party in the armed forces.[58]

However, the internal reaction against the Military Organization apparently did not end here. In his last known memoir on the revolutionary period Nevsky credits Sverdlov, then in charge of party organizational matters, with having confided to him that in the aftermath of the July days the Bolshevik Military Organization had been the accused in what Sverdlov referred to as a "trial," during the course of which A. S. Bubnov, F. E. Dzerzhinsky, V. R. Menzhinsky, and Ia. M. Sverdlov were delegated by the Central Committee to inspect and oversee various aspects of the Military Organization's activities. According to Nevsky's account of his conversation with Sverdlov, which apparently took place sometime in late August, the Military Organization was ultimately cleared of the charges against it, perhaps partly as a result of Lenin's personal intervention. Nevsky quotes Sverdlov as having said that when Lenin learned that Sverdlov had been delegated to acquaint himself with the Military Organization, Lenin told him: "To acquaint yourself is necessary. It is necessary to help them, but there should be no pressure and no reprimands. To the contrary, they should be supported: those who don't take risks never win; without defeats there are no victories."[59]

While there is little evidence, save Nevsky's memoir, in regard to a party trial involving the leadership of the Military Organization,[60] the published protocols of the Bolshevik Central Committee for the August-September period contain some details of specific measures adopted by the Central Committee to curb the Military Organization's autonomy in the aftermath of the July days. One such measure was directed toward preventing the Military Organization from publishing its own newspaper. The first regular Bolshevik paper to appear after the July days was the Military Organization's *Rabochii i soldat*, but at its very first meeting after the Sixth Congress (on August 4) the Central Committee decreed that *Rabochii i soldat* should become the party's central organ as a replacement for *Pravda*, which had been shut down by the Provisional Government on July 5.[61] At this same time it also resolved that for the time being neither the Military Organization nor the

Petersburg Committee would be allowed to have its own news-paper. A short time later, after the Military Organization had some-how contrived to organize yet another newspaper, *Soldat*, and the Central Committee made moves to take it over as well, the Military Organization angrily insisted on what it considered its just preroga-tives. In no uncertain terms it affirmed its right to publish an inde-pendent newspaper and formally protested what is referred to as "a system of persecution and repression of an extremely peculiar character which had begun with the election of the new Central Committee [i.e., with the conclusion of the Sixth Congress]."[62] In response to this protest the Central Committee, at its meeting of August 16, bluntly reaffirmed the Military Organization's subordi-nate position within the party hierarchy, declaring:

> The Military Bureau is an organization conducting work among the soldiers. At the same time . . . according to the party rules, an independently directed party organization parallel with other [regular] party organizations cannot exist. This goes for local as well as All-Russian organizations. Because of this, the All-Russian Military Organization Bureau cannot be an inde-pendent political center.[63]

Yet having delivered this rebuke, the Central Committee agreed to let the Military Organization continue publishing *Soldat*, with the proviso that a member of the Central Committee with the right of veto be a member of its editorial board. According to the Central Committee protocols for the August 16 meeting, it also delegated Sverdlov and Dzerzhinsky to conduct discussions with the Military Bureau, to establish a proper relationship between it and the Cen-tral Committee, and to keep tabs on *Soldat*. Whether this action was connected with the "trial" referred to by Sverdlov, as seems likely, is uncertain. In any event barely two weeks later, evidently on the heels of the Military Organization's strikingly successful effort in connection with the mobilization of the Petrograd garrison against Kornilov, Sverdlov presented a very favorable progress re-port to the Central Committee on the current state of the Military Organization. He declared that the latter was at that time "not an independent political organization but a military commission under the Central Committee. At the same time," he continued, "the work of the Military Organization is gradually becoming closely associated with regular party work. The work of the Military Organization is being supervised by the Central Committee: Comrade Bubnov is working with the staff of *Soldat* and [Military Organization] work in general is being supervised by Dzerzhinsky and Sverdlov."[64] The latter is the last reference in the Central Committee protocols to the Military Organization's difficulties with the party as a result of its activities in connection with the July uprising. Only a few weeks later, under the supervision of the Central Committee and with Lenin's full approval, the Military Organization had become primarily concerned with preparing the fighting forces that would be required to implement Lenin's call for an immediate armed uprising.

VIII

Conclusion: The Party Divided

From the time of the October revolution, the writing of Bolshevik Party history has been rigidly controlled by the Communist Party of the Soviet Union in accordance with the changing requirements of politics and ideology. One apparently fixed axiom of Soviet historiography, however, is the basically unified character of the party's leadership during the revolution. Thus, Soviet historians must either ignore such deviations from the revolutionary course prescribed by Lenin as the "right opportunism" of Kamenev and Zinoviev or the leftism of Latsis and Semashko, or present them as the insignificant actions of isolated obstructionists. Consequently, one searches Soviet secondary sources is vain for frank discussions of the very real differences in outlook and policy between the Bolshevik Petersburg Committee and the party Central Committee from April to July, 1917, or the apparently uncoordinated but by no means insignificant activities of the Bolshevik Military Organization during this time. Yet the evidence suggests that precisely these kinds of problem hold the key to an understanding of the Bolshevik role and objectives in the preparation and development of the abortive June 10 demonstration and the July uprising of 1917.

The fissures which plagued the Bolshevik Party throughout 1917 developed almost immediately after the February revolution, when, in spite of the relatively small size of the Petrograd organization (party membership in the capital was then barely over two thousand[1]), conservative and radical wings rapidly emerged. Differing sharply on the crucial issues of the war and the Provisional

Government, representatives of these two groups occasionally pursued mutually contradictory policies. Lenin, observing the split in the Petrograd organization at the time of his return to Russia, wasted no time in criticizing this condition. It will be recalled that he warned in his first major speech that the Bolsheviks' former "discipline" and "unity of thought" were missing.

Although Soviet historians today acknowledge some of the disunity prevailing within the party in the aftermath of the February revolution, they suggest that for practical purposes all serious differences were eliminated upon Lenin's return in April. At the First Petrograd City Conference and at the April All-Russian Party Conference, it is true, Lenin succeeded in obtaining formal acceptance of his radical course by an overwhelming majority of the Bolshevik Party. But this was at least partly because his resolutions on the Provisional Government and on the war were ambiguous enough both to allay the immediate fears of the moderates and to inspire the hopes of the radicals. In essence, the major resolutions of the April conferences pointed the party toward the socialist revolution, but left the key questions of how and when unanswered. Right-wing Bolshevik leaders apparently came away from these conferences with the feeling that the extended educational campaign envisioned by Lenin as a prerequisite to transfer of power to the Soviets might not differ much in practice from their own program of action based on their belief in the inevitability of an indefinitely prolonged bourgeois-democratic stage in the revolution. Moreover, they probably hoped that Lenin's position would mellow after longer exposure to Russian conditions. And in the meantime their representation in the Central Committee and on *Pravda's* editorial board appeared to assure them a significant voice in the formulation of policy. On the other hand, party radicals evidently left the same meetings convinced that Lenin shared their overwhelming impatience and their will to seize power. Thus, while the April conferences confirmed Lenin's ideological and political leadership, fundamental intra-party differences were by no means eliminated. Many basic organizational questions were left unanswered, and more important, the party was provided with only the haziest of blue-prints as a guide for future action.

In the meantime Russian workers, peasants, and soldiers were showing the first signs of disenchantment with the results of the February revolution. In Petrograd the April-June period witnessed the striking spurt in party membership that enabled the Bolsheviks to play such an important role in the subsequent political life of the capital. It is unfortunate that historical literature has paid so little attention to the changing composition of the Bolshevik Party at this time. However, even on the basis of the fragmentary materials available it appears clear that during this period of rapid growth the requirements for party membership were all but suspended in order to obtain a militant mass following in the shortest possible time. At the opening of the April All-Russian Conference party membership in Petrograd was already about 16,000.[2] By late June it had doubled again to reach 32,000, while during these same months 2,000 garrison soldiers joined the Military Organization and 4,000 soldiers became associated with "Club Pravda."[3]

The inevitable price of this enormous growth was a significant increase in problems of control. To be sure, some of these additional members were long-time Bolsheviks returning from exile or emigration, but the bulk were green recruits from among the most impatient and dissatisfied elements in the factories and garrison who knew little, if anything, about Marxism and cared less about party discipline. Thus, besides having to overcome the conservatism of the Central Committee Lenin was now faced with the problem of keeping his thousands of impetuous new followers in the fold (and attracting others), while at the same time controlling them and the increasingly radical Petersburg Committee and Military Organization until a propitious moment for the seizure of power had arrived.

First signs that this would not be an easy task emerged during the April crisis when elements of the Petrograd party organization, without the authorization of the Central Committee, initiated steps to overthrow the Provisional Government. Precisely the same thing occurred during the preparations for the June 10 demonstration.

Granted that the full extent of Lenin's aims in connection with the latter is open to question, it appears clear that no more than a peaceful demonstration was authorized by the Central Committee. Yet on June 9 the Military Organization prepared its forces for a possible armed clash, and the powerful Vyborg District Bolshevik Committee, under the leadership of M. Ia. Latsis, armed itself and laid plans to seize vital public services. As we have seen, these activities were halted only at the eleventh hour upon the insistence of conservative members of the Central Committee and the party's delegation in the First Congress of Soviets, without the Bolshevik Petersburg Committee and Military Organization having been consulted. By his own admission, Lenin chose to see the demonstration go by the boards rather than risk an open break with the Soviet. And conscious of the danger of a premature uprising in the revolutionary capital, Lenin now seemed considerably more insistent on the immediate need for organization, patience, and discipline. He emphasized this point in his address at the critical Petersburg Committee meeting of June 11; this was the crux of his message to the All-Russian Conference of Bolshevik Military Organizations, where demands for the immediate overthrow of the Provisional Government were particularly emphatic; and this was a theme of some editorials which Lenin wrote for *Pravda* at this time.

The few weeks between the June crisis and the July days, however, witnessed a sharp rise of unrest in Petrograd factories and military regiments and a concomitant increase in impatience and a desire for direct action on the part of radical elements within the Bolshevik Petersburg Committee and Military Organization. As a result, the divergence between the activities of district and unit level Bolsheviks and the course advocated by the Central Committee widened, and in this process the events of June 18 had special significance.

It will be remembered that on June 18 the Bolsheviks were able to turn the mass street demonstration sponsored by the First All-Russian Congress of Soviets of Workers' and Soldiers' Deputies into an impressive expression of support for the Bolshevik program. On that day as well Russian military forces on the Southwestern front launched their long heralded offensive. To Bolsheviks of Kamenev's persuasion the victory exacted by the party in the Soviet demonstration paled considerably beside the Provisional Government's evident success in uniting a large portion of the population behind the dramatic assault of the Russian army. Indeed, to them it seemed more apparent than ever that an extended bourgeois-liberal stage in the revolution could not be avoided and thus that the correct course for the party was a moderate one.

More radically inclined party members from the Petersburg Committee, the Military Organization, and the Kronstadt Bolshevik Committee, on the other hand, drew quite different conclusions from the events of June 18. For people like Podvoisky, Nevsky, Beliakov, Semashko, and Sakharov of the Military Organization and Latsis, Stukov, and Zalutsky of the Petersburg Committee, the mass support for the Bolshevik program which emerged in the June 18 parade seemed evidence enough that the forces already at the disposal of the party were more than adequate for the seizure of power, while the launching of the offensive and the subsequent call for garrison troops were indications that the revolution was in danger. Moreover, not a few Bolsheviks were evidently genuinely concerned about losing the support of the masses if the party proved unwilling to act. At the All-Russian Conference of Bolshevik Military Organizations, in sessions of the Petersburg Committee, in mass rallies at the Kronstadt naval base, and at meetings of the Military Organization they criticized the role of "fireman" being pressed on them by the Central Committee and insisted on the need for immediate direct action. Although on June 20 the leadership of the Military Organization cooperated in squelching efforts by the First Machine Gun Regiment to organize an uprising of the garrison, we have Nevsky's word that on the twenty-second, apparently without authorization from the Central Committee, the Military Organization began to lay plans for an uprising of its own.

As we have seen, a little over a week later the explosive First Machine Gun Regiment touched off the July uprising. Organized with the help of Bolshevik Military Organization members in the First Machine Gun Regiment, it was almost immediately supported by rank-and-file party members throughout the capital and in Kronstadt. Evidently only after the Military Organization, the Executive Commission of the Petersburg Committee, and the Second City Conference had formally approved participation in the movement, and then only very belatedly and reluctantly, did the Central Committee agree to stand at its head. To sum up the Bolshevik role in the preparation and organization of the July uprising, then, it seems that the movement was in part an outgrowth of months-long Bolshevik anti-government propaganda and agitation, that rank-and-file Bolsheviks from Petrograd factories and military regiments played a leading role in its organization, and that the leadership of the Military Organization and part of the Petersburg Committee probably encouraged it against the wishes of Lenin and the Central Committee.

Finally, it should be noted that Lenin's role in the July events appears to have been a secondary one. His conviction of the need for a socialist revolution, particularly as expressed in the slogan "All power to the Soviets," undoubtedly helped inspire the uprising. Moreover, those radical Bolsheviks from the Military Organization and the Petersburg Committee who joined with the Anarchist-Communists in initiating the July movement may well have been convinced that as Lenin differed with them only in regard to timing, he would ultimately approve of their activities. But in any event, judging by available evidence, Lenin appears to have honestly tried to control the rising mood of rebellion in Petrograd until it could be supported in the provinces and at the front. In this task he was unsuccessful. Thus before dawn on July 5, with his forces compromised and with all hope of immediate victory extinguished, Lenin was left with no choice but to sound the call for an ignominious, albeit temporary, retreat.

Lenin emerged from the July experience more convinced than ever of the need for an armed uprising against the Provisional Government. The defeat suffered by the Bolsheviks proved to be much less serious than might have been expected. At the time of the abortive Kornilov affair the party more than recouped its losses. On the last day of August the resurgent Bolsheviks won a majority in the Petrograd Soviet for the first time, and barely two weeks later Lenin was exhorting the Bolshevik leadership in the capital to overthrow the Provisional Government at once. It is significant that during the second half of September and in October, when the Bolshevik Party was once again divided over the question of seizing power, the high command of the Military Organization insisted on the absolute necessity of careful and thorough preparation before taking the offensive against the Provisional Government.[4] Referring to this development in his memoirs, Nevsky recalls that "some comrades felt then that we [the leaders of the Military Organization] were too cautious. . . . But our experience (especially in the July days) showed us what an absence of thorough preparation and a preponderance of strength means."[5] As the October revolution was to show, for the leadership of the Military Organization, as for Petrograd Bolsheviks generally, the lessons of July were not without value.

Selected Bibliography

Chronologies

AKHUN, M. I., and PETROV, V. A. *1917 god v Petrograde: Khronika sobytii i bibliografiia* (1917 in Petrograd: Chronicle of Events and Bibliography). Leningrad: Lenpartizdat, 1933.

AVDEEV, N. *Revoliutsiia 1917 goda: Khronika sobytii* (The Revolution of 1917: Chronicle of Events). Vol. I: *Ianvar'-aprel'* (January-April). Vol. II: *Aprel'-mai* (April-May). Moscow: Gosizdat, 1923.

KONSTANTINOV, A. P. *Bol'sheviki Petrograda v 1917 godu: Khronika sobytii* (The Petrograd Bolsheviks in 1917: Chronicle of Events). Leningrad: Lenizdat, 1957.

MAKSANOV, V., and NELIDOV, N. *Khronika revoliutsii. Vypusk I: 1917 god* (Chronicle of the Revolution. Issue I: 1917). Moscow-Petrograd: Gosizdat, 1923.

VLADIMIROVA, V. *Revoliutsiia 1917 goda: Khronika sobytii* (The Revolution of 1917: Chronicle of Events). Vol. III: *Iiun'-iiul'* (June-July). Moscow: Gosizdat, 1923.

ZASLAVSKY, D. O., and KANTOROVICH, V. A. *Khronika fevral'skoi revoliutsii* (Chronicle of the February Revolution). Vol. I: *1917 god, fevral'-mai* (1917, February-May). Petrograd: Byloe, 1924.

Documentary Materials

AKADEMIIA NAUK SSSR. Institut istorii, et al. *Baltiiskie moriaki v podgotovke i provedenii velikoi oktiabr'skoi sotsialisticheskoi revoliutsii* (Baltic Sailors in the Preparation and Execution of the Great October Socialist Revolution). Edited by P. N. Mordvinov. Moscow-Leningrad: Izd-vo Akademii nauk SSSR, 1957.

236

———. *Revoliutsionnoe dvizhenie v Rossii v aprele 1917 g.: Aprel'skii krizis* (The Revolutionary Movement in Russia in April 1917: The April Crisis). Edited by L. S. Gaponenko, et al. Moscow: Izd-vo Akademii nauk SSSR, 1958.

———. *Revoliutsionnoe dvizhenie v Rossii v iiule 1917 g.: Iiul'skii krizis* (The Revolutionary Movement in Russia in July 1917: The July Crisis). Edited by D. A. Chugaev, et al. Moscow: Izd-vo Akademii nauk SSSR, 1959.

———. *Revoliutsionnoe dvizhenie v Rossii v mae-iiune 1917 g.: Iiun'skaia demonstratsiia* (The Revolutionary Movement in Russia in May-June 1917: The June Demonstration). Edited by D. A. Chugaev, et al. Moscow: Izd-vo Akademii nauk SSSR, 1959.

BELKOV, A. K., and VEREVKIN, B. P. (eds.). *Bol'shevistskaia pechat': Sbornik materialov* (The Bolshevik Press: Collection of Materials). Vol. IV. Moscow: Vysshaia partinaia shkola, 1960.

BROWDER, ROBERT P., and KERENSKY, ALEXANDER F. (eds.). *The Russian Provisional Government, 1917.* 3 vols. Stanford: Stanford University Press, 1961.

DREZEN, A. K. (ed.). *Bol'shevizatsiia Petrogradskogo garnizona: Sbornik materialov i dokumentov* (The Bolshevization of the Petrograd Garrison: Collection of Materials and Documents). Leningrad: Lenoblizdat, 1932.

———. *Burzhuaziia i pomeshchiki v 1917 godu: Chastnye soveshchaniia chlenov Gosudarstvennoi dumy* (The Bourgeoisie and the Landlords in 1917: Unofficial Meetings of the Members of the State Duma). Moscow-Leningrad: Partiinoe Izd-vo, 1932.

ELOV, B. (ed.). "Petrogradskaia organizatsiia RSDRP(b) nakanune iiul'skikh sobytii" (The Petrograd Organization of the RSDLP(b) on the Eve of the July Events), in *3-5 iiulia 1917 g.* (July 3-5, 1917). Petrograd, 1922, pp. 53-74.

———. "Posle iiul'skikh sobytii" (After the July Events), *Krasnaia letopis'*, No. 7, 1923, pp. 95-127.

GOLDER, FRANK A. (ed.). *Documents of Russian History, 1914-1917.* New York: Century, 1927.

IAKOVLEVA, IA. A. (ed.). *Razlozhenie armii v 1917 g.* (The Disintegration of the Army in 1917). Moscow-Leningrad: Gosizdat, 1925.

[ILIN-] ZHENEVSKY, A. (ed.). "Arest Viktora Chernova v iiul'skie dni 1917 g." (The Arrest of Victor Chernov during the July Days of 1917), *Krasnaia letopis'*, No. 6 (21), 1926, pp. 68-75.

ILIN-ZHENEVSKY, A. F. (ed.). "Vystuplenie polkov v Petrograde v iiul'skie dni 1917 goda: Materialy 'Dela 3-5 iiulia' " (The Demonstration of Regiments in Petrograd during the July Days of 1917: Materials on the "Affair of July 3-5"), *Krasnaia letopis'*, No. 3 (30), 1929, pp. 105-19.

INSTITUT MARKSA-ENGEL'SA-LENINA-STALINA PRI TsK KPSS. *Kommunisticheskaia Partiia Sovetskogo Soiuza v rezoliutsiiakh i resheniiakh s"ezdov, konferentsii i plenumov TsK, 1898-1954* (The Communist Party of the Soviet Union in Resolutions and Decisions of its Congresses, Conferences, and Central Committee Plenums, 1898-1954). 4 vols. 7th ed. Moscow: Gospolitizdat, 1954.

INSTITUT MARKSIZMA-LENINIZMA PRI TsK KPSS. *Protokoly Tsentral'nogo komiteta RSDRP(b): Avgust 1917-fevral' 1918* (Protocols of the Central Committee of the RSDLP(b): August, 1917-February, 1918). Moscow: Gospolitizdat, 1958.

———. *Sed'maia (Aprel'skaia) Vserossiiskaia konferentsiia RSDRP(bol'shevikov); Petrogradskaia obshchegorodskaia konferentsiia RSDRP(bol'shevikov), aprel' 1917 goda: Protokoly* (Seventh [April] All-Russian Conference of the RSDLP [Bolshevik]; Petrograd City Conference of the RSDLP [Bolshevik]; April, 1917: Protocols). Moscow: Gospolitizdat, 1958.

———. *Shestoi s"ezd RSDRP(bol'shevikov), avgust 1917 goda: Protokoly* (Sixth Congress of the RSDLP [Bolshevik], August, 1917: Protocols). Moscow: Gospolitizdat, 1958.

KOMMUNISTICHESKAIA PARTIIA SOVETSKOGO SOIUZA. *Protokoly s"ezdov i konferentsii Vsesoiuznoi kommunisticheskoi partii (bol'shevikov): Shestoi s"ezd, 8-16 avgust 1917* (Protocols of the Congresses and Conferences of the All-Union Communist Party [Bolshevik]: Sixth Congress, August 8-16, 1917). Edited by A. S. Bubnov. Moscow: Gosizdat, 1927.

LENINGRAD. Sovet deputatov trudiashchikhsia. *Petrogradskii Sovet rabochikh i soldatskikh deputatov: Protokoly zasedanii Ispolnitel'nogo komiteta i Biuro Ispolnitel'nogo komiteta* (Petrograd Soviet of Workers' and Soldiers' Deputies: Protocols of the Sessions of the Executive Committee and the Bureau of the Executive Committee). Moscow: Gosizdat, 1925.

Leninskii sbornik (Lenin Collection). Vol. I. Moscow: Gosizdat, 1924. Vol. VII. Moscow: Gosizdat, 1928.

LUR'E, M. L. (ed.). "Kronshtadtskie moriaki v iiul'skom vystuplenii 1917 goda" (Kronstadt Sailors in the July Demonstration of 1917), *Krasnaia letopis'*, No. 3 (48), 1932, pp. 76-105.

"Morskoe Ministerstvo Kerenskogo v iiul'skie dni" (Kerensky's Naval Ministry during the July Days), *Petrogradskaia pravda*, July 17, 1921, p. 2.

Okun, S. B. (ed.). *Putilovets v trekh revoliutsiiakh: Sbornik materialov po istorii Putilovskogo zavoda* (The Putilov Worker in Three Revolutions: Collection of Materials on the History of the Putilov Factory). Moscow-Leningrad: Ogiz, 1933.

Pervyi Vserossiiskii s"ezd Sovetov rabochikh, soldatskikh i krest'ianskikh deputatov (First All-Russian Congress of Workers', Soldiers', and Peasants' Deputies). Leningrad: Gosizdat, 1930.

Rossiiskaia Sotsial-Demokraticheskaia Rabochaia Partiia. Tsentral'nyi komitet. *Perepiska sekretariata TsK RSDRP (b) s mestnymi partiinymi organizatsiiami: Sbornik dokumentov* (Correspondence of the Secretariat of the Central Committee of the RSDLP(b) with Local Party Organizations: Collection of Documents). Vol. I: *Mart-oktiabr' 1917 g.* (March-October, 1917). Moscow: Gospolitizdat, 1957.

Russia. 1917 Provisional Government. *Zhurnaly zasedanii Vremennogo pravitel'stva* (Journals of the Sessions of the Provisional Government). Petrograd, 1917.

Tobolin, I. (ed.). "Iiul'skie dni v Petrograde" (The July Days in Petrograd), *Krasnyi arkhiv*, No. 4 (23), 1927, pp. 1-63, and No. 5 (24), 1927, pp. 3-70.

Vsesoiuznaia Kommunisticheskaia Partiia (Bol'shevikov). *Vtoraia i tret'ia obshchegorodskie konferentsii bol'shevikov v iiule i oktiabre 1917 goda: Protokoly* (Second and Third Bolshevik Petrograd City Conferences in July and October, 1917: Protocols). Moscow-Leningrad: Gosizdat, 1927.

———. Leningradskii Istpart. *Pervyi legal'nyi Peterburgskii komitet bol'shevikov v 1917 g.: Sbornik materialov i protokolov zasedanii Peterburgskogo komiteta RSDRP(b) i ego Ispolnitel'noi komissii za 1917 g.* (The First Legal Bolshevik Petersburg Committee in 1917: Collection of Materials and Protocols of the Meetings of the Petersburg Committee of the RSDLP(b) and its Executive Commission for 1917). Edited by P. F. Kudelli. Moscow-Leningrad: Gosizdat, 1927.

Zeman, Z. A. B. (ed.). *Germany and the Revolution in Russia, 1915-1918: Documents from the Archives of the German Foreign Ministry.* London: Oxford University Press, 1958.

1917 Newspapers

Bakiinskii rabochii (Baku Worker). Baku. Daily newspaper of the Baku Bolshevik Committee.

Birzhevye vedomosti (Stock Exchange Gazette). Petrograd. Non-party daily.

Biulleten' Vserossiiskoi konferentsii frontovykh i tylovykh voennykh organizatsii RSDRP(b) (Bulletin of the All-Russian Conference of Front and Rear Military Organizations of the RSDLP(b)). Petrograd. Published by the Bolshevik Military Organization as a special supplement to *Soldatskaia pravda,* June 16-24, 1917.

Delo naroda (The People's Cause). Petrograd. Newspaper of the Socialist-Revolutionary Party.

Edinstvo (Unity). Petrograd. Published by Edinstvo, G. V. Plekhanov's political organization.

Golos pravdy (Voice of Truth). Kronstadt. Kronstadt Bolshevik organ.

Izvestiia Kronshtadtskogo Soveta rabochikh i soldatskikh deputatov (News of the Kronstadt Soviet of Workers' and Soldiers' Deputies). Kronstadt. Kronstadt Soviet organ.

Izvestiia Petrogradskogo Soveta rabochikh i soldatskikh deputatov (News of the Petrograd Soviet of Workers' and Soldiers' Deputies). Petrograd. Daily newspaper of the Petrograd Soviet until the First All-Russian Congress of Soviets of Workers' and Soldiers' Deputies, when it became joint organ of the Petrograd Soviet and the All-Russian Central Executive Committee.

Listok pravdy (Leaflet of Truth). Petrograd. Published on July 6, 1917, in place of *Pravda.*

Malenkaia gazeta (Little Gazette). Petrograd. Right-wing daily.

Novaia zhizn' (New Life). Petrograd. Socialist newspaper edited by Maxim Gorky.

Novoe vremia (New Times). Petrograd. Ultra-conservative daily.

Okopnaia pravda (Trench Truth). Riga. Bolshevik Military Organization newspaper for the Northern front.

Pravda (Truth). Petrograd. Central Bolshevik Party organ.

Rabochaia gazeta (Workers' Gazette). Petrograd. Central Menshevik Party organ.

Riech' (Speech). Petrograd. Constitutional Democratic Party organ.

Sibirskaia pravda (Siberian Truth). Krasnoiarsk. Bolshevik daily.

Soldatskaia pravda (Soldiers' Truth). Petrograd. Organ of the Bolshevik Military Organization.

Volia naroda (The People's Will). Petrograd. Right Socialist-Revolutionary Party newspaper.

Volna (The Wave). Helsingfors. Organ of the Helsingfors Bolshevik Committee.

Vpered (Forward). Petrograd. Interdistrict Committee newspaper.

Zhivoe slovo (Living Word). Petrograd. Right-wing newspaper.

Zvezda (Star). Ekaterinoslav. Newspaper published by the Ekaterinoslav Bolshevik Committee.

Bolshevik Memoirs

A. I-ZH. [ILIN-ZHENEVSKY, A. F.]. "Bol'sheviki v tiurme Kerenskogo" (The Bolsheviks in Kerensky's Prison), *Krasnaia letopis'*, No. 2 (26), 1928, pp. 43-65.

ANTONOV-OVSEENKO, V. A. *Stroitel'stvo Krasnoi Armii v revoliutsii* (The Building of the Red Army in the Revolution). Moscow: Izd-vo Krasnaia Nov', 1923.

BADAEV, A. *Bol'sheviki v gosudarstvennoi dume* (The Bolsheviks in the State Duma). Moscow: Gospolitizdat, 1954.

BONCH-BRUEVICH, V. *Na boevykh postakh fevral'skoi i oktiabr'skoi revoliutsii* (At the Fighting Posts of the February and October Revolutions). Moscow: Federatsiia, 1931.

BURSIN. "Piterskie rabochie ob iiul'skikh dniakh: Zavod Erikson" (Petrograd Workers on the July Days: The Erickson Factory), *Krasnaia letopis'*, No. 9, 1924, p. 26.

EGOROV, V. I. "Iiul'skie dni 1917 goda" (The July Days of 1917), *Leningradskaia pravda*, July 18, 1926, p. 3.

EGOROVA, E. N. "Iunkeram plevali v litso" (They Spat in the Cadets' Faces), *Leningradskaia pravda*, July 18, 1926, p. 3.

EREMEEV. "Iiul'skii pogrom 1917 goda" (The July Pogrom of 1917), *Pravda*, July 17, 1927, p. 4.

FLEROVSKY, I. P. "Iiul'skii politicheskii urok" (The Political Lesson of July), *Proletarskaia revoliutsiia*, No. 7 (54), 1926, pp. 57-90.

———. "Predmetnyi urok" (An Object Lesson), *Pravda*, July 16, 1922, p. 2.

GAVRILOV, I. *Ocherki po istorii Vyborgskoi partorganizatsii goroda Leningrada* (Essays on the History of the Vyborg Party Organization in the City of Leningrad). Leningrad: Lenpartizdat, 1933.

GRAF, TATIANA. "V iiul'skie dni 1917 g." (During the July days of 1917), *Krasnaia letopis'*, No. 2 (26), 1928, pp. 66-75.

IABLONSKY, V. "3-5 iiulia" (July 3-5), *Krasnaia letopis'*, No. 2-3, 1922, pp. 158-64.

ILIN-ZHENEVSKY, A. F. *Iiul' 1917 goda* (July 1917). Moscow: Gosizdat, 1927.

———. "Na rubezhe russkoi revoliutsii" (On the Brink of the Russian Revolution), *Krasnyi Petrograd*, 1919, pp. 34-44.

———. *Ot fevralia k zakhvatu vlasti: Vospominaniia o 1917 g.* (From February to the Seizure of Power: Memoirs of 1917). Leningrad: Priboi, 1927.

———. "Voennaia organizatsiia RSDRP i *Soldatskaia pravda*" (The Military Organization of the RSDLP and *Soldiers' Truth*), *Krasnaia letopis'*, No. 1 (16), 1926, 57-73.

ITKINA, A. M. "Oplot bol'shevizma" (Stronghold of Bolshevism), in *Narvskaia zastava v 1917 godu v vospominaniiakh i dokumentakh* (The Narva Gates [District] in 1917 in Memoirs and Documents). Edited by M. I. Protopopov, et al. Leningrad: Lenizdat, 1960, pp. 145-58.

KALININ, M. I. "Vladimir Il'ich o dvizhenii" (Vladimir Ilich on the Movement), *Krasnaia gazeta*, July 16, 1920, p. 2.

KEDROV, M. "Iz krasnoi tetradi ob Il'iche" (From the Red Notebook about Ilich), *Proletarskaia revoliutsiia*, No. 1 (60), 1927, pp. 36-69.

———. "Vserossiiskaia konferentsiia voennykh organizatsii RSDRP(b)" (All-Russian Conference of Military Organizations of the RSDLP-(b)), *Proletarskaia revoliutsiia*, No. 6 (65), 1927, pp. 216-31. Also contained in *Velikaia oktiabr'skaia sotsialisticheskaia revoliutsiia: Sbornik vospominanii* (The Great October Socialist Revolution: Collection of Memoirs). Moscow: Gosizdat, 1957, pp. 71-82.

KHOKHRIAKOV, A. [BONNER, S.]. "Iz zhizni Petrogradskogo garnizona v 1917 godu" (From the Life of the Petrograd Garrison in 1917), *Krasnaia letopis'*, No. 2 (17), 1926, pp. 29-50.

KOLBIN, I. N. "Kronshtadt organizuetsia, gotovitsia k boiu" (Kronstadt Organizes, Prepares for Battle), in *Oktiabr'skii shkval: Moriaki Baltiiskogo flota v 1917 g.* (October Squall: The Sailors of the Baltic Fleet in 1917). Edited by P. F. Kudelli and I. V. Egorov. Leningrad: Izd-vo Krasnaia gazeta, 1927, pp. 23-50.

———. "Kronshtadt ot fevralia do kornilovskikh dnei" (Kronstadt from February to the Kornilov Days), *Krasnaia letopis'*, No. 2 (23), 1927, pp. 134-61.

KRUPSKAIA, N. K. *Lenin i partiia* (Lenin and the Party). Moscow: Gospolitizdat, 1963.

KUDELLI, P. F. (ed.). *Leningradskie rabochie v bor'be za vlast' Sovetov 1917 g.* (Leningrad Workers in the Struggle for [Transfer of] Power to the Soviets in 1917). Leningrad: Gosizdat, 1924.

LASHEVICH, M. M. "Iiul'skie dni" (The July Days), *Petrogradskaia pravda*, July 17, 1921, p. 1.

LATSIS, M. Ia. "Iiul'skie dni v Petrograde: Iz dnevnika agitatora" (The July Days in Petrograd: From an Agitator's Diary), *Proletarskaia revoliutsiia*, No. 5 (17), 1923, pp. 102-16.

———. "Nakanune oktiabr'skikh dnei" (On the Eve of the October Days), *Izvestiia*, November 6, 1918, p. 2.

LIUBOVICH, A. M. "3-5 iiulia" (July 3-5), *Leningradskaia pravda*, July 16, 1925, p. 3.

LUNACHARSKY, A. V. "Iz vospominanii ob iiul'skikh dniakh 1917 g." (Recollections of the July Days, 1917), *Petrogradskaia pravda*, July 16, 1922, p. 3.

MEKHONOSHIN, K. "Iiul'skie dni v Petrograde" (The July Days in Petrograd), *Izvestiia*, July 16, 1922, p. 1.

———. "Iz vospominanii o tov. Lenine" (Recollections of Comrade Lenin), *Politrabotnik*, No. 2-3, 1924, pp. 7-9.

———. "Iz vospominanii o V. I. Lenine" (Recollections of V. I. Lenin), in *O Vladimire Il'iche Lenine: Vospominaniia 1900-1922 gody* (On Vladimir Ilich Lenin: Memoirs, 1900-1922). Edited by L. V. Ivanova and N. I. Krutikova. Moscow: Gospolitizdat, 1963, pp. 243-45.

METELEV, A. "Iiul'skoe vosstanie v Petrograde" (The July Uprising in Petrograd), *Proletarskaia revoliutsiia*, No. 6, 1922, pp. 158-77.

MINCHEV, A. "Boevye dni" (Fighting Days), *Krasnaia letopis'*, No. 9, 1924, pp. 5-10.

NEVSKY, V. I. "Dve vstrechi" (Two Meetings), *Krasnaia letopis'*, No. 4, 1922, pp. 142-46.

———. "Narodyne massy v oktiabr'skoi revoliutsii" (The Masses in the October Revolution), *Rabotnik prosveshcheniia*, No. 8, 1922, pp. 20-22.

———. "Organizatsiia mass" (Organization of the Masses), *Krasnaia gazeta*, July 16, 1922, p. 3.

———. *V bure deianii: Petrograd za piat' let Sovetskoi raboty* (In the Storm of Action: Petrograd after Five Years of Soviet Work). Moscow-Petrograd: Gosizdat, 1922.

———. "V oktiabre: Beglye zametki pamiati" (In October: Brief Notes from Memory), *Katorga i ssylka*, No. 11-12 (96-97), 1932, pp. 27-45.

———. "Voennaia organizatsiia i oktiabr'skaia revoliutsiia" (The Military Organization and the October Revolution), *Krasnoarmeets*, No. 10-15, 1919, pp. 34-44.

———. "Zamechaniia k soobshcheniiu B. Elova i stat'e F. Raskol'nikova" (Remarks on the Communication of B. Elov and the Article of F. Raskolnikov), *Krasnaia letopis'*, No. 7, 1923, pp. 128-30.

--ov. "Vyborgskaia raionnaia Duma 1917 goda" (The Vyborg District Duma in 1917), *Leningradskaia pravda*, November 4, 1927, p. 3.

PODVOISKY, N. I. *God 1917* (The Year 1917). Moscow: Gospolitizdat, 1958.

———. "Iiul'skie dni: Tri momenta" (The July Days: Three Moments), *Pravda*, July 18, 1925, p. 2.

———. "Voennaia organizatsiia TsK RSDRP(b) i voenno-revoliutsionnyi komitet 1917 g." (The Military Organization of the Central Committee of the RSDLP(b) and the Military Revolutionary Committee of 1917), *Krasnaia letopis'*, No. 6, 1923, pp. 64-97 and No. 8, 1923, pp. 7-43.

POKROVSKY, M. N. "Grazhdanin Chernov v iiul'skie dni" (Citizen Chernov in the July Days), *Pravda*, July 16, 1922, p. 1.

RASKOLNIKOV, F. F. *Kronshtadt i Piter v 1917 godu* (Kronstadt and Petrograd in 1917). Moscow-Leningrad: Gosizdat, 1925.

———. "Kronshtadt v iiul'skie dni" (Kronstadt in the July Days), *Pravda*, July 16, 1927, p. 3.

———. *Na boevykh postakh* (At the Fighting Posts). Moscow: Voenizdat, 1964.

———. "Vooruzhennoe vosstanie ili vooruzhennoe demonstratsiia?" (Armed Uprising or Armed Demonstration?), *Pravda*, July 27, 1927, p. 3.

———. "Zasedaniia pervogo legal'nogo Peka" (The Meetings of the First Legal Petersburg Committee), *Proletarskaia revoliutsiia*, No. 8, 1922, pp. 48-54.

ROZANOV, A. "Pervyi pulemetnyi polk" (The First Machine Gun Regiment), *Petrogradskaia pravda*, July 16, 1922, p. 3.

S. M. "Na putilovskom zavode v iiul'skie dni" (At the Putilov Factory during the July Days), *Petrogradskaia pravda*, July 18, 1922, p. 3.

SAVELIEV, M. "Lenin v iiul'skie dni" (Lenin in the July Days), *Pravda*, July 17, 1930, p. 2.

SHLIAPNIKOV, A. "Iiul'skie dni v Petrograde" (The July Days in Petrograd), *Proletarskaia revoliutsiia*, No. 4 (51), 1926, pp. 46-89, and No. 5 (52), 1926, pp. 5-60.

———. *Kanun semnadtsatogo goda* (The Eve of 1917). 2 vols. Moscow-Petrograd: Gosizdat, 1923.

———. *Semnadtsatyi god* (The Year '17). 4 vols. Moscow-Petrograd: Gosizdat, 1923.

SHUMIATSKY, B. "Pervyi s"ezd Sovetov (The First Congress of Soviets), in V *dni velikoi proletarskoi revoliutsii: Epizody bor'by v Petrograde v 1917 godu* (In the Days of the Great Proletarian Revolution: Episodes from the Struggle in Petrograd in 1917). Edited by I. P. Tovstukha. Moscow: Ogiz, 1937, pp. 52-60.

———. "Shestoi s"ezd partii i rabochii klass" (The Sixth Party Congress and the Working Class), in *V dni velikoi proletarskoi revoliutsii: Epizody bor'by v Petrograde v 1917 godu* (In the Days of the Great

Proletarian Revolution: Episodes from the Struggle in Petrograd in 1917). Edited by I. P. Tovstukha. Moscow: Ogiz, 1937, pp. 88-95.

SMIRNOV, P., et al. Review of F. F. Raskolnikov's *Kronshtadtsy: Iz vospominanii bol'shevika* (The Kronstadters: From the Memoirs of a Bolshevik), *Krasnaia letopis'*, No. 5-6 (50-51), 1933, pp. 214-15.

SULIMOVA, M. "Eto budet poslednii i reshitel'nyi boi" (This Will Be the Last and Decisive Battle), in *Letopis' velikogo oktiabria* (Chronicle of the Great October). Edited by A. Iu. Krivitsky. Moscow: Sovetskaia Rossiia, 1958, pp. 101-107.

SVERDLOVA, K. T. *Iakob Mikhailovich Sverdlov*. Moscow: Molodaia gvardiia, 1960.

TARASOV-RODIONOV, A. "3-5 iiulia" (July 3-5), *Izvestiia*, July 18, 1922, p. 2.

TROTSKY, LEON. *The History of the Russian Revolution*. Translated by Max Eastman. 3 vols. Ann Arbor: University of Michigan Press, 1957.

VEINBERG, G. D. "Preddverie oktiabr'skoi revoliutsii: Moi vospominaniia o iiul'skikh dniakh" (The Threshhold of the October Revolution: My Recollections of the July Days), *Petrogradskaia pravda*, July 17, 1921, p. 3.

ZALEZHSKY, V. N. *Iz vospominanii podpol'shchika* (From the Memoirs of a Member of the Underground). Moscow: Gosizdat, 1931.

ZINOVIEV, G. "Lenin i iiul'skie dni" (Lenin and the July Days), *Proletarskaia revoliutsiia*, No. 8-9 (67-68), 1927, pp. 55-72.

Non-Bolshevik Memoirs

ARONSON, G. *Rossiia nakanune revoliutsii* (Russia on the Eve of Revolution). New York, 1962.

ARSKY, N. "Tragikomediia 3-go iiulia" (The Tragicomedy of July 3), in *Perezhitoe* (Past Experiences). Moscow: Verf, [1918], pp. 33-45.

CHERNOV, V. M. *The Great Russian Revolution*. Translated and abridged by Philip E. Mosely. New Haven: Yale University Press, 1936.

IARCHUK, E. *Kronshtadt v russkoi revoliutsii* (Kronstadt in the Russian Revolution). New York: Izdanie Ispolnitel'nogo komiteta professional'nykh soiuzov, 1923.

KERENSKY, A. F. *Russia and History's Turning Point*. New York: Duell, Sloan, and Pearce, 1965.

———, *The Catastrophe: Kerensky's Own Story of the Russian Revolution*. New York: Appleton, Century, Crofts, 1927.

MILIUKOV, P. N. *Istoriia vtoroi russkoi revoliutsii* (History of the Second Russian Revolution). 3 vols. Sofia: Rossiisko-Bolgarskoe knigoizd-vo, 1921-1924.

———. *Rossiia na perelome* (Russia at the Turning Point). 3 vols. Paris: Imprimerie d'art Voltaire, 1927.

———. *Vospominaniia, 1859-1917* (Memoirs, 1859-1917). New York: Izd-vo im. Chekhova, 1955.

NIKITINE, B. V. *The Fatal Years*. London: William Hodge, 1938.

POLOVTSEV, P. A. *Dni zatmeniia* (Days of Eclipse). Paris: Vozrozhdenie, n.d.

RODZIANKO, M. V. "Gosudarstvennaia duma i fevral'skaia 1917 goda revoliutsiia" (The State Duma and the February, 1917 Revolution), *Arkhiv russkoi revoliutsii* (Archive of the Russian Revolution). Vol. VI. Berlin, 1922.

STANKEVICH, B. V. *Vospominaniia 1914-1919 gg.* (Memoirs 1914-1919). Berlin: I. P. Ladyzhnikov, 1920.

SUKHANOV, N. N. *The Russian Revolution, 1917*. Edited, abridged, and translated by Joel Carmichael. 2 vols. New York: Harper and Row, 1962.

———. *Zapiski o revoliutsii* (Notes on the Revolution). 7 vols. Berlin-Petersburg-Moscow: Z. I. Grzhebin, 1922-1923.

TSERETELI, I. G. *Vospominaniia o fevral'skoi revoliutsii* (Memoirs of the February Revolution). 2 vols. Paris: Mouton and Co., 1963.

WOYTINSKY, W. S. "Gody pobed i porazhenii: 1917" (Years of Victories and Defeats: 1917). Berlin, 1922-1923. Nicolaevsky archives, The Hoover Institution, Stanford, California.

———. *Stormy Passage*. New York: Vanguard Press, 1961.

Museum Collections

GOSUDARSTVENNYI MUZEI VELIKOI OKTIABR'SKOI SOTSIALISTICHESKOI REVOLIUTSII (State Museum of the Great October Socialist Revolution), Leningrad. Photograph and leaflet collections.

MUZEI REVOLIUTSII SSSR (Museum of the Revolution USSR), Moscow. Photograph and leaflet collections.

TSENTRAL'NYI VOENNO-MORSKOI MUZEI (Central Military-Naval Museum), Leningrad. Photograph collection.

Soviet Dissertations

BYKOV, G. D. "Revoliutsionnaia deiatel'nost' bol'shevikov Vyborgskoi storony goroda Petrograda v period podgotovki i provedeniia oktiabr'skoi sotsialisticheskoi revoliutsii" (The Revolutionary Activity of the Bolsheviks of the Vyborg Side of the City of Petrograd during the Period of the Preparation and Execution of the October Socialist Revolution). *Kandidat* dissertation, Leningrad State University, Leningrad, 1951.

MIRONOV, T. G. "Bor'ba bol'shevikov za Petrogradskii garnizon v period dvoevlastiia 1917 goda" (The Bolshevik Struggle for the Petrograd Garrison during the Period of Dual Power in 1917). *Kandidat* dissertation, Leningrad State University, Leningrad, 1954.

PCHELKO, F. P. "Voennaia organizatsiia bol'shevistskoi partii v period bor'by za massy v 1917 godu" (The Military Organization of the Bolshevik Party in the Period of the Struggle for the Masses in 1917). *Kandidat* dissertation, Moscow State Pedagogical Institute, Moscow, 1946.

PETROV, I. F. "Strategiia i taktika partii bol'shevikov v period podgotovki i pobedy sotsialisticheskoi revoliutsii: Mart-oktiabr' 1917 g." (The Strategy and Tactics of the Bolshevik Party in the Preparation and Victory of the Socialist Revolution: March-October, 1917). Doctoral dissertation, Academy of Social Sciences under the Central Committee of the CPSU, Moscow, 1961.

ZHELEZKOV, N. "Iiul'skii politicheskii krizis 1917 goda" (The July Political Crisis of 1917). *Kandidat* dissertation, Tomsk State University, Tomsk, 1955.

ZNAMENSKY, O. N. "Iiul'skii krizis 1917 goda." (The July Crisis of 1917). *Kandidat* dissertation, Leningrad State University, Leningrad, 1962.

Soviet Secondary Sources

AKADEMIIA NAUK SSSR, Institut istorii, et al. *Ocherki istorii Leningrada* (Essays on the History of Leningrad). 4 vols. Moscow-Leningrad: Izd-vo Akademii nauk SSSR, 1955-1964.

AKHUN, M. I. and PETROV, V. A. *Bol'sheviki i armiia v 1905-1917 gg.* (The Bolsheviks and the Army, 1905-1917). Leningrad: Izd-vo Krasnaia gazeta, 1929.

BALABANOV, M. *Ot 1905 k 1917: Massovoe rabochee dvizhenie* (From 1905 to 1917: The Mass Workers' Movement). Moscow-Leningrad: Gosizdat, 1927.

BURDZHALOV, E. N. "O taktike bol'shevikov v marte-aprele 1917 goda" (On Bolshevik Tactics in March and April 1917), *Voprosy istorii*, No. 4, 1956, pp. 38-56.

CENTRAL COMMITTEE OF THE CPSU. *History of the Communist Party of the Soviet Union (Bolshevik): Short Course.* New York: International Publishers, 1939.

D'OR, O. L. *Krasnyi chasovoi Kronshtadt* (Kronstadt, the Red Sentinel). Moscow: Literaturno-izdatel'skii otdel politicheskogo upravleniia revoliutsionnogo voennogo soveta respubliki, 1920.

DREZEN, A. K. "Petrogradskii garnizon v iiule i avguste 1917 g." (The Petrograd Garrison in July and August, 1917), *Krasnaia letopis'*, No. 3 (24), 1927, pp. 191-223.

FLEER, M. G. *Peterburgskii komitet bol'shevikov v gody voiny 1914-1917* (The Bolshevik Petersburg Committee during the War Years, 1914-1917). Leningrad: Priboi, 1927.

GOREV, B. I. *Anarkhizm v Rossii* (Anarchism in Russia). Moscow: Molodaia Gvardiia, 1930.

IGNATOV, E. "I Vserossiiskii s"ezd Sovetov rabochikh i soldatskikh deputatov" (First All-Russian Congress of Soviets of Workers' and Soldiers' Deputies), *Proletarskaia revoliutsiia*, No. 6 (65), 1927, pp. 72-126.

ILIN, M. S. "Demonstratsiia i miting na marsovom pole v Petrograde 4 iiunia 1917 g." (The Demonstration and Meeting on Mars Field in Petrograd on June 4, 1917), *Voprosy istorii*, No. 6, 1957, pp. 126-30.

INSTITUT ISTORII PARTII PRI LENINGRADSKOM OBKOME KPSS. *Ocherki istorii Leningradskoi organizatsii KPSS* (Essays on the History of the Leningrad Organization of the CPSU). Part I: *1883-oktiabr' 1917 gg.* (1883-October, 1917). Leningrad: Lenizdat, 1962.

IUGOV, M. S. "Sovety v pervyi period revoliutsii" (The Soviets in the First Period of the Revolution), in *Ocherki po istorii oktiabr'skoi revoliutsii* (Essays on the History of the October Revolution). Edited by M. N. Pokrovsky. 2 vols. Moscow-Leningrad: Gosizdat, 1927, Vol. II, pp. 113-253.

KARAMYSHEVA, L. F. *Bor'ba bol'shevikov za Petrogradskii Sovet: Mart-oktiabr' 1917 g.* (The Bolshevik Struggle for the Petrograd Soviet: March-October, 1917). Leningrad: Lenizdat, 1964.

KNIAZEV, S. P. (ed.). *Petrogradskie bol'sheviki v oktiabr'skoi revoliutsii* (The Petrograd Bolsheviks in the October Revolution). Leningrad: Lenizdat, 1957.

KOCHAKOV, V. M. "Sostav Petrogradskogo garnizona v 1917 g." (The Composition of the Petrograd Garrison in 1917), *Uchenye zapiski Leningradskogo gosudarstvennogo universiteta* (Scholarly Communications of Leningrad State University), Vyp. 24, No. 205, 1956, pp. 60-86.

KRIVOSHEINA, E. P. *Dve demonstratsii* (Two Demonstrations). Moscow-Leningrad: Gosudarstvennoe Sotsial'no–Ekonomicheskoe Izd-vo, 1931.

LEVI, E. "Moskovskaia organizatsiia bol'shevikov v iiule 1917 g." (The Moscow Bolshevik Organization in July, 1917), *Proletarskaia revoliutsiia*, No. 2-3 (85-86), 1929, pp. 123-51.

LIDAK, O. A. "Iiul'skie sobytiia 1917 goda" (The July Events of 1917), in *Ocherki po istorii oktiabr'skoi revoliutsii* (Essays on the History of the October Revolution). Edited by M. N. Pokrovsky. 2 vols. Moscow-Leningrad: Gosizdat, 1927, Vol. I, pp. 257-346.

———. *1917 god: Ocherk istorii oktiabr'skoi revoliutsii* (The Year 1917: An Essay on the History of the October Revolution). Moscow-Leningrad: Partizdat, 1932.

NEVSKY, V. I. *Ocherki po istorii Rossiiskoi kommunisticheskoi partii* (Essays on the History of the Russian Communist Party). 2d ed. Leningrad: Priboi, 1925.

PETROV, I. F. *Strategiia i taktika partii bol'shevikov v podgotovke pobedy oktiabr'skoi revoliutsii* (Bolshevik Party Strategy and Tactics in Preparing the Triumph of the October Revolution). Moscow: Gospolitizdat, 1964.

POPOV, N. G. "Putilovets v iiul'skie dni" (A Putilovite in the July Days), *Bor'ba klassov*, No. 11-12, 1932, pp. 280-98.

RABINOVICH, S. E. "Bol'shevistskie voennye organizatsii v 1917 g." (The Bolshevik Military Organizations in 1917), *Proletarskaia revoliutsiia*, No. 6-7 (77-78), 1928, pp. 179-98.

———. *Bor'ba za armiiu 1917 g.* (The Struggle for the Army in 1917). Leningrad: Gosizdat, 1930.

———. "Rabota bol'shevikov v armii v 1917 g." (Bolshevik Work in the Army in 1917), *Voina i revoliutsiia*, No. 6, 1927, pp. 96-108.

———. "Vserossiiskaia konferentsiia bol'shevistskikh voennykh organizatsii 1917 g." (The All-Russian Conference of the Bolshevik Military Organizations in 1917), *Krasnaia letopis'*, No. 5 (38), 1930, pp. 105-32.

———. *Vserossiiskaia voennaia konferentsiia bol'shevikov 1917 g.* (The All-Russian Military Conference of Bolsheviks in 1917). Moscow: Gosvoenizdat, 1931.

SHELAVIN, K. "K voprosu o podgotovke iiul'skikh dnei" (On the Problem of the Preparation of the July Days), *Zvezda*, No. 3 (9), 1925, pp. 143-49.

———. *Ocherki russkoi revoliutsii 1917 g.* (Essays on the Russian Revolution of 1917). Part I: *Fevral'-iiul'skie dni* (February-July Days). Petrograd: Priboi, 1923.

SOVOKIN, A. M. "K istorii iiun'skoi demonstratsii 1917 g." (On the History of the June Demonstration of 1917), *Voprosy istorii KPSS*, No. 5, 1966, pp. 45-54.

———. "Rasshirennoe soveshchanie TsK RSDRP(b), 13-14 iiulia 1917 g." (The Expanded Meeting of the Central Committee of the RSDLP(b), July 13-14, 1917), *Voprosy istorii KPSS*, No. 4, 1959, pp. 125-38.

STARTSEV, V. I. *Ocherki po istorii Petrogradskoi krasnoi gvardii i rabochei militsii* (Essays on the History of the Petrograd Red Guard and Workers' Militia). Moscow-Leningrad: Nauka, 1965.

STULOV, P. M. "Pervyi pulemetnyi polk v iiul'skie dni 1917 g." (The First Machine Gun Regiment in the July Days of 1917), *Krasnaia letopis'*, No. 3 (36), 1930, pp. 64-125.

TSUKERMAN, S. I. "Petrogradskii raionnyi komitet bol'shevikov v 1917 g." (The Petrograd District Bolshevik Committee in 1917), *Krasnaia letopis'*, No. 5-6 (51-52), 1932, pp. 213-40.

VAVILIN, I. "Lenin i Peterburgskaia organizatsiia bol'shevikov v 1917 g. do iiulia" (Lenin and the Petersburg Bolshevik Organization in 1917 prior to July), in *Lenin kak rukovoditel' Leningradskoi organizatsii bol'shevikov* (Lenin as Leader of the Leningrad Bolshevik Organization). Edited by O. A. Lidak. Leningrad: Lenpartizdat, 1934, pp. 75-95.

VLADIMIROVA, V. "Iiul'skie dni 1917 goda" (The July Days of 1917), *Proletarskaia revoliutsiia*, No. 5 (17), 1923, pp. 3-52.

ZALESSKAIA, F. "Iiun'skaia demonstratsiia 1917 g." (The June Demonstration of 1917), *Proletarskaia revoliutsiia*, No. 6 (65), 1927, pp. 127-63.

ZNAMENSKY, O. N. *Iiul'skii krizis 1917 goda* (The July Crisis of 1917). Moscow-Leningrad: Nauka, 1964.

Non-Soviet Secondary Sources

BARON, SAMUEL H. *Plekhanov, The Father of Russian Marxism*. Stanford University Press, 1963.

CARR, EDWARD H. *The Bolshevik Revolution, 1917-1923*. 3 vols. New York, Macmillan, 1951-1953.

CHAMBERLIN, W. H. *The Russian Revolution, 1917-1921*. 2 vols. New York: Macmillan, 1935.

CURTISS, JOHN S. *The Russian Revolutions of 1917*. Princeton: Van Nostrand, 1957.

DANIELS, ROBERT V. *The Conscience of the Revolution.* Cambridge: Harvard University Press, 1960.

DEUTSCHER, ISAAC. *The Prophet Armed.* New York: Oxford University Press, 1954.

FAINSOD, MERLE. *How Russia Is Ruled.* Cambridge: Harvard University Press, 1958.

FISCHER, LOUIS. *The Life of Lenin.* New York: Harper and Row, 1964.

FLORINSKY, MICHAEL T. *The Fall of the Russian Empire.* New York: Collier Books, 1961.

FUTRELL, MICHAEL. *Northern Underground.* London: Faber and Faber, 1963.

HAIMSON, LEOPOLD. "The Problem of Social Stability in Urban Russia, 1905-1917," *Slavic Review,* XXIII, No. 4 (1964), pp. 619-42, and XXIV, No. 1 (1965), pp. 1-22.

KARPOVICH, MICHAEL. *Imperial Russia, 1801-1917.* New York: Holt, Rinehart and Winston, 1932.

KEEP, J. L. H. *The Rise of Social Democracy in Russia.* London: Oxford University Press, 1963.

MEYER, ALFRED G. *Leninism.* New York: Praeger, 1957.

NICOLAEVSKY, BORIS I. "I G. Tsereteli i ego vospominaniia o 1917 g." (I. G. Tsereteli and his Memoirs on 1917), *Sotsialisticheskii vestnik,* No. 9-10, 1962, pp. 132-36.

PARES, BERNARD. *The Fall of the Russian Monarchy.* New York: Vintage Books, 1961.

PIPES, RICHARD. *The Formation of the Soviet Union.* 1st ed. rev. Cambridge: Harvard University Press, 1964.

RADKEY, OLIVER H. *The Agrarian Foes of Bolshevism.* New York: Columbia University Press, 1958.

SCHAPIRO, LEONARD B. *The Communist Party of the Soviet Union.* New York: Random House, 1959.

SCHMITT, B. E. *The Coming of the War, 1914.* 2 vols. New York: Charles Scribner's Sons, 1930.

SHUB, DAVID. *Lenin.* New York: Mentor, 1948.

TREADGOLD, DONALD W. *Twentieth Century Russia.* Chicago: Rand McNally, 1959.

ULAM, ADAM B. *The Bolsheviks.* New York: Macmillan, 1965.

VON LAUE, THEODORE H. *Why Lenin? Why Stalin?* Philadelphia: Lippincott, 1964.

WARTH, ROBERT D. *The Allies and the Russian Revolution.* Durham: Duke University Press, 1954.

WOLFE, BERTRAM D. *Three Who Made a Revolution*. Boston: Beacon, 1948.

Other Works Cited

A. SH. [SHAPIRO] "Anarkhizm-kommunizm i anarkho-sindikalizm" (Anarchism-Communism and Anarcho-Syndicalism), *Golos truda*, January 27, 1918, p. 3.

LENIN, V. I. *Sochineniia* (Works). 40 vols. 4th ed. Moscow: Gospolitizdat, 1941-1957.

TROTSKY, L. D. *Sochineniia* (Works). Vol. III, Part I: *Ot fevralia do oktiabria* (From February to October). Moscow: Gosizdat, 1925.

TROTSKY, LEON. *The Stalin School of Falsification*. Translated by John G. Wright. New York: Pioneer Publishers, 1962.

ZINOVIEV, G. E. *God revoliutsii* (Year of Revolution). Leningrad: Gosizdat, 1926.

Notes

Full citations are given in the bibliography. The following abbreviations are used in the notes:

> KA: *Krasnyi arkhiv*
> KL: *Krasnaia letopis'*
> PR: *Proletarskaia revoliutsiia*

Prologue

1. O. N. Znamensky, *Iiul'skii krizis 1917 goda* (Moscow-Leningrad: Nauka, 1964) is the latest of these studies.
2. W. H. Chamberlin, *The Russian Revolution, 1917-1921* (2 vols.; New York: Macmillan, 1935).
3. N. N. Sukhanov, *Zapiski o revoliutsii* (7 vols.; Berlin-Petersburg-Moscow: Z. I. Grzhebin, 1922-1923). Unless otherwise specified, all references to Sukhanov's memoirs in this study are to the abridged English translation, N. N. Sukhanov, *The Russian Revolution, 1917*, ed. and trans. Joel Carmichael (2 vols.; Harper and Row, 1962).

I. The Historical Background

1. Cited in B. E. Schmitt, *The Coming of the War, 1914* (2 vols.; New York: Charles Scribner's Sons, 1930), II, 245.
2. *Novoe vremia*, July 19, 1914, pp. 1-2.
3. Bernard Pares, *The Fall of the Russian Monarchy* (New York: Vintage Books, 1961), p. 187.

4. *Leninskii sbornik*, Vol. I (Moscow: Gosizdat, 1924), p. 137.

5. Frank A. Golder, *Documents of Russian History, 1914-1917* (New York: Century, 1927), pp. 3-23.

6. Theodore H. Von Laue, *Why Lenin? Why Stalin?* (Philadelphia: Lippincott, 1964), p. 79.

7. Leopold Haimson, "The Problem of Social Stability in Urban Russia, 1905-1917," *Slavic Review*, XXIII, No. 4 (1964), 620-642, and XXIV, No. 1 (1965), 1-22, contains a persuasive analysis of the revolutionary situation prevailing among Russian workers on the eve of World War I. See also M. Balabanov, *Ot 1905 k 1917: Massovoe rabochee dvizhenie* (Moscow-Leningrad, Gosizdat, 1927), 275-327.

8. O. H. Gankin and H. H. Fisher, *The Bolsheviks and the War: The Origins of the Third International* (Stanford: Stanford University Press, 1940), p. 134.

9. P. N. Miliukov, *Vospominaniia, 1859-1917* (2 vols.; New York: Izd-vo im. Chekhova, 1955), II, 191.

10. Samuel H. Baron, *Plekhanov, The Father of Russian Marxism* (Stanford: Stanford University Press, 1963), p. 324.

11. G. Aronson, *Rossiia nakanune revoliutsii* (New York, 1962), pp. 182-84.

12. For a thorough analysis of the SR internationalist program, see Oliver H. Radkey, *The Agrarian Foes of Bolshevism* (New York: Columbia University Press, 1958), pp. 103-13.

13. V. I. Lenin, *Sochineniia* (40 vols.; 4th ed.; Moscow: Gospolitizdat, 1941-1957), XXI, 1-4.

14. Radkey, *The Agrarian Foes of Bolshevism*, pp. 90-91.

15. Thus, in early November, 1914, a gathering of Bolshevik leaders held outside Petrograd to discuss Lenin's theses and to formulate policies in regard to the war was broken up by the police. A number of participants in the meeting, including the five-man Bolshevik Duma delegation, were subsequently arrested, tried, and exiled to Siberia. A. Badaev, *Bol'sheviki v gosudarstvennoi dume* (Moscow: Gospolitizdat, 1954), pp. 369-419.

16. During the course of the World War Russia sent some fifteen million men to the front. By May 1, 1917, according to Russian General Staff figures, total Russian casualties, including those killed, wounded, captured, or missing, were 66,154 officers and 6,226,005 soldiers. Ia. A. Iakovleva, *Razlozhenie armii v 1917 g.* (Moscow-Leningrad: Gosizdat, 1925), p. iii.

17. M. V. Rodzianko, "Gosudarstvennaia duma i fevral'skaia 1917 goda revoliutsiia," *Arkhiv russkoi revoliutsii* (Berlin, 1922), VI, 43.

18. M. I. Akhun and V. A. Petrov, *Bol'sheviki i armiia v 1905-1917 gg.* (Leningrad: Krasnaia gazeta, 1929), p. 22.

19. Akademiia nauk SSSR, Institut istorii, et al., *Ocherki istorii Leningrada* (4 vols.; Moscow-Leningrad: Izd-vo Akademii nauk SSSR, 1955-1964), III, 979.

20. A. K. Drezen, *Bol'shevizatsiia Petrogradskogo garnizona: Sbornik materialov i dokumentov* (Leningrad: Lenoblizdat, 1932), p. iv; Akhun and Petrov, *Bol'sheviki i armiia*, pp. 174-75.

21. A. F. Kerensky, *Russia and History's Turning Point* (New York: Duell, Sloan and Pearce, 1965), p. 17.

22. P. N. Miliukov, *Istoriia vtoroi russkoi revoliutsii* (3 vols.; Sofia: Rossiisko-Bolgarskoe knigoizd-vo, 1921-1924), I, 24.

23. Michael T. Florinsky, *The Fall of the Russian Empire* (New York: Collier Books, 1961), p. 88.

24. The economic effects of the war on Russia are discussed in some detail in Florinsky, *The Fall of the Russian Empire*.

25. Miliukov, *Istoriia vtoroi russkoi revoliutsii*, I, 33-34.

26. *Ibid.*, p. 35.

27. This description of the February revolution in Petrograd is based on material from N. Avdeev, *Revoliutsiia 1917 goda: Khronika sobytii*, Vol. I: *Ianvar'-aprel'* (Moscow: Gosizdat, 1923); D. O. Zaslavsky and V. A. Kantorovich, *Khronika fevral'skoi revoliutsii*, Vol. I: *1917 god, fevral'-mai* (Petrograd: Byloe, 1924); A. Shliapnikov, *Semnadtsatyi god* (4 vols.; Moscow-Petrograd: Gosizdat, 1923), Vol. I; *Ocherki istorii Leningrada*, Vol. III; and Chamberlin, *The Russian Revolution*, Vol. I.

28. Akademiia nauk SSSR, Institut istorii, et al., *Baltiiskie moriaki v podgotovke i provedenii velikoi oktiabr'skoi sotsialisticheskoi revoliutsii*, ed. P. N. Mordvinov (Moscow-Leningrad: Izd-vo Akademii nauk SSSR, 1957), p. 21.

II. The Struggle Begins

1. E. N. Burdzhalov, "O taktike bol'shevikov v marte-aprele 1917 goda," *Voprosy istorii*, No. 4, 1956, p. 39.

2. M. G. Fleer, *Peterburgskii komitet bol'shevikov v gody voiny 1914-1917* (Leningrad: Priboi, 1927), p. 116. See the report of V. V. Shmidt at the Seventh All-Russian Party Conference in Institut marksizma-leninizma pri TsK KPSS, *Sed'maia (aprel'skaia) Vserossiiskaia konferentsiia RSDRP(bol'shevikov); Petrogradskaia obshchegorodskaia konferentsiia RSDRP(bol'shevikov), aprel' 1917 goda: Protokoly* (Moscow: Gospolitizdat, 1958), pp. 200-201.

3. Shliapnikov, *Semnadtsatyi god*, I, 225.

4. Lenin, *Sochineniia*, XXXV, 238-41.

5. Ibid., XXIII, 287.

6. Burdzhalov, *Voprosy istorii*, No. 4, 1956, p. 42.

7. M. Ia. Latsis, "Nakanune oktiabr'skikh dnei," *Izvestiia*, November 6, 1918, p. 2.

8. Shliapnikov, *Semnadtsatyi god*, I, 256.

9. Burdzhalov, *Voprosy istorii*, No. 4, 1956, p. 41.

10. Vsesoiuznaia Kommunisticheskaia partiia (bol'shevikov), Leningradskii Istpart, *Pervyi legal'nyi Peterburgskii komitet bol'shevikov v 1917 g.: Sbornik materialov i protokolov zasedanii Peterburgskogo komiteta RSDRP (b) i ego Ispolnitel'noi komissii za 1917 g.*, ed. P. F. Kudelli (Moscow-Leningrad: Gosizdat, 1927), p. 19.

11. Ibid.

12. See *Pravda*, March 5-13, 1917, all issues.

13. *Pervyi legal'nyi Peterburgskii komitet*, pp. 49-52.

14. Lenin, *Sochineniia*, XXIII, 299.

15. F. F. Raskolnikov, *Kronshtadt i Piter v 1917 godu* (Moscow-Leningrad: Gosizdat, 1925), p. 54.

16. N. I. Podvoisky, *God 1917* (Moscow: Gospolitizdat, 1958) p. 23. A somewhat different recollection of this speech is contained in Sukhanov, *The Russian Revolution*, II, 273; See also Shliapnikov, *Semnadtsatyi god*, III, 249-59.

17. Tight organizational discipline and unity of thought were, of course, always foremost Leninist goals, but they were seldom attained. Leonard Schapiro and Robert V. Daniels in their respective invaluable studies, *The Communist Party of the Soviet Union* (New York: Random House, 1959) and *The Conscience of the Revolution* (Cambridge: Harvard University Press, 1960), reveal the degreee to which ideological conflict and factionalism prevailed within the Bolshevik organization from the time of its inception.

18. W. S. Woytinsky, "Gody pobed i porazhenii: 1917 god" (Nicolaevsky archives, The Hoover Institution, Stanford, California), p. 48. This substantial memoir on 1917, written in Berlin in 1922-1923, was intended as Volume III of the author's *Gody pobed i porazhenii* (2 vols.; Berlin-Petersburg-Moscow: Z. I. Grzhebin, 1923-1924).

19. Sukhanov, *The Russian Revolution*, I, 285.

20. A detailed record of these Bolshevik meetings is contained in L. Trotsky, *The Stalin School of Falsification*, trans. John G. Wright (New York: Pioneer Publishers, 1962), pp. 231-301.

21. Schapiro, *The Communist Party of the Soviet Union*, p. 162.

22. Burdzhalov, *Voprosy istorii*, No. 4, 1956, p. 47.

23. Trotsky, *The Stalin School*, pp. 289-99.

24. Schapiro, *The Communist Party of the Soviet Union*, pp. 163-64.

25. Woytinsky, "Gody pobed i porazhenii," p. 50.

26. Sukhanov, *The Russian Revolution*, I, 286-87; David Shub, *Lenin* (New York: Mentor, 1948), p. 109.

27. Burdzhalov, *Voprosy istorii*, No. 4, 1956, p. 41.

28. *Pervyi legal'nyi Peterburgskii komitet*, p. 88.

29. Sukhanov, *The Russian Revolution*, I, 290.

30. Thus, Lenin's resolution on the Provisional Government at the First Petrograd City Conference in mid-April spoke of the need for an extended indoctrination campaign among the masses before power could be transferred to the Soviets. *Sed'maia konferentsiia: Protokoly*, p. 291.

31. Ibid., pp. 35-37. In this connection Kamenev proposed an amendment to Lenin's resolution which, while acknowledging the basic class character of the Provisional Government, specifically warned against the "disorganizing effects" of the slogan "Down with the Provisional Government," which Kamenev believed was implicit in the Lenin resolution. This slogan, affirmed the amendment, could "slow down the long-term job of educating and organizing the masses, which was the primary task of the party." The amendment was rejected 20 votes to 6 with 9 abstentions.

32. Avdeev, *Khronika sobytii*, I, 117.

33. Ibid., II, 47-59.

34. Akademiia nauk SSSR, Institut istorii, et al., *Revoliutsionnoe dvizhenie v Rossii v aprele 1917 goda: Aprel'skii krizis*, ed. L. S. Gaponenko, et al. (Moscow: Izd-vo Akademii nauk SSSR, 1958), p. 726.

35. Ibid., p. 737.

36. M. S. Iugov, "Sovety v pervyi period revoliutsii," in *Ocherki po istorii oktiabr'skoi revoliutsii*, ed. M. N. Pokrovsky (Moscow-Leningrad: Gosizdat, 1927), II, 189.

37. *Sed'maia konferentsiia: Protokoly*, pp. 42-44.

38. Ibid., p. 204; see also I. Vavilin, "Lenin i Peterburgskaia organizatsiia bol'shevikov v 1917 g. do iiulia," in *Lenin kak rukovoditel' Leningradskoi organizatsii bol'shevikov*, ed. O. A. Lidak (Leningrad: Lenpartizdat, 1934), pp. 83-87.

39. S. P. Kniazev (ed.), *Petrogradskie bol'sheviki v oktiabr'skoi revoliutsii* (Leningrad: Lenizdat, 1957), p. 100.

40. *Sed'maia konferentsiia: Protokoly*, p. 111.

41. Ibid., pp. 241-43.

42. V. M. Kochakov, "Sostav Petrogradskogo garnizona v 1917 g.," *Uchenye zapiski Leningradskogo gosudarstvennogo universiteta*, Vyp. 24, No. 205, 1956, pp. 67-68; see also T. G. Mironov, "Bor'ba bol'she-vikov za Petrogradskii garnizon v period dvoevlastiia 1917 goda" *Kandidat* dissertation, Leningrad University, Leningrad, 1954), pp. 70-71.

43. S. E. Rabinovich, "Bol'shevistskie voennye organizatsii v 1917 g.," PR, No. 6-7 (77-78), 1928, pp. 181-82.

44. See V. I. Nevsky, "Voennaia organizatsiia i oktiabr'skaia revoliut-siia," *Krasnoarmeets*, No. 10-15, 1919, p. 34.

45. Vsesoiuznaia Kommunisticheskaia partiia (bol'shevikov), *Vtoraia i tret'ia Petrogradskie obshchegorodskie konferentsii bol'shevikov v iiule i oktiabre 1917 goda: Protokoly* (Moscow-Leningrad: Gosizdat, 1927), p. 15.

46. V. I. Nevsky, *V bure deianii: Petrograd za piat' let sovetskoi raboty* (Moscow-Leningrad: Gosizdat, 1922), p. 7.

47. Akhun and Petrov, *Bol'sheviki i armiia*, p. 217.

48. *Soldatskaia pravda*, June 2, 1917, p. 2.

49. Leon Trotsky, *The History of the Russian Revolution*, trans. Max Eastman (3 vols.; Ann Arbor: University of Michigan Press, 1957), II, 31.

50. F. F. Raskolnikov, "Zasedaniia pervogo legal'nogo Peka," PR, No. 8, 1922, p. 50.

51. Trotsky, *History of the Russian Revolution*, II, 31.

52. See, for example, Institut marksizma-leninizma pri TsK KPSS, *Protokoly Tsentral'nogo komiteta RSDRP(b): Avgust 1917-fevral' 1918* (Moscow: Gospolitizdat, 1958), p. 326.

53. Akhun and Petrov, *Bol'sheviki i armiia*, p. 224.

54. This is a very rough approximation based on an estimate of Military Organization strength for mid-June in S. E. Rabinovich, "Vserossiiskaia konferentsiia bol'shevistskikh voennykh organizatsii 1917 g.," KL, No. 5 (38), 1930, p. 109.

55. See, for example, Podvoisky's report to the Petrograd Bolshevik City Conference, *Vtoraia i tret'ia Petrogradskie obshchegorodskie konferentsii*, pp. 17-19.

56. Ibid., pp. 14-22.

III. The Abortive June 10 Demonstration

1. Nevsky, *Krasnoarmeets*, No. 10-15, 1919, p. 35.

2. *Pervyi legal'nyi Peterburgskii komitet*, pp. 136-37, 159. See also

N. I. Podvoisky, "Voennaia organizatsiia TsK RSDRP(b) i voenno-revoliutsionnyi komitet 1917 g.," KL, No. 6, 1923, p. 74.

3. I. F. Petrov, "Strategiia i taktika partii bol'shevikov v period podgotovki i pobedy sotsialisticheskoi revoliutsii: Mart-oktiabr' 1917 g." (doctoral dissertation, Akademiia obshchestvennykh nauk pri TsK KPSS, Moscow, 1961), p. 415. The published version of this work is I. F. Petrov, *Strategiia i taktika partii bol'shevikov v podgotovke pobedy oktiabr'skoi revoliutsii: Mart-oktiabr' 1917 g.* (2d ed.; Moscow: Izdatel'-stvo politicheskoi literatury, 1964). At a Petersburg Committee meeting in early June Nevsky referred to a Central Committee stipulation that the Military Organization not make any final decisions regarding a demonstration without its sanction. *Pervyi legal'nyi Peterburgskii komitet*, p. 136.

4. Ibid., pp. 136-37; *Soldatskaia pravda*, June 13, 1917, p. 3. Garrison troops were particularly bitter about Kerensky's "Declaration of Soldiers' Rights" issued on May 11, which *Pravda* called the "Declaration of no rights."

5. Akademiia nauk SSSR, Institut istorii, et al., *Revoliutsionnoe dvizhenie v Rossii v mae-iiune 1917 g.: Iiun'skaia demonstratsiia*, ed. D. A. Chugaev, et al. (Moscow: Izd-vo Akademii nauk SSSR, 1959), pp. 483-85. The fragmentary protocol of this meeting, published here for the first time, is the only one I have been able to find dealing with the initial discussions regarding a demonstration within the Military Organization itself. The document is interesting because it mirrors the way in which individual Military Organization unit representatives, speaking for their regiments, exerted influence on Military Organization policy. The document also bears witness to the Military Organization leadership's early interest in encouraging and organizing a demonstration.

6. Petrov, "Strategiia i taktika," p. 415.

7. A. M. Sovokin, "K istorii iiun'skoi demonstratsii 1917 g.," *Voprosy istorii KPSS*, No. 5, 1966, p. 46.

8. *Soldatskaia pravda*, June 6, 1917, p. 1. See also *Novaia zhizn'*, June 7, 1917, p. 2. For a detailed Soviet interpretation of the June 4 demonstration, see M. S. Ilin, "Demonstratsiia i miting na marsovom pole v Petrograde 4 iiunia 1917 g.," *Voprosy istorii*, No. 6, 1957, pp. 126-30.

9. *Revoliutsionne dvizhenie: Iiun'skaia demonstratsiia*, pp. 485-87. The very fragmentary protocol of this important meeting has been published here for the first time. See also Petrov, "Strategiia i taktika," p. 415; Vavilin, *Lenin kak rukovoditel' Leningradskoi organizatsii bol'shevikov*, p. 9; K. T. Sverdlova, *Iakob Mikhailovich Sverdlov* (Mos-

cow: Molodaia Gvardiia, 1960), p. 259; and Podvoisky's defense of the Military Organization at the Sixth Party Congress, in Institut marksizma-leninizma pri TsK KPSS, *Shestoi s"ezd RSDRP(bol'shevikov), avgust 1917 goda: Protokoly* (Moscow: Gospolitizdat, 1958), p. 62.

10. For a full exposition of Lenin's attitudes toward the offensive at this time, see Lenin, *Sochineniia*, XXV, 3-28.

11. Kamenev incorporated these arguments in a memorandum which he later submitted to the party leadership. Petrov, "Strategiia i taktika," p. 415.

12. The protocol of this meeting is contained in *Pervyi legal'nyi Peterburgskii komitet*, pp. 136-45.

13. Party membership in the Vyborg District was the largest in Petrograd, totalling 5,000 at the end of May, 1917. *Ocherki istorii Leningradskoi organizatsii KPSS, Chast' I: 1883-oktiabr' 1917 gg.* (Leningrad: Lenizdat, 1962), p. 502.

14. The Vyborg District Duma contained a large Bolshevik majority. Kozlovsky and Molotov (both Bolsheviks) were the Duma's chairman and secretary, respectively. —ov, "Vyborgskaia raionnaia duma 1917 goda," *Leningradskaia pravda*, November 4, 1927, p. 3.

15. V. I. Gorev, *Anarkhizm v Rossii* (Moscow: Molodaia Gvardiia, 1930), p. 105; A. Sh. [Shapiro], "Anarkhizm-kommunizm i anarkhosindikalizm," *Golos truda* (organ of the Anarcho-Syndicalists), January 27, 1918, p. 3.

16. Below, p. 108.

17. An Anarchist-Syndicalist writer, undoubtedly with justification, labeled the Anarchist-Communist program "a collection of empty phrases." *Golos truda*, January 27, 1918, p. 3. It should be noted that the two anarchist groups were at odds with each other during most of the revolutionary period. Gorev, *Anarkhizm v Rossii*, p. 105.

18. Gosudarstvennyi Muzei Velikoi Oktiabr'skoi Sotsialisticheskoi Revoliutsii, fond listovok, f. 2, No. 11641.

19. V. N. Zalezhsky, *Iz vospominanii podpol'shchika* (Moscow: Gosizdat, 1931), pp. 180-81.

20. See below, p. 129, for M. M. Lashevich's comment in regard to the similarity between Bolsheviks and Anarchists in the First Machine Gun Regiment.

21. P. M. Stulov, "Pervyi pulemetnyi polk v iiul'skie dni 1917 g.," KL, No. 3 (36), 1930, p. 73.

22. This account is based in part on reports in *Riech'* and *Izvestiia*, June 6-10, 1917.

23. In May the Anarchist-Communists began publishing a newspaper called *Kommuna*. After *Kommuna* was shut down by the Provisional

Government, the name of the Anarchist-Communist organ was changed to *Svobodnaia kommuna*. I did not have access to either newspaper in the Soviet Union and have been unable to locate any issues in Western libraries.

24. Apparently Vyborg workers went out on strike at least partly in the belief that the Pereverzev eviction order applied to all organizations using the villa, including the bakers' union and the workers' militia. They were disturbed as well because use of the public park surrounding the villa also appeared to be threatened. At the Soviet Congress evening session on June 8 Pereverzev made it clear that his order applied only to the Anarchists. *Pervyi Vserossiiskii s"ezd Sovetov rabochikh, soldatskikh i krest'ianskikh deputatov* (Leningrad: Gosizdat, 1930), p. 267.

25. Miliukov, *Istoriia vtoroi russkoi revoliutsii*, I, 214.

26. Leningrad, Sovet deputatov trudiashchikhsia, *Petrogradskii Sovet rabochikh i soldatskikh deputatov: Protokoly zasedanii Ispolnitel'nogo komiteta i Biuro Ispolnitel'nogo komiteta* (Moscow: Gosizdat, 1925), p. 274.

27. I. G. Tsereteli, *Vospominaniia o fevral'skoi revoliutsii* (Paris: Mouton and Co., 1963), II, 197-201. From the time of his return from Siberia to Petrograd in the middle of March, 1917, Tsereteli, a Georgian Menshevik, was the most influential figure in the Soviet. His memoirs are of great value in understanding the role of the Soviets and particularly the political situation within the Petrograd Soviet, the All-Russian Congress of Soviets, and the All-Russian Executive Committee of the Soviets during this period. In the absence of adequate archival materials, they constitute the only really detailed source available for study of this important subject. See also *Pervyi Vserossiiskii s"ezd Sovetov*, pp. 262-64; Sukhanov, *The Russian Revolution*, II, 387-88; and Miliukov, *Istoriia vtoroi russkoi revoliutsii*, I, 214.

28. Tsereteli, *Vospominaniia*, II, 202.

29. *Pervyi legal'nyi Peterburgskii komitet*, p. 157; M. Ia. Latsis, "Iiul'skie dni v Petrograde: Iz dnevnika agitatora," PR, No. 5 (17), 1923, p. 103. See also F. D. Stasova's letter dated June 9 informing the Moscow party organization of the Central Committee's plans, in Rossiiskaia sotsial-demokraticheskaia rabochaia partiia, Tsentral'nyi komitet, *Perepiska sekretariata TsK RSDRP(b) s mestnymi partiinymi organizatsiiami: Sbornik dokumentov, Vol. I: Mart-oktiabr' 1917 g.* (Moscow: Gospolitizdat, 1957), p. 13.

30. Latsis, PR, No. 5 (17), 1923, pp. 103-104. Latsis kept a detailed diary beginning with the February revolution in order to keep track of his agitational work. Apparently only a very small portion of it has been published.

31. *Revoliutsiia 1917 goda: Khronika sobytii*, Vol. III: *Iiun'-iiul'*, compiled by V. Vladimirova (Moscow: Gosizdat, 1923), p. 42.

32. *Pravda* on June 11 stated that the meeting on June 8 indicated that the demonstration movement enjoyed very broad support among both workers and soldiers, and this, of course, has been the official Soviet interpretation. In his diary, however, Latsis suggests that some worker representatives were enthusiastic, while others were uncertain of the prevailing mood. In a speech to the Sixth Congress in late July Stalin reported that it appeared clear that although the soldiers were bursting to rush into the streets, this mood was not yet shared by the workers. *Shestoi s"ezd*, p. 15.

33. *Pervyi legal'nyi Peterburgskii komitet*, p. 158.

34. *Soldatskaia pravda*, June 10, 1917.

35. This claim was later to acquire particular significance as one of the justifications for opposition to garrison troop levies, the primary cause of unrest in the garrison in late June and early July.

36. Latsis, PR, No. 5 (17), 1923, p. 103.

37. Ibid., p. 104.

38. I. P. Flerovsky, "Iiul'skii politicheskii urok," PR, No. 7 (54), 1926, p. 62.

39. Trotsky, *History of the Russian Revolution*, I, 443; I. Iurenev, "Ocherednaia lozh'," *Vpered*, June 17, 1917, p. 8. See also *Pervyi legal'nyi Peterburgskii komitet*, p. 156, and I. Deutscher, *The Prophet Armed* (New York: Oxford University Press, 1954), p. 267.

40. Miliukov, *Istoriia vtoroi russkoi revoliutsii*, I, 216; Sukhanov, *The Russian Revolution*, II, 390.

41. On the basis of materials presently available it is not possible to exclude the possibility that Miliukov is correct in his contention that the Provisional Revolutionary Committee was a joint Anarchist-Bolshevik administrative center for the demonstration. *Istoriia vtoroi russkoi revoliutsii*, I, 216. In the immediate aftermath of the abortive demonstration Lunacharsky and Liber made similar allegations in regard to the role of the special committee organized in the Durnovo villa; see *Pervyi Vserossiiskii s"ezd Sovetov*, p. 444; *Izvestiia*, June 11, 1917, p. 2, and June 15, 1917, p. 5.

42. *Baltiiskie moriaki*, pp. 88-89.

43. An announcement to the Helsingfors party committee, dated June 9 and signed by Boky, is contained in ibid., p. 88.

44. G. D. Bykov, "Revoliutsionnaia deiatel'nost' bol'shevikov Vyborgskoi storony goroda Petrograda v period podgotovki i provedeniia oktiabr'skoi sotsialisticheskoi revoliutsii" (*Kandidat* dissertation, Leningrad University, Leningrad, 1951), p. 112.

45. Trotsky calls this the simplest possible expression for liquidation of the Provisional Government. *History of the Russian Revolution*, I, 443.

46. The text of the leaflet, as it was posted on June 9, appeared in *Soldatskaia pravda*, June 10, 1917, p. 1; reprinted in *Revoliutsionnoe dvizhenie: Iiun'skaia demonstratsiia*, pp. 494-95.

47. Material contained in *Izvestiia*, June 10-16, 1917, was especially useful in preparing this section.

48. *Revoliutsionnoe dvizhenie: Iiun'skaia demonstratsiia*, p. 495.

49. The text of the Congress resolution supporting the Provisional Government was published in *Izvestiia* on June 9, 1917.

50. Above, pp. 60-61.

51. Tsereteli, *Vospominaniia*, II, 205.

52. *Petrogradskii Sovet: Protokoly*, pp. 186-87.

53. Tsereteli, *Vospominaniia*, II, 205-206.

54. *Pervyi legal'nyi Peterburgskii komitet*, p. 156; E. Ignatov, "I Vserossiiskii s"ezd Sovetov rabochikh i soldatskikh deputatov," PR, No. 6 (65), 1927, p. 115.

55. At the evening session of the First Congress on June 9, Kerensky vehemently denied these rumors: "No Cossack regiments are moving to Petrograd and could not be because our task is to send troops to the front and not the rear." *Pervyi Vserossiiskii s"ezd Sovetov*, pp. 382-83.

56. *Pervyi legal'nyi Peterburgskii komitet*, pp. 158-66; Latsis, PR, No. 5 (17), 1923, p. 104.

57. Latsis, PR, No. 5 (17), 1923, pp. 104-105; *Pervyi legal'nyi Peterburgskii komitet*, p. 164; see also Chamberlin, *The Russian Revolution*, I, 161.

58. Below, pp. 94-96.

59. Trotsky, *History of the Russian Revolution*, I, 443. See also E. P. Krivosheina, *Dve Demonstratsii* (Moscow: Gos. Sotsial'no-ekonomicheskoe izd-vo, 1931), p. 29.

60. Tsereteli, *Vospominaniia*, II, 205-211; *Pervyi Vserossiiskii s"ezd Sovetov*, pp. 375-78. See also Vladimirova, *Khronika sobytii*, III, 48.

61. Particularly important sources for this study include *Pervyi legal'nyi Peterburgskii komitet*, pp. 152-66; Sverdlova, *Ia. M. Sverdlov*, p. 259; and Sovokin, *Voprosy istorii KPSS*, No. 5, 1966, p. 49.

62. Ignatov, PR, No. 6 (65), 1927, p. 115; B. Shumiatsky, "Pervyi s"ezd sovetov," in *V dni velikoi proletarskoi revoliutsii* (Moscow: Ogiz, 1937), p. 59. For an inside view of what was occurring within the Soviet Congress at this time, see Tsereteli, *Vospominaniia*, II, 206-209 and *Pervyi Vserossiiskii s"ezd Sovetov*, p. 382.

63. *Pervyi legal'nyi Peterburgskii komitet*, p. 156. One of the members of the Bolshevik delegation, Kuzmin, voiced his personal bitterness at the Congress session on June 9: "Comrades, as sad as it may be, I must state: most of us, the Bolshevik representatives here, representatives of three million workers and soldiers, as it turns out, did not even know that all this was being organized. Here I, a representative, only now found out that such a demonstration was being organized." *Pervyi Vserossiiskii s"ezd Sovetov*, p. 382.

64. Sverdlova, *Ia. M. Sverdlov*, p. 259; *Pervyi legal'nyi Peterburgskii komitet*, p. 158; Sovokin, *Voprosy istorii KPSS*, No. 5, 1966, p. 49.

65. Below, p. 86.

66. For the official Bolshevik explanation of the demonstration decision and call-off, see *Pravda*, June 11, 1917, p. 1.

67. At an unofficial meeting of the First Congress of Soviets on June 10, an unnamed Bolshevik announced that in the early morning he had been assigned by the party delegation to inform the gathering in the Durnovo villa of the Central Committee's decision. He stated that the Bolsheviks and SR Maximalists, immediately upon receiving news of the cancellation, left the Provisional Revolutionary Committee meeting, and only the Anarchists remained. *Pervyi Vserossiiskii s"ezd Sovetov*, p. 445; *Izvestiia*, June 11, 1917, p. 6. See also Ignatov, PR, No. 6 (65), 1927, p. 115.

68. *Birzhevye vedomosti*, June 10, 1917, p. 2. See also *Pravda*, June 11, 1917, p. 1, and *Petrogradskii Sovet: Protokoly*, p. 192.

69. Some memoirists, such as Tsereteli, have tended to emphasize the acquiescence of the masses and their basic loyalty to the Soviet and the Provisional Government, while more radically inclined observers, such as Trotsky and Sukhanov, have made use of roughly the same evidence (i.e., summaries of observations by Soviet representatives) in stressing the mass disaffection unearthed in the aftermath of the cancellation. Significantly, even Miliukov sides with the latter. The events immediately succeeding the cancellation (i.e., the June 18 demonstration and the July uprising) suggest that the Trotsky-Sukhanov-Miliukov appraisals of latent radical strength more closely approximate the situation actually prevailing. Tsereteli, *Vospominaniia*, II, 219-25; Trotsky, *History of the Russian Revolution*, I, 446; Sukhanov, *Zapiski*, IV, 300-301; Miliukov, *Istoriia vtoroi russkoi revoliutsii*, I, 217-19.

70. Quoted in Trotsky, *History of the Russian Revolution*, I, 445-46.

71. *Izvestiia*, June 11, 1917, pp. 6-12; *Revoliutsionnoe dvizhenie: liun'skaia demonstratsiia*, pp. 499-503.

72. Latsis, PR, No. 5 (17), 1923, p. 106; *Pervyi legal'nyi Peterburgskii komitet*, p. 164.

73. *Rabochaia gazeta*, June 13, 1917, pp. 1-2.

74. Flerovsky, PR, No. 7 (54), 1926, p. 63.

75. *Shestoi s"ezd*, pp. 77-78. In his memoirs Flerovsky remembers that the colorful Anarchist-Communist leader Asnin strove to persuade the sailors to act immediately. PR, No. 7 (54), 1926, p. 66. In a critique of F. F. Raskolnikov's *Kronshtadtsy: Iz vospominanii bol'shevika*, a group of reviewers, six former Kronstadt Bolsheviks, describe the radical spirit prevailing in the Kronstadt Bolshevik organization at this time: "The Kronstadt Committee had to fight leftist tendencies within its own organization and to straighten out the lines of many, even prominent party members on the subject of an armed uprising. . . . All Kronstadt got used so quickly to power being in the Soviets that this seemed right for Russia. Enormous stores of arms, matériel, and fighters gave rise to strong and dangerous moods regarding the need for an immediate move on Leningrad in full strength to overthrow the Provisional Government. . . . Finally, in June, to the Kronstadt party headquarters came many thousands of sailors and soldiers with the demand that the Bolsheviks lead the fleet and the Kronstadt sailors to Leningrad to overthrow the Provisional Government. At the head of this crowd was Kiril Orlov [a Bolshevik leader] who led the crowd to the committee from Iakornaia Square. Someone sounded the general garrison alarm. The affair just missed ending in disaster. All strength was mobilized and the giddiness liquidated." P. Smirnov, D. Kondakov, A. Liubovich, A. Gertsburg, M. Pozdeeva, S. Emmin, in KL, No. 5-6 (56-57), 1933, pp. 214-15.

76. Flerovsky, PR, No. 7 (54), 1926, p. 67.

77. Tsereteli, *Vospominaniia*, II, 228.

78. Ibid., pp. 226-28. Tsereteli's is apparently the only detailed published account of this meeting. See also Vladimirova, *Khronika sobytii*, III, 56.

79. *Pravda*, June 13, 1917. See also Sukhanov, *Zapiski*, IV, 303. Apparently because the meeting was closed there were no newspaper accounts of it other than that which appeared in *Pravda*.

80. Sukhanov, *Zapiski*, IV, 305; *Pravda*, June 13, 1917; Vladimirova, *Khronika sobytii*, III, 56.

81. See also Sukhanov, *Zapiski*, IV, 306, and Trotsky, *History of the Russian Revolution*, I, 447-51.

82. Quotations from this debate are taken from Tsereteli, *Vospominaniia*, II, 231-38.

83. *Shestoi s"ezd*, pp. 21-23.

84. Flerovsky, PR, No. 7 (54), 1926, p. 67; see also Sukhanov, *Zapiski*, IV, 322.

85. *Golos pravdy*, June 14, 1917, p. 3.

86. Sovokin, *Voprosy istorii KPSS*, No. 5, 1966, p. 52.

87. *Pervyi legal'nyi Peterburgskii komitet*, p. xv. The following account of this meeting is based on ibid., pp. 153-68.

88. Presumably Boky was referring to the continuing difficulties between the Central Committee and Petersburg Committee in regard to the direction of party activity in the capital. The interrelation of the organizations was most recently on the agenda of the May 30 meeting, but was not discussed because of a drawn-out debate on the question of a separate newspaper for the Petersburg Committee.

89. The City Conference convened on July 1.

90. Tsereteli, *Vospominaniia*, II, 203.

91. Sukhanov, *The Russian Revolution*, II, 402-406. B. I. Nicolaevsky claims that Nevsky was the source of Sukhanov's information. "I. G. Tsereteli i ego vospominaniia o 1917 g.," *Sotsialisticheskii vestnik*, No. 9-10, 1962, p. 135. In a conversation with this writer Nicolaevsky asserted that this was disclosed to him by Sukhanov.

92. E. H. Carr, *The Bolshevik Revolution, 1917-1923* (3 vols.; New York: Macmillan, 1951-1953), I, 90.

IV. The Rise of Unrest

1. Tsereteli, *Vospominaniia*, II, 246.

2. *Izvestiia*, June 17, 1917, p. 1.

3. Petrov, "Strategiia i taktika," p. 429.

4. The protocol of this meeting is contained in *Pervyi legal'nyi Peterburgskii komitet*, pp. 168-84.

5. Vladimirova, *Khronika sobytii*, III, 66.

6. *Revoliutsionnoe dvizhenie: Iiun'skaia demonstratsiia*, p. 518; *Petrogradskii Soviet: Protokoly*, pp. 278-79; see also Tsereteli, *Vospominaniia*, II, 250-51.

7. Miliukov, *Istoriia vtoroi russkoi revoliutsii*, I, 222; *Riech'*, June 13, 1917, p. 5.

8. *Pervyi legal'nyi Peterburgskii komitet*, p. 173.

9. For the minutes of this discussion, see ibid., pp. 173-78.

10. Gorky's *Novaia zhizn'* (June 15, 1917, p. 1) hailed this appeal as a long overdue sign that the Bolsheviks might be willing to separate themselves from the Anarchists in the future.

11. For a detailed Soviet interpretation of the June 18 demonstration, see Krivosheina, *Dve demonstratsii.*

12. W. S. Woytinsky, *Stormy Passage* (New York: Vanguard Press, 1961), p. 293; Tsereteli, *Vospominaniia*, II, 247.

13. Vladimirova, *Khronika sobytii*, III, 69.

14. In this regard M. Ia. Latsis, on the eve of the July days, made an extremely relevant point in criticizing the organizational work of the Military Organization: "In the question of an uprising in the streets [and presumably also a demonstration]," he said, "the majority of regiments will follow us, but in ordinary situations—as in elections to the Soviets, etc.—leadership is not in our hands." See B. Elov, "Petrogradskaia organizatsiia RSDRP(b) nakanune iiul'skikh sobytii," in *3-5 iiulia 1917 g.* (Petrograd, 1922), p. 60.

15. Latsis, PR, No. 5 (17), 1923, p. 108.

16. *Revoliutsionnoe dvizhenie: Iiun'skaia demonstratsiia*, p. 525.

17. Accounts in *Pravda, Izvestiia, Novaia zhizn', Rabochaia gazeta, Volia naroda,* and *Riech'* were consulted in preparing this account of the June 18 demonstration.

18. Sukhanov, *The Russian Revolution*, II, 416-17.

19. P. N. Miliukov, *Rossiia na perelome* (3 vols.; Paris: Imprimerie d'art Voltaire, 1927), I, 73.

20. The Kronstadt sailors were among those invited to participate in the Congress demonstration and on June 16 the Kronstadt Soviet voted to accept. *Izvestiia Kronshtadtskogo Soveta*, June 18, 1917, p. 1. Flerovsky recalls, however, that the sailors were still bitter at the Bolshevik Central Committee for cancelling the June 10 demonstration and with the Congress for scheduling one of their own and so voted against a large turnout. PR, No. 7 (54), 1926, p. 68. A. F. Ilin-Zhenevsky, who edited *Golos pravdy* at this time, suggests that the problem was that the sailors had no interest in an unarmed demonstration. "Na rubezhe russkoi revoliutsii," *Krasnyi Petrograd*, 1919, p. 36.

21. Official and special reports in *Pravda, Malenkaia gazeta, Izvestiia, Novaia zhizn', Rabochaia gazeta, Volia naroda,* and *Riech'*, June 19-23, 1917, were used in preparing the following section.

22. Raskolnikov, *Kronshtadt i Piter*, p. 188. In Khaustov's statements, remembers Raskolnikov, "there could be sensed almost no Marxist influence whatever."

23. *Biulleten' Vserossiiskoi konferentsii frontovykh i tylovykh voennykh organizatsii RSDRP(b)*, No. 3, June 18, 1917, p. 2.

24. F. Zalesskaia, "Iiun'skaia demonstratsiia 1917 g.," PR, No. 6 (65), 1927, p. 159.

25. The pertinent Congress resolution stated that "until the war is brought to an end by the efforts of the revolutionary democracy, the Russian revolutionary democracy is obliged to keep its army in condition to take either the offensive or defensive. . . . The question of whether to take the offensive should be decided from a purely military and strategic point of view." Golder, *Documents of Russian History*, p. 371.

26. *Izvestiia*, June 20, 1917, p. 4.

27. See, for example, the resolution of the First Reserve Infantry Regiment signed by Lieutenant Sakharov (as chairman of the meeting that passed the motion) in *Soldatskaia pravda*, June 25, 1917, p. 3. Sentiment against the offensive was especially high in Kronstadt, where the local Soviet passed two resolutions (one Bolshevik, the other left SR) condemning the move by votes of 195 in favor, 1 opposed, with 65 abstentions. *Golos pravdy*, June 21, 1917, p. 1.

28. See several such documents in *Revoliutsionnoe dvizhenie: Iiun'-skaia demonstratsiia*, pp. 366-68, 377-81.

29. Ibid., p. 373.

30. The most valuable records of the conference proceedings and of the mood prevailing at the meetings are contained in the five bulletins (*Biulleten' Vserossiiskoi konferentsii frontovykh i tylovykh voennykh organizatsii RSDRP(b)*, No. 1-5, June 16, 17, 18, 21, and 24, 1917) published during the conference as a special supplement to *Soldatskaia pravda*. Sometimes useful eyewitness accounts were also published in provincial Bolshevik Party organs. The best memoir account is M. Kedrov, "Vserossiiskaia konferentsiia voennykh organizatsii RSDRP(b)," PR, No. 6 (65), 1927, pp. 216-31, reprinted in *Velikaia oktiabr'skaia sotsialisticheskaia revoliutsiia: Sbornik vospominanii* (Moscow: Gosizdat, 1957), pp. 71-82. An extremely useful detailed secondary account containing many important documents is S. E. Rabinovich, *Vserossiiskaia voennaia konferentsiia bol'shevikov 1917 g.* (Moscow: Gosvoenizdat, 1931). The resolutions of the conference are contained in Institut Marksa-Engel'sa-Lenina-Stalina pri TsK KPSS, *Kommunistich-eskaia Partiia Sovetskogo Soiuza v rezoliutsiiakh i resheniiakh s"ezdov, konferentsii i plenumov TsK, 1898-1954* (4 vols.; 7th ed.; Moscow: Gospolitizdat, 1954), I, 354-67.

31. The aims of the conference were outlined in a leaflet originally distributed in May. Muzei Revoliutsii SSSR, Moscow, fond listovok, A49134.

32. "Politicheskii moment i zadachi Vserossiiskoi konferentsii VO," *Biulleten'*, No. 1, June 16, 1917, p. 1.

33. *Shestoi s"ezd*, p. 62; V. A. Antonov-Ovseenko, *Stroitel'stvo Krasnoi Armii v revoliutsii* (Moscow: Izd-vo Krasnaia Nov', 1923), p. 10.

34. Rabinovich, KL, No. 5 (38), 1930, p. 110.

35. A specific decision to employ delegates as agitators in the garrison was taken at a preliminary session of the conference on June 15. *Biulleten'*, No. 1, June 16, 1917, p. 1.

36. Kedrov, *Velikaia Oktiabr'skaia sotsialisticheskaia revoliutsiia*, p. 74; M. Sulimova, "Eto budet poslednii i reshitel'nyi boi," in *Letopis' velikogo oktiabria*, ed. A. Iu. Krivitsky (Moscow: Sovetskaia Rossiia, 1958), p. 104.

37. A. F. Ilin-Zhenevsky, "Voennaia organizatsiia RSDRP i *Soldatskaia pravda*," KL, No. 1 (16), 1926, p. 70; Petrov, "Strategiia i taktika," p. 447.

38. *Shestoi s"ezd*, p. 63.

39. *Biulleten'*, No. 3, June 18, 1917, pp. 1-2; see also Rabinovich, KL, No. 5 (38), 1930, pp. 113-16.

40. A. Ia. Arosev, a long-time Bolshevik, was a member of the *Biulleten'*'s five-man editorial board and at the close of the conference was elected to the Military Organization's ruling All-Russian Bureau.

41. *Birzhevye vedomosti*, June 19, 1917, p. 1, reported that word of the offensive first began circulating at about 2:00 in the afternoon.

42. *Okopnaia pravda*, July 9, 1917; *Biulleten'*, No. 4, June 21, 1917, p. 2.

43. Kedrov, *Velikaia Oktiabr'skaia sotsialisticheskaia revoliutsiia*, pp. 75-76.

44. Podvoisky, *God 1917*, p. 59; see also Petrov, "Strategiia i taktika," p. 447. The account of the meeting in the *Biulleten'* (No. 4, June 21, 1917) disclosed that a proposal to change the program was made and rejected just before the last speech of the evening.

45. Podvoisky, KL, No. 6, 1923, p. 76. For a later, substantially similar version of this conversation, see N. I. Podvoisky, "Iiul'skie dni: Tri momenta," *Pravda*, July 18, 1925, p. 2. The conversation is omitted from the most recent edition of Podvoisky's memoirs (*God 1917*).

46. *Biulleten'*, No. 4, June 21, 1917; *Okopnaia pravda*, July 9, 1917, p. 2. It was in support of this objective that it was decided at one of the last conference sessions to initiate publication of a special soldier-peasant newspaper under the control of the Military Organization All-Russian Bureau. *KPSS v rezoliutsiiakh*, I, 354-65. Due to the events and consequences of the July days, the first issue of this newspaper, *Derevenskaia bednota*, did not come out until October 12, 1917.

47. Though Nevsky recognized the need for the best possible organization, he was not one of those who felt at this time that organizational weakness precluded an attempt to seize power. Below, pp. 130, 137-138.

48. *Biulleten'*, No. 4, June 21, 1917, p. 1; *Volna*, July 4, 1917, p. 2. Nevsky demanded, however, that the Military Organization be given a vote in the Central Committee. The demand was rejected and according to the rules adopted at the conference, the Military Organization was given only a "consultive" vote in the Central Committee. *KPSS v rezoliutsiiakh*, I, 367. The frankest and most detailed discussions of the All-Russian Military Organization's "separatist" tendencies before and after the July days are contained in Rabinovich, PR, No. 6-7 (77-78), 1928, pp. 187-88, and the same author's "Rabota bol'shevikov v armii v 1917 g.," *Voina i revoliutsiia*, No. 6, 1927, pp. 96-108.

49. Latsis, PR, No. 5 (17), 1923, p. 109; I. Gavrilov, *Ocherki po istorii Vyborgskoi part-organizatsii goroda Leningrada* (Leningrad: Lenpartizdat, 1953), p. 109. A major strike at the Putilov factory on the same day was not concerned with the unrest in the Vyborg District. The Putilov workers struck in support of pay increase demands though the movement also had ominous political overtones. *Delo naroda*, June 20, 1917, p. 2.

50. *Novaia zhizn'*, June 20, 1917, p. 3.

51. *Pervyi legal'nyi Peterburgskii komitet*, pp. 185-86; Bykov, "Revoliutsionnaia deiatel'nost' bol'shevikov Vyborgskoi storony," p. 125. The text of the First Machine Gun Regiment's resolution of rejection was published in *Soldatskaia pravda*, June 22, 1917, p. 3.

52. Mironov, "Bor'ba bol'shevikov za Petrogradskii garnizon," p. 211; A. P. Konstantinov, *Bol'sheviki Petrograda v 1917 godu: Khronika sobytii* (Leningrad: Lenizdat, 1957), p. 292. In a letter to the regimental committee of the First Machine Gun Regiment, the Military Section of the Petrograd Soviet emphasized the emergency nature of the request and urged that it be fulfilled. Bykov, "Revoliutsionnaia deiatel'nost' bol'shevikov Vyborgskoi storony," p. 135.

53. Mironov, "Bor'ba bol'shevikov za Petrogradskii garnizon," p. 211; Stulov, KL, No. 3 (36), 1930, p. 87.

54. In regard to the movement toward an uprising at this time, P. M. Stulov, basing his work on thorough archival study, writes that "regimental Bolsheviks were already carried away by the common stream and did not try to restrict the movement, especially since it was actually formulated out of Bolshevik slogans." KL, No. 3 (36), 1930, p. 93.

55. Ibid.

56. *Novaia zhizn'*, June 21, 1917, p. 4; *Delo naroda*, June 22, 1917, p. 4.

57. A recently published protocol of a Petrogradsky Regiment meeting on June 20 indicates that the First Machine Gun Regiment was represented there by Ia. M. Golovin, a member of the Bolshevik Military Organization. He appealed for the Petrogradsky Regiment's support of the decision to organize a demonstration and claimed that the approval of some garrison units and factories had already been obtained. According to this source, the meeting voted unanimous approval of Golovin's proposal and chose two members of the regiment to coordinate planning with the First Machine Gun Regiment. *Revoliutsionnoe dvizhenie: liun'skaia demonstratsiia*, pp. 567-68.

58. *Novaia zhizn'*, June 21, 1917, p. 4; *Delo naroda*, June 22, 1917, p. 4.

59. Stulov, KL, No. 3 (36), 1930, p. 88; A. Shliapnikov, "Iiul'skie dni v Petrograde," PR, No. 4 (51), 1926, p. 60. That Bolshevik representatives attempted to keep the First Machine Gun Regiment from going into the streets is supported by a protocol of a meeting of the Petrogradsky Regiment's soldiers' committee on June 21. *Revoliutsionnoe dvizhenie: liun'skaia demonstratsiia*, p. 569.

60. *Revoliutsionnoe dvizhenie: liun'skaia demonstratsiia*, p. 576.

61. *Golos pravdy*, June 21, 1917, p. 4, and June 25, 1917, p. 2; *Novaia zhizn'*, June 24, 1917, p. 3; *Rabochaia gazeta*, June 25, 1917. See also Flerovsky, PR, No. 7 (54), 1926, pp. 71-72.

62. Flerovsky, PR, No. 7 (54), 1926, p. 71; V. Vladimirova, "Iiul'skie dni 1917 goda," ibid., No. 5 (17), 1923, p. 7.

63. The proposed agenda was first published in *Pravda*, June 20, 1917.

64. *Pervyi legal'nyi Peterburgskii komitet*, p. 181.

65. Sulimova, *Letopis' velikogo oktiabria*, p. 105.

66. Kedrov, *Velikaia oktiabr'skaia sotsialisticheskaia revoliutsiia*, p. 78. In another memoir, Kedrov identifies himself as one of the "hotheads." He recalls that to the Military Organization the seizure of power seemed a simple matter, and on the basis of discussions with Lenin prior to the June 10 demonstration, he had expected him to feel the same way. "In this," remembers Kedrov, "I was deeply mistaken." "Iz krasnoi tetradi ob Il'iche," PR, No. 1 (60), 1927, pp. 38-40.

67. Kedrov, *Velikaia oktiabr'skaia sotsialisticheskaia revoliutsiia*, pp. 77-78. This speech is not contained in any editions of Lenin's complete works. An abridged account appeared in *Novaia zhizn'*, June 21, 1917; Kedrov's record is much fuller. The *Novaia zhizn'* account and that of Kedrov were both reprinted in *Zapiski Instituta Lenina*, Vol. II, 1927, pp. 48-49. According to the Lenin Institute these were the only detailed accounts of the speech to be preserved. Interestingly, the *Biulleten'*, *Volna*, and *Okopnaia pravda* all ignored it. Very short accounts were

contained in *Zvezda*, July 1, 1917, p. 1, and *Bakiinskii rabochii*, June 27, 1917, p. 3.

68. *KPSS v rezoliutsiiakh*, I, 356.

69. Kaganovich and Krylenko were both elected to the All-Russian Military Organization Bureau at the close of the conference. The members of this organ (they were to remain in Petrograd to direct the work of the Military Organization), in addition to Kaganovich and Krylenko, were: V. I. Nevsky, N. I. Podvoisky, E. F. Rozmirovich, K. A. Mekhonoshin, I. Ia. Arosev, F. P. Khaustov, and I. I. Dzevaltovsky. Rabinovich, KL, No. 5 (38), 1930, p. 124. Included were some of the most radical Bolsheviks—indeed, on the surface it appears as if the Bureau was weighted in their favor.

70. Vasiliev, Khaustov's successor as editor of *Okopnaia pravda*, the Bolshevik frontline newspaper, was one of three delegates representing the front in the conference Presidium. He and Shemaev, who represented military units in Arensburg, emphasized Bolshevik strength in their areas throughout the conference. See for example *Biulleten'*, No. 3, June 18, 1917, p. 1.

71. Ibid.

72. On the subject of the offensive, the conference passed a moderate Krylenko-sponsored resolution by a vote of 32 in favor with 21 abstentions. *KPSS v rezoliutsiiakh*, I, 356-57. Apparently, the bulk of the conference was not present for the vote, and the position was for practical purposes never really implemented by the Military Organization.

73. *Pervyi legal'nyi Peterburgskii komitet*, pp. 185-99. These minutes are also contained in *Revoliutsionnoe dvizhenie: Iiun'skaia demonstratsiia*, pp. 556-65.

74. V. I. Nevsky, "Narodnye massy v oktiabr'skoi revoliutsii," *Rabotnik proveshcheniia*, No. 8, 1922, pp. 20-21.

75. A complete list of participants is contained in *Revoliutsionnoe dvizhenie: Iiun'skaia demonstratsiia*, p. 614.

76. *Pervyi legal'nyi Peterburgskii komitet*, p. 205; these minutes are contained in ibid., pp. 200-205, and in *Revoliutsionnoe dvizhenie: Iiun'skaia demonstratsiia*, pp. 570-74.

77. Nevsky, *Rabotnik prosveshcheniia*, No. 8, 1922, p. 21.

78. There was no issue of *Pravda* on Monday, June 19, and no mention of the offensive appeared in the June 20 issue.

79. *Golos pravdy*, the Kronstadt Bolshevik newspaper, echoed Lenin's rejection of immediate action and his appeal for a sustained propaganda and organizational campaign in large-type page-one editorials on June 22 and 23. Both editorials directly rejected the immediate over-

throw of the Provisional Government. On July 2, the eve of the July days, *Golos pravdy* seemed primarily concerned with the coming elections to the Kronstadt Duma.

80. Vladimirova, *Khronika sobytii*, III, 293-94.

81. In addition to backing the position of the returning Grenadiers in *Soldatskaia pravda*, leaders of the Bolshevik Military Organization personally campaigned among units of the Petrograd garrison in behalf of the mutinous soldiers. Their role in fomenting unrest is particularly evident in the case of the garrison Reserve Grenadier Regiment, where agitation by members of the Military Organization All-Russian Bureau stimulated passage on July 1 of a resolution inviting all Petrograd military units and factories to join in supporting the Grenadier position. See I. Tobolin (ed.), "Iiul'skie dni v Petrograde," KA, No. 5 (24), 1927, p. 26, and Mironov, "Bor'ba bol'shevikov za Petrogradskii garnizon," p. 193.

82. *Soldatskaia pravda*, July 2, 1917, p. 1. V. Iablonsky, a rank-and-file member of the Military Organization, also recalls the appearance at this time (that is, before July 3) of Military Organization leaflets calling for an early uprising (*vosstanie*) against the Provisional Government. "3-5 iiulia," KL, No. 2-3, 1922, p. 160.

V. The July Uprising Begins

1. Below, pp. 141-44.

2. Soviet historians have generally treated the July uprising as a spontaneous mass protest movement originating in the wake of the resignation of the Kadets from the coalition government and in response to news of reverses at the front. The most significant exception to this official interpretation is Stulov, KL, No. 3 (36), 1930, pp. 64-125, which convincingly documents the pre-July 3 origins of the rebellion within the First Machine Gun Regiment.

3. Above, pp. 117-119.

4. *Izvestiia*, June 23, 1917, p. 2.

5. For General Polovtsev's recollection of these difficulties, see P. A. Polovtsev, *Dni zatmeniia* (Paris: Vozrozhdenie, n.d.), pp. 116-19.

6. Quoted from the archives on the Provisional Government's investigation of the July uprising by Stulov, KL, No. 3 (36), 1930, p. 92. Stulov emphasizes that the material from the Provisional Government investigations pertaining to the First Machine Gun Regiment published in 1927 (Tobolin, KA, No. 4 (23), 1927, pp. 1-63 and No. 5 (24), 1927,

pp. 3-70) is extremely incomplete and does not by any means represent the most important documents.

7. Stulov, KL, No. 3 (36), 1930, p. 94.

8. Ibid., p. 95.

9. V. I. Nevsky, "Organizatsiia mass," *Krasnaia gazeta*, July 16, 1922, p. 3.

10. *Shestoi s"ezd*, p. 64. In a previous explanation to the Second City Conference several days before, Podvoisky denied knowing of the machine gunners' plans until July 3 (B. Elov, "Posle iiul'skikh sobytii," KL, No. 7, 1923, p. 100). A footnote to the 1927 edition of the Sixth Congress protocols justifies this discrepancy on the grounds that it was necessary for the Military Organization's protection. The footnote adds that in agreement with Sverdlov and other members of the Central Committee, some inaccuracies were also contained in Podvoisky's explanations to the Sixth Congress (*Protokoly s"ezdov i konferentsii vsesoiuznoe kommunisticheskoi partii (b): Shestoi s"ezd avgust 1917*, ed. A. S. Bubnov [Moscow: Gosizdat, 1927], p. 329).

11. Nevsky, *Krasnoarmeets*, No. 10-15, 1919, p. 39.

12. A. F. Ilin-Zhenevsky, *Ot fevralia k zakhvatu vlasti* (Leningrad: Priboi, 1927), p. 68.

13. Nevsky, *Krasnoarmeets*, No. 10-15, 1919, p. 39.

14. Ibid.

15. *Pervyi legal'nyi Peterburgskii komitet*, pp. 244-45.

16. Nevsky, *Krasnoarmeets*, No. 10-15, 1919, p. 39.

17. V. I. Nevsky, "V oktiabre: beglye zametki pamiati," *Katorga i ssylka*, No. 11-12 (96-97), 1932, pp. 29-30.

18. Elov, KL, No. 7, 1923, p. 100.

19. Cited by Znamensky (*Iiul'skii krizis 1917 goda*, p. 46) from the unpublished memoirs of A. Fedorov in the Leningrad Party Archives. Znamensky calls Fedorov's memoirs the only existing record of Anarchist plans on the eve of the July days. According to a memoir by Bolshevik I. Lebedev, the Anarchists also organized an all-night planning session of worker and soldier delegates in the Durnovo villa in connection with the proposed uprising. Lebedev claims to have been a participant. *Pravda*, July 16, 1937, p. 4.

20. *Pravda*, July 4, 1917, p. 4.

21. Above, pp. 133-34.

22. F. F. Raskolnikov, "Kronshtadt v iiul'skie dni," *Pravda*, July 16, 1927.

23. Trotsky, *History of the Russian Revolution*, II, 12.

24. *Pravda*, July 4, 1917, p. 4.

25. Stulov, KL, No. 3 (36), 1930, p. 96.

26. Miliukov, *Istoriia vtoroi russkoi revoliutsii*, I, 238.

27. V. I. Nevsky, "Zamechaniia k soobshcheniiu B. Elova i stat'e F. Raskol'nikova," KL, No. 7, 1923, pp. 128-30.

28. Above, p. 130.

29. Nevsky, *Krasnoarmeets*, No. 10-15, 1919, p. 39.

30. Richard Pipes's valuable survey, *The Formation of the Soviet Union* (1st ed. rev.; Cambridge: Harvard University Press, 1964), pp. 50-61, and Tsereteli, *Vospominaniia*, II, 133-61, were particularly useful in preparing this account of the Ukraine crisis. A translation of pertinent documents may be found in R. P. Browder and A. Kerensky (eds.), *The Russian Provisional Government 1917* (Stanford: Stanford University Press, 1961), Vol. I.

31. A. K. Drezen (ed.), *Burzhuaziia i pomeshchiki v 1917 godu: Chastnye soveshchaniia chlenov gosudarstvennoi dumy* (Moscow-Leningrad: Partiinoe Izd-vo, 1932), p. 157.

32. Pipes, *The Formation of the Soviet Union*, p. 61.

33. Miliukov, *Istoriia vtoroi russkoi revoliutsii*, I, 235-36.

34. *Birzhevye vedomosti*, July 3, 1917, evening edition, p. 1. "Over-forties" refers to those soldiers (all over 40) who had been furloughed for agricultural field work, then called back in preparation for the offensive. Many of them protested their recall with demonstrations.

35. A. Rozanov, "Pervyi pulemetnyi polk," *Petrogradskaia pravda*, July 16, 1922, p. 3.

36. According to five witnesses, A. Poliakov, a member of the Bolshevik Military Organization, in the name of that organization called upon his company (the Fourth) to participate in the meeting and to join the rest of the garrison and the Military Organization in overthrowing the Provisional Government. Tobolin, KA, No. 4 (23), 1927, p. 20.

37. Ibid., pp. 13-14; Stulov, KL, No. 3 (36), 1930, p. 96.

38. Tobolin, KA, No. 4 (23), 1927, p. 14.

39. Ibid.; Stulov, KL, No. 3 (36), 1930, p. 97.

40. Trotsky, *History of the Russian Revolution*, II, 13-14.

41. Tobolin, KA, No. 4 (23), 1927, p. 14.

42. Ibid. It is interesting that at the Second City Conference and later at the Sixth Congress Podvoisky stated that between 10 A.M. and 5:00 P.M. on July 3 the Military Organization sent twenty-three comrades to restrain the First Machine Gun Regiment. Rejecting this claim,

Stulov states categorically that no agitators sent by the Military Organization appeared in the regiment during this period. Stulov, KL, No. 3 (36), 1930, p. 100.

43. Stulov, KL, No. 3 (36), 1930, pp. 99-101.

44. It is characteristic that after 1923, when Semashko fled the Soviet Union, Soviet writers suddenly stopped absolving him of blame for starting the July uprising. Thus, Ilin-Zhenevsky writes that "he [Semashko] enjoyed great influence and undoubtedly could have restrained the masses had he wanted to. Now," continues Ilin-Zhenevsky, "this behavior of Lt. Semashko should ont surprise us." *Ot fevralia k zakhvatu vlasti*, p. 68.

45. Stulov, KL, No. 3 (36), 1930, pp. 99-104. A recent history of the Petrograd Red Guard (V. I. Startsev, *Ocherki po istorii Petrogradskoi krasnoi gvardii i rabochei militsii* [Moscow-Leningrad: Nauka, 1965]) suggests that the Workers' Militia, a modest Bolshevik-Anarchist led forerunner of the Red Guard, also played a prominent role in the expansion of the movement at this point. Startsev's study contains much new information, but if his evaluation of the importance of the Workers' Militia on July 3 is correct, it is difficult to understand the absence of any attention to the activities of the Workers' Militia in earlier literature on the organization and expansion of the July uprising.

46. Tobolin, KA, No. 4 (23), 1927, p. 58.

47. Znamensky, *liul'skii krizis 1917 goda*, pp. 57-58.

48. See General Polovtsev's report of July 3 to Kerensky. Akademiia nauk SSSR, Institut istorii, et al., *Revoliutsionnoe dvizhenie v Rossii v iiule 1917 g.: liul'skii krizis*, ed. D. A. Chugaev, et al. (Moscow: Izd-vo Akademii nauk SSSR, 1959), p. 15.

49. *Birzhevye vedomosti*, July 4, 1917, morning edition, p. 3.

50. The news apparently first appeared in the July 3 evening edition of *Birzhevye vedomosti*.

51. Woytinsky, "Gody pobed i porazhenii," p. 183.

52. Akhun and Petrov, *Bol'sheviki i armiia*, p. 225.

53. Tobolin, KA, No. 5 (24), 1927, p. 26.

54. N. G. Popov, "Putilovets v iiul'skie dni," *Bor'ba klassov*, No. 11-12, 1932, p. 280.

55. *Birzhevye vedomosti*, July 4, 1917, morning edition, p. 2.

56. Latsis, PR, No. 5 (17), 1923, p. 111.

57. K. Shelavin, "K voprosu o podgotovke iiul'skikh dnei," *Zvezda*, No. 3 (9), 1925, p. 149. See also O. A. Lidak, *1917 god: Ocherk istorii oktiabr'skoi revoliutsii* (Moscow-Leningrad: Partizdat, 1932), p. 49.

58. M. I. Kalinin, "Vladimir Il'ich o dvizhenii," *Krasnaia gazeta*, July 16, 1920, p. 2. To cite but one specific example from the many re-flected in memoirs, according to a Bolshevik from the Novyi Lessner factory, immediately after the First Machine Gun Regiment's repre-sentative A. I. Zhilin (a member of the Military Organization and fre-quent contributor to *Soldatskaia pravda*) finished appealing for support, "rank-and-file party members decided on their own to join the machine gunners." P. F. Kudelli (ed.), *Leningradskie rabochie v bor'be za vlast' Sovetov 1917* (Leningrad: Gosizdat, 1924), p. 57.

59. Latsis, PR, No. 5 (17), 1923, p. 112.

60. N. K. Krupskaia, *Lenin i partiia* (Moscow: Gospolitizdat, 1963), p. 118.

61. S. M., "Na putilovskom zavode v iiul'skie dni," *Petrogradskaia pravda*, July 18, 1922, p. 4. This is the Bogdatiev who was ejected from the Petersburg Committee (but allowed to retain his membership in the Bolshevik Party) in April after calling for the overthrow of the Provi-sional Government in the name of the Petersburg Committee. Above, p. 45. According to L. M. Mikhailov-Politikus and P. F. Kudelli, on the eve of the July days Bogdatiev wrote a leaflet (over the signature of the Petersburg Committee) calling for a demonstration on July 3. The leaflet was evidently widely circulated in all districts. Tatiana Graf, "V iiul'skie dni 1917 g.," KL, No. 5-6 (50-51), 1932, p. 232.

62. I. Kazakov and E. Koshelev, both members of the Military Or-ganization, were the delegates sent to Kronstadt by the First Machine Gun Regiment. Tobolin, KA, No. 4 (23), 1927, pp. 19-20.

63. E. Iarchuk, *Kronshtadt v russkoi revoliutsii* (New York: Izdanie Ispolnitel'nogo komiteta professional'nykh soiuzov, 1923), p. 11.

64. O. L. D'or, *Krasnyi chasovoi Kronshtadt* (Moscow: Literaturno-izdatel'skii otdel politicheskogo upravleniia revoliutsionnogo voennogo soveta respubliki, 1920), p. 40.

65. M. L. Lur'e, "Kronshtadtskie moriaki v iiul'skom vystuplenii 1917 goda," KL, No. 3 (48), 1932, pp. 93-94. Other Investigating Com-mission documents dealing with Kronstadt appear in Tobolin, KA, No. 5 (24), 1927, pp. 40-48, and *Baltiiskie moriaki*, pp. 162-74.

66. V. I. Nevsky, "Dve vstrechi," KL, No. 4, 1922, p. 144.

67. Flerovsky, PR, No. 7 (54), 1926, p. 58.

68. Significant in this connection is Woytinsky's contention that delegates from the provinces were the strongest supporters of the coali-tion government at the All-Russion Congress. "Gody pobed i pora-zhenii," pp. 186-87.

69. Tsereteli, *Vospominaniia*, II, 261.

70. Ibid., p. 266.

71. Tobolin, KA, No. 4 (23), 1927, p. 14.

72. *Izvestiia*, July 4, 1917, p. 1.

73. *Novaia zhizn'*, July 4, 1917, p. 3.

74. The basic source for the study of this conference is *Vtoraia i tret'ia Petrogradskie obshchegorodskie konferentsii bol'shevikov v iule i oktiabre 1917 goda: Protokoly* (Moscow-Leningrad: Gosizdat, 1927). These protocols have not been republished. Study of this work can be supplemented profitably with Elov, *3-5 iiulia 1917 g.*, pp. 53-74.

75. For the development of this controversy, see *Pervyi legal'nyi Peterburgskii komitet*, pp. 106, 114-22, 127-32.

76. *Vtoraia i tret'ia Petrogradskie obshchegorodskie konferentsii*, p. 43.

77. Ibid., p. 53; E. N. Egorova, "Iunkeram plevali v litso," *Leningradskaia pravda*, July 18, 1926, p. 3; V. I. Egorov, "Iiul'skie dni 1917 goda," ibid.

78. *Shestoi s"ezd*, p. 17.

79. Elov, KL, No. 7, 1923, p. 96.

80. *Vtoraia i tret'ia Petrogradskie obshchegorodskie konferentsii*, p. 47.

81. Egorov, *Leningradskaia pravda*, July 18, 1926, p. 3.

82. Egorova, ibid.

83. Below, pp. 167-70.

84. *Shestoi s"ezd*, p. 17; see also Elov, KL, No. 7, 1923, p. 96.

85. Mironov, "Bor'ba bol'shevikov za Petrogradskii garnizon," p. 234. During the Stalin period Soviet sources often identified Smilga as one of those who along with Latsis supported the idea of leaning on the First Machine Gun Regiment to seize power in Petrograd.

86. Lidak, *1917 god*, p. 49.

87. Flerovsky, PR, No. 7 (54), 1926, p. 72.

88. Nogin broke the news of the government crisis to a meeting of the Moscow Party Committee on July 3, emphasizing that the Central Committee "had decided to continue its restrained policy and was appealing to party members for discipline." E. Levi, "Moskovskaia organizatsiia bol'shevikov v iiule 1917 goda," PR, No. 2-3 (85-86), 1929, p. 127.

89. *Shestoi s"ezd*, p. 17; Tsereteli, *Vospominaniia*, II, 266-67.

90. *Vtoraia i tret'ia Petrogradskie obshchegorodskie konferentsii*, p. 50. In official party histories published after Tomsky and Latsis fell from favor in the 1930's their opposition to the policies of the Central

Committee during the July days was acknowledged. However, these sources treat Latsis and Tomsky as exceptions to the rule, ignoring the fact that Latsis was spokesman for the Vyborg District and the elected chairman of the Second City Conference and that Tomsky's speech of July 3 was made at the behest of the Presidium, of which he was a member.

91. Elov, *3-5 iiulia 1917 g.*, p. 73.

92. *Vtoraia i tret'ia Petrogradskie obshchegorodskie konferentsii*, pp. 50-52.

93. *Volia naroda*, July 4, 1917, pp. 3-4.

94. *Izvestiia*, July 4, 1917, p. 3.

95. Stulov, KL, No. 3 (36), 1930, p. 105; see also M. M. Lashevich, "Iiul'skie dni," *Petrogradskaia pravda*, July 17, 1921, p. 1.

96. A. Metelev, "Iiul'skoe vosstanie v Petrograde," PR, No. 6, 1922, p. 161.

97. Tobolin, KA, No. 5 (24), 1927, pp. 56-59.

98. Stulov, KL, No. 3 (36), 1930, pp. 105-106.

99. Nevsky, *Krasnoarmeets*, No. 10-15, 1919, p. 39. This gathering is sometimes referred to as an unofficial Petersburg Committee meeting or as a gathering of the Military Organization.

100. A. Tarasov-Rodionov, "3-5 iiulia," *Izvestiia*, July 18, 1922, p. 2.

101. Kalinin, *Krasnaia gazeta*, July 16, 1920, p. 2; see also G. D. Veinberg, "Preddverie oktiabr'skoi revoliutsii: Moi vospominaniia o iiul'-skikh dniakh," *Petrogradskaia pravda*, July 17, 1921, p. 3.

102. See Podvoisky's speech at the Second City Conference and those of Podvoisky and Stalin at the Sixth Congress in Elov, KL, No. 7, 1923, p. 101, and *Shestoi s"ezd*, pp. 17, 65.

103. Ibid.; see also K. Shelavin, *Ocherki russkoi revoliutsii 1917 g.*: Part I, *Fevral'-iiul'skie dni* (Petrograd: Priboi, 1923), p. 142, and Metelev, PR, No. 6, 1922, p. 161.

104. Elov, KL, No. 7, 1923, p. 101.

105. Ibid., p. 96.

106. Kalinin, *Krasnaia gazeta*, July 16, 1920, p. 2.

107. Ilin-Zhenevsky, *Krasnyi Petrograd*, 1919, p. 37.

108. Latsis, PR, No. 5 (17), 1923, p. 113.

109. Petrov, "Strategiia i taktika," p. 464, citing documents from the Institute of Marxism-Leninism.

110. Latsis, PR, No. 5 (17), 1923, p. 113.

111. Vladimirova, *Khronika sobytii*, III, 133. See also Trotsky, *History of the Russian Revolution*, II, 21.

112. *Revoliutsionnoe dvizhenie: Iiul'skii krizis*, p. 23.

113. Tobolin, KA, No. 4 (23), 1927, p. 58; Tarasov-Rodionov, *Izvestiia*, July 16, 1922, pp. 2-3.

114. Tobolin, KA, No. 4 (23), 1927, p. 32. An excellent example of the implementation of these instructions is contained in the published investigation documents on the Third Reserve Infantry Regiment. Ibid., No. 5 (24), pp. 16-19.

115. Ibid., No. 4 (23), p. 26; Elov, KL, No. 7, 1923, p. 101, and *Izvestiia*, July 4, 1917, p. 3. It should be noted that the fortress was occupied with no resistance.

116. Vladimirova, PR, No. 5 (17), 1923, p. 18. In this connection see N. Arsky, "Tragikomediia 3-go iiulia," in *Perezhitoe* (Moscow: Verf, [1918]), p. 37.

117. G. Zinoviev, "Lenin i iiul'skie dni," PR, No. 8-9 (67-68), 1927, p. 62.

118. See *Ocherki istorii Leningradskoi organizatsii KPSS*, p. 491, and L. F. Karamysheva, *Bor'ba bol'shevikov za Petrogradskii Sovet: Mart-oktiabr', 1917 g.* (Leningrad: Lenizdat, 1964), p. 80.

119. *Vtoraia i tret'ia Petrogradskie obshchegorodskie konferentsii,* p. 47.

120. A protocol of this meeting was published in *Izvestiia*, July 5, 1917. See also A. Shliapnikov, "Iiul'skie dni v Petrograde," PR, No. 4 (51), 1926, pp. 68-72.

121. To be sure, Trotsky's views on the revolutionary situation were not akin to those of the Kamenev-Zinoviev wing of the Bolshevik Party. Rather, Trotsky, like Lenin, apparently felt that direct action had to be postponed until support for the Bolsheviks was greater in the provinces and at the front.

122. In this connection, see V. V. Sakharov's testimony in Tobolin, KA, No. 4 (23), 1927, p. 51.

123. *Izvestiia*, July 4, 1917, p. 5.

124. It should be noted that troops mobilized by the government did not become engaged with insurgent elements until late the next day. It appears fairly well established that para-military rightist organizations were directly involved in some of the confused street battles of July 3 and 4. In this connection, see Znamensky, *Iiul'skii krizis 1917 goda*, p. 66, and Polovtsev, *Dni zatmeniia*, pp. 123-24.

125. *Leningradskie rabochie v bor'be*, pp. 71-72; see also A. F. Ilin-Zhenevsky, "Vystuplenie polkov v Petrograde v iiul'skie dni 1917 goda," KL, No. 3 (30), 1929, pp. 112-13, and *Volia naroda*, July 4, 1917, p. 4.

126. Stulov, KL, No. 3 (36), 1930, pp. 111-12.

127. Woytinsky "Gody pobed i porazhenii," p. 193; see also Woytinsky's report to the All-Russian Executive Committees on July 6. *Izvestiia*, July 7, 1917, p. 3.

128. Woytinsky, "Gody pobed i porazhenii," p. 191; see also *Novaia zhizn'*, July 5, 1917, p. 3, and Sukhanov, *The Russian Revolution*, II, 431-32.

129. *Izvestiia*, July 5, 1917, p. 1.

130. Flerovsky, PR, No. 7 (54), 1926, p. 75; see also Petrov, "Strategiia i taktika," p. 469.

131. L. D. Trotsky, *Sochineniia*, Vol. III, Part I: *Ot fevralia do oktiabria* (Moscow: Gosizdat, 1925), pp. 165-66.

132. G. E. Zinoviev, *God revoliutsii* (Leningrad: Gosizdat, 1926), pp. 189-90. This may be the way the situation appeared to Zinoviev (and this is the way it appears in official Soviet histories), but it was far from the whole story. According to Raskolnikov's own reluctant admission during a meeting of the Kronstadt Soviet on July 7, Liubovich had phoned Raskolnikov from Petrograd (evidently from the Kshesinskaia mansion) with a request for troops well before the Zinoviev conversation. Evidently, after talking to Liubovich, Raskolnikov called Zinoviev in the Taurida Palace and then took charge of arranging a massive, early morning move on Petrograd. *Izvestiia Kronshtadtskogo Soveta*, July 14, 1917, p. 2.

133. Zinoviev, PR, No. 5 (17), 1923, p. 62.

134. Muzei Revoliutsii SSSR, fond listovok, 1519.

135. Nevsky, *Krasnoarmeets*, No. 10-15, 1919, pp. 39-40.

136. F. F. Raskolnikov, "Vooruzhennoe vosstanie ili vooruzhennoe demonstratsiia?" *Pravda*, July 27, 1927, p. 3.

137. Nevsky, *Krasnoarmeets*, No. 10-15, 1919, p. 40.

VI. The July Uprising: Culmination
and Collapse

1. *Riech'*, July 5, 1917, p. 2; *Novaia zhizn'*, July 6, 1917, pp. 2-3.

2. *Volia naroda*, July 5, 1917, p. 2.

3. Mironov, "Bor'ba bol'shevikov za Petrogradskii garnizon," p. 238, *Birzhevye vedomosti*, July 5, 1917, morning edition, p. 3.

4. See for example Nevsky, *Krasnoarmeets*, No. 10-15, 1919, pp. 39-40.

5. Significant in this connection is the following passage from Podvoisky's report to the Second City Conference: "On the night before

the fourth the mood in the regiments was undoubtedly deflated while the spirit of the workers and of the regiments which had not yet gone out [presumably those from the suburbs] was high. . . . As late as 12:45 the Military Organization could not answer the question of whether the regiments would be out soon." Elov, KL, No. 7, 1923, p. 101.

6. The Pavlovsky and Finliandsky Regiments, for example, refused to participate in the demonstration on July 4.

7. Woytinsky, "Gody pobed i porazhenii," p. 193.

8. Miliukov, *Istoriia vtoroi russkoi revoliutsii*, I, 243.

9. Woytinsky, "Gody pobed i porazhenii," p. 194.

10. Late on the evening of July 3, Pereverzev first suggested the possibility of attempting to discredit the Bolsheviks by immediately publishing some documents in the government's possession purporting to show that the Bolsheviks were working for the Germans.

11. Miliukov, *Istoriia vtoroi russkoi revoliutsii*, I, 243; see also Woytinsky, "Gody pobed i porazhenii," p. 193.

12. Vladimirova, *Khronika sobytii*, III, 140.

13. Vladimirova, PR, No. 5 (17), 1923, p. 12; Woytinsky, "Gody pobed i porazhenii," pp. 206-208.

14. Ibid.; Tsereteli, *Vospominaniia*, II, 317-18. It appears clear that the Northern front at this time was still solidly supporting the Executive Committee of the Soviet.

15. B. V. Stankevich, *Vospominaniia 1914-1919 gg.* (Berlin: I. P. Ladyzhnikov, 1920), pp. 184-85.

16. Woytinsky, "Gody pobed i porazhenii," p. 208. The Provisional Government specifically issued its first direct order for troops late on July 3, but according to Tsereteli, the Fifth Army Committee awaited official authorization from the Soviet before sending them.

17. V. Bonch-Bruevich, *Na boevykh postakh fevral'skoi i oktiabr'skoi revoliutsii* (Moscow: Federatsiia, 1931), p. 72.

18. *Birzhevye vedomosti*, July 7, 1917, evening edition, p. 2.

19. Bonch-Bruevich, *Na boevykh postakh*, p. 73.

20. M. Saveliev, "Lenin v iiul'skie dni," *Pravda*, July 17, 1930, p. 2.

21. *Izvestiia*, July 5, 1917, p. 2.

22. Raskolnikov, *Kronshtadt i Piter*, p. 120.

23. Estimates of the number of Kronstadters arriving in Petrograd on July 4 range from ten to thirty thousand. *Izvestiia*, July 5, 1917, p. 2. It should be noted that in Kronstadt the July demonstration had the support of the Anarcho-Syndicalist-Communists, the Bolsheviks, and with less enthusiasm, the Left SR's and some non-party members.

24. Lur'e, KL, No. 3 (48), 1932, p. 96.

25. Ibid., pp. 96-97; *Novaia zhizn'*, July 5, 1917, p. 2; I. P. Flerovsky, "Predmetnyi urok," *Pravda*, July 16, 1922, p. 2.

26. A. M. Liubovich, like Flerovsky, was a Kronstadt Bolshevik. Both had spent the night in Petrograd. Judging by their memoirs, Flerovsky spent much of the night at the Taurida Palace (from there he informed Kronstadt of the resolution adopted by the Workers' Section), while Liubovich maintained contact with the Military Organization in the Kshesinskaia mansion.

27. This was the reason given to non-Bolshevik leaders who protested the change. See the critical comments of the Anarchist Iarchuk and the Left SR Smoliansky in *Izvestiia Kronshtadtskogo Soveta*, July 7, 1917, p. 1, and July 14, 1917, p. 2.

28. I. N. Kolbin, "Kronshtadt ot fevralia do kornilovskikh dnei," KL, No. 2 (23), 1927, p. 149.

29. *Novaia zhizn'*, July 5, 1917, p. 2.

30. Flerovsky, PR, No. 7 (54), 1926, p. 77.

31. *Birzhevye vedomosti.* July 5, 1917, morning edition; Raskolnikov, *Kronshtadt i Piter*, p. 123.

32. The Left SR, A. Baranov, commenting on this episode in the Kronstadt Soviet after the July days, said that "it seemed peculiar that people who were angered because others carried portraits of Kerensky themselves had led us to receive Lenin's blessing." *Izvestiia Kronshtadtskogo Soveta*, July 14, 1917, pp. 2-3.

33. Podvoisky, *God 1917*, p. 62.

34. *Birzhevye vedomosti*, July 5, 1917, morning edition, p. 3.

35. Kalinin, *Krasnaia gazeta*, July 16, 1920, p. 2.

36. Lenin, *Sochineniia*, XXV, 190.

37. A. M. Liubovich, "3-5 iiulia," *Leningradskaia pravda*, July 16, 1925, p. 3.

38. A. V. Lunacharsky, "Iz vospominanii ob iiul'skikh dniakh 1917 g.," *Petrogradskaia pravda*, July 16, 1922, p. 3.

39. Reports in *Riech'*, *Izvestiia*, and *Novaia zhizn'* were used in preparing this account.

40. Sukhanov, *The Russian Revolution*, II, 443-44.

41. *Putilovets v trekh revoliutsiiakh: Sbornik materialov po istorii Putilovskogo zavoda*, ed. S. B. Okun' (Moscow-Leningrad: Ogiz, 1933), p. 355.

42. *Izvestiia*, July 5, 1917, p. 2.

43. Some of these clashes of July 4 involved military patrols (generally made up of Cossacks and military school cadets) attempting to carry out Polovtsev's order to arrest and disarm rebelling soldiers and

workers. But as on the previous evening, indignant private citizens and rightist organizations were also involved. See Znamensky, *Iiul'skii krizis 1917 goda*, pp. 66-67.

44. Raskolnikov, *Kronshtadt i Piter*, p. 124.

45. Flerovsky, PR, No. 7 (54), 1926, p. 78.

46. Iarchuk, *Kronshtadt v russkoi revoliutsii*, p. 13.

47. *Izvestiia Kronshtadtskogo Soveta*, July 7, 1917, p. 1.

48. Lur'e, KL, No. 3 (48), 1932, p. 98.

49. *Izvestiia Kronshtadtskogo Soveta*, July 14, 1917, p. 2.

50. Flerovsky, PR, No. 7 (54), 1926, p. 79.

51. The lack of unity prevailing among the Kronstadt leaders is vividly reflected in the heated arguments over the demonstrations which took place in the Kronstadt Soviet after the July days. See *Izvestiia Kronshtadtskogo Soveta*, July 7-18, 1917, all issues.

52. "Our task was to go to the Taurida Palace to present our demands," stated the Left SR, G. Smoliansky, in the Kronstadt Soviet the next day. "We wanted to nudge it into taking power and when our protests were ignored, we considered it impossible to remain." Ibid., July 7, 1917, p. 2.

53. "The Anarcho-Syndicalist-Communist organization considered that the armed demonstration would turn into an uprising," writes Iarchuk. "The government would thus be given a decisive and powerful blow from which it would be unable to recover. In the course of the future struggle, the local Soviets of Workers', Soldiers', and Peasants' Deputies would bring about its complete liquidation." *Kronshtadt v russkoi revoliutsii*, p. 11.

54. Sukhanov implies that at this time Raskolnikov was empowered to dissolve the Executive Committees of the All-Russian Soviets "if conditions appeared favorable." *Zapiski*, IV, 426. Although this possibility cannot be excluded, it seems much more likely that this crucial decision was at all times up to the Bolshevik Central Committee. This would appear to be the sense of the following passage from Nevsky's memoirs: "Events developed so rapidly that every moment of indecision was a loss. The Military Organization, whose military operations were directed by Podvoisky and Mekhonoshin, carried out the orders of the Central Committee, but its directives were such that to carry the affair to its conclusion and to set our forces into motion were impossible. Because of this the Bolshevik military masses were indecisive." *Krasnoarmeets*, No. 10-15, 1919, p. 40.

55. *Izvestiia*, July 5, 1917, p. 3.

56. A. [Ilin-] Zhenevsky, "Arest V. Chernova v iiul'skie dni 1917 g.," *KL*, No. 6 (21), 1926, p. 70.

57. Miliukov, *Istoriia vtoroi russkoi revoliutsii*, I, 244.

58. I. N. Kolbin, "Kronshtadt organizuetsia, gotovitsia k boiu," in *Oktiabr'skii shkval: Moriaki Baltiiskogo flota v 1917 g.*, ed. P. F. Kudelli and I. V. Egorov (Leningrad: Izd-vo Krasnaia gazeta, 1927), p. 41.

59. [Ilin-] Zhenevsky, *KL*, No. 5 (20), 1926, p. 70.

60. Sukhanov, *The Russian Revolution*, II, 445; see also M. Pokrovsky, "Grazhdanin Chernov v iiul'skie dni," *Pravda*, July 16, 1922, p. 1.

61. *Izvestiia Kronshtadtskogo Soveta*, July 13, 1917, p. 2.

62. Sukhanov, *The Russian Revolution*, II, 446-47.

63. Radkey, *The Agrarian Foes of Bolshevism*, p. 284.

64. Above, p. 74.

65. Tsereteli, *Vospominaniia*, II, 318.

66. *Baltiiskie moriaki*, p. 122.

67. Ibid., p. 123. The chairman of Tsentrobalt at this time was the Bolshevik P. Dybenko.

68. Ibid., p. 346.

69. "Morskoe Ministerstvo Kerenskogo v iiul'skie dni," *Petrograd-skaia pravda*, July 17, 1921, p. 2.

70. Polovtsev, *Dni zatmeniia*, p. 125.

71. O. A. Lidak, "Iiul'skie sobytiia 1917 goda," in *Ocherki po istorii oktiabr'skoi revoliutsii*, ed. M. N. Pokrovsky (2 vols.; Moscow-Leningrad: Gosizdat, 1927), II, 331.

72. These telegrams are translated in B. V. Nikitine, *The Fatal Years* (London: William Hodge, 1938), pp. 119-22. The connection between Lenin's revolutionary activities and the German government's efforts to subvert the Provisional Government and the Russian war effort is one of the more controversial episodes of the revolutionary period. A few of the captured documents of the German Foreign Office support the charge that German funds were channeled to the Bolsheviks. Among the most damning of these is a letter dated December 3, 1917, from the German Foreign Minister Kuhlmann to the Kaiser asserting that "it was not until the Bolsheviks had received from us a steady flow of funds through various channels and under different labels" that they were able to build up their propaganda effort. Z. A. B. Zeman (ed.), *Germany and the Revolution in Russia, 1915-1918: Documents from the Archives of the German Foreign Ministry* (London: Oxford University Press, 1958), pp. 94-95. The fact that substantial amounts of German money were pumped to the Bolsheviks in the summer of 1917 now seems cer-

tain. But nowhere in the vast literature on the subject does there appear to be any evidence to support the thesis that Lenin's policies or tactics were in any way directed or even influenced by the Germans.

73. See Pereverzev's letter to the editor in *Birzhevye vedomosti,* July 9, 1917, evening edition, p. 7.

74. Woytinsky, "Gody pobed i porazhenii," p. 198.

75. Latsis, PR, No. 5 (17), 1923, p. 113.

76. *Izvestiia,* July 6, 1917, p. 3.

77. Ibid.

78. Ibid., p. 4.

79. Woytinsky, "Gody pobed i porazhenii," p. 193.

80. *Izvestiia,* July 6, 1917, p. 4.

81. *Izvestiia Kronshtadtskogo Soveta,* July 7, 1917, p. 2, and July 13, 1917, p. 2. Upon leaving the Taurida Palace some of the sailors, accompanied by Menshevik and SR leaders, returned to their boats and departed for Kronstadt. However, the majority stayed in Petrograd for the night. According to Iarchuk the purpose of the delay in the departure of most of the sailors was to promote intensification and prolongation of the demonstrations. *Kronshtadt v russkoi revoliutsii,* p. 13.

82. Podvoisky, KL, No. 6, 1923, p. 80.

83. Sukhanov, *The Russian Revolution,* II, 455.

84. Arsky, *Perezhitoe,* p. 43. See also Miliukov, *Istoriia vtoroi russkoi revoliutsii,* I, 246, and Shliapnikov, PR, No. 4 (51), 1926, p. 84.

85. Tsereteli, *Vospominaniia,* II, 330.

86. *Izvestiia,* July 7, 1917, p. 3.

87. Sukhanov, *The Russian Revolution,* II, 479-82. Lunacharsky (then People's Commissar for Education) denied Sukhanov's version of this conversation in a letter dated March 30, 1920. In the letter Lunacharsky wrote: "It is clear, Nikolai Nikolayevich, that you have fallen into a profound error. . . . It never, of course, occurred to Comrade Lenin, Comrade Trotsky, or myself to agree on the seizure of power, nor was there even a hint of anything in the nature of a triumvirate. . . . Of course, we did not conceal from ourselves that if the Menshevik-SR Soviet had seized the power, it would have slipped away to more resolute revolutionary groups further to the Left. Your error was probably caused by my telling you that at a decisive moment of the July Days, I told Trotsky in conversation that I should consider it calamitous for us to be in power just then, to which Comrade Trotsky, who was always far more resolute than I and surer of victory, replied that in his opinion that would not have been so bad at all, since the masses would of course have supported us." Ibid., pp. 480-81.

88. Lidak, *Ocherki*, II, 331.

89. See Raskolnikov, *Pravda*, July 27, 1927, p. 3.

90. Bonch-Bruevich, *Na boevykh postakh*, pp. 83-86.

91. Tsereteli, *Vospominaniia*, II, 329.

92. Lidak, *Ocherki*, II, 297.

93. K. Mekhonoshin, "Iz vospominanii o tov. Lenine," *Politrabotnik*, No. 2-3, 1924, p. 7.

VII. The July Uprising: Retreat
and Reaction

1. Woytinsky, "Gody pobed i porazhenii," p. 209.

2. Lidak, *Ocherki*, II, 298.

3. *Izvestiia*, July 6, 1917, p. 7; Eremeev, "Iiul'skii pogrom 1917 g.," *Pravda*, July 17, 1927, p. 4.

4. Raskolnikov, *Kronshtadt i Piter*, pp. 135-37; Ilin-Zhenevsky, *Ot fevralia k zakhvatu vlasti*, pp. 71-72.

5. A meeting of the Kronstadt Soviet on the afternoon of July 5 rejected this request, limiting itself to the dispatch of a delegation to help arrange for the sailors' evacuation without a struggle. The indecision prevailing in Bolshevik ranks at this time is reflected by the fact that initially even some Bolsheviks opposed sending the requested artillery on the grounds that the party Central Committee had decided against any further action and had appealed to all units to return to their quarters. After a break, these same Bolsheviks suddenly reversed themselves because "Raskolnikov was not the type of person to call for help unless it was absolutely necessary." *Izvestiia Kronshtadtskogo Soveta*, July 7, 1917, pp. 1-2.

6. Lur'e, KL, No. 3 (48), 1932, pp. 84-85; Raskolnikov, *Kronshtadt i Piter*, pp. 136-38.

7. A note from Ter-Arutuniants to Kudelko, apparently written at about this time, suggests that in the minds of some unit level Military Organization leaders a resumption of the street demonstrations was then still a possibility. In the message Ter-Arutuniants stated that he was on his way to a joint meeting of the Petersburg Committee and Military Organization, that Vasilievsky Island and the Petrograd side were in Bolshevik hands, and that the question of whether the soldiers would go out again would probably be decided toward evening. Tobolin, KA, No. 4 (23), 1927, p. 32.

8. Raskolnikov, *Kronshtadt i Piter*, p. 137.

9. Lidak, *Ocherki*, II, 298. An editor's footnote to this statement declares that "this characterization of the Military Organization's position is not sufficiently substantiated."

10. Trotsky, *History of the Russian Revolution*, II, 53.

11. Latsis, PR, No. 5 (17), 1923, p. 114.

12. Metelev, PR, No. 6, 1922, p. 173.

13. Stulov, KL, No. 3 (36), 1930, p. 115.

14. *Birzhevye vedomosti*, July 6, 1917, morning edition, p. 3.

15. *Novaia zhizn'*, July 6, 1917, p. 2.

16. Zinoviev, PR, No. 8-9 (67-68), 1927, p. 64.

17. Znamensky, *Iiul'skii krizis 1917 goda*, pp. 123-32. A protocol of the Moscow Committee meeting of July 5 which discussed the demonstration is contained in *Revoliutsionnoe dvizhenie: Iiul'skii krizis*, pp. 106-112.

18. Stulov, KL, No. 3 (36), 1930, p. 116.

19. Akhun and Petrov, *1917 god v Petrograde*, p. 67. See also *Novaia zhizn'*, July 6, 1917, p. 2.

20. *Listok pravdy*, July 6, 1917, p. 1.

21. K. Mekhonoshin, "Iiul'skie dni v Petrograde," *Izvestiia*, July 16, 1922, p. 1.

22. Podvoisky, KL, No. 6, 1923, p. 81; see also *Shestoi s"ezd*, p. 65.

23. Nevsky, *Rabotnik prosveshcheniia*, No. 8, 1922, p. 21.

24. Tobolin, KA, No. 5 (24), 1927, pp. 35-36.

25. *Izvestiia Kronshtadtskogo Soveta*, July 8, 1917, p. 2.

26. Raskolnikov, *Kronshtadt i Piter*, pp. 141-42.

27. Lidak, *Ocherki*, II, 298.

28. *Izvestiia Kronshtadtskogo Soveta*, July 11, 1917, p. 2; Raskolnikov, *Kronshtadt i Piter*, p. 142; Iarchuk, *Kronshtadt v russkoi revoliutsii*, p. 14.

29. Eye-witness reports from *Izvestiia* and *Birzhevye vedomosti* on July 7 were used in preparing this account of the raid on the Kshesinskaia mansion and the Fortress of Peter and Paul.

30. Podvoisky, KL, No. 6, 1923, p. 82.

31. *Izvestiia Kronshtadtskogo Soveta*, July 15, 1917, p. 2.

32. Metelev, PR, No. 6, 1922, p. 174.

33. Ilin-Zhenevsky, *Ot fevralia k zakhvatu vlasti*, p. 82.

34. Lidak, *Ocherki*, II, 344.

35. *Leninskii sbornik*, Vol. VII (Moscow: Gosizdat, 1928), pp. 317-18. See also Latsis, PR, No. 5 (17), 1923, p. 115.

36. Podvoisky, KL, No. 6, 1923, p. 84.

37. Lenin, "Politicheskoe polozhenie," *Sochineniia*, XXV, 157-59, and "K lozungam," ibid., pp. 164-70.

38. In conversations at this time Lenin evidently spoke in terms of a possible uprising in a few weeks and at least no later than the fall. Lidak, *Ocherki*, II, 331-32.

39. A. M. Sovokin, "Rasshirennoe soveshchanie TsK RSDRP(b) 13-14 iiulia 1917 g.," *Voprosy istorii KPSS*, No. 4, 1959, pp. 125-38.

40. *Shestoi s"ezd*, pp. 110-46, 255-57.

41. Russia, 1917 Provisional Government, *Zhurnaly zasedanii Vremennogo Pravitel'stva* (Petrograd, 1917), meeting of July 6, 1917, p. 1.

42. Ibid., meeting of July 7, 1917, p. 4.

43. "We know of no counterrevolutionary instigators among us or in the whole of Kronstadt, and so we can't do any arresting" was the Kronstadt Soviet's reply to this order. Kolbin, KL, No. 2 (23), 1927, pp. 153-54.

44. Tobolin, KA, No. 4 (23), 1927, pp. 2-5.

45. See the district committee reports at the Petersburg Committee meeting of July 10. *Pervyi legal'nyi Peterburgskii komitet*, pp. 210-16.

46. Ibid.

47. *Izvestiia*, July 16, 1917, p. 7.

48. See Podvoisky's report at the continuation of the Second City Conference on July 16. Elov, KL, No. 7, 1923, p. 102.

49. Tobolin, KA, No. 4 (23), 1927, pp. 6-13. For an interesting account of the life of Military Organization members in prison see A. I-Zh. [Ilin-Zhenevsky], "Bol'sheviki v tiurme Kerenskogo," KL, No. 2 (26), 1928, pp. 43-65. The best biographical dictionary for use in identifying Military Organization members is contained in Akhun and Petrov, *Bol'sheviki i armiia*.

50. Stulov, KL, No. 3 (36), 1930, p. 122.

51. A. K. Drezen, "Petrogradskii garnizon v iiule i avguste 1917 g.," KL, No. 3 (24), 1927, p. 218.

52. *Revoliutsionnoe dvizhenie: Iiul'skii krizis*, pp. 73-74.

53. Evidently the only measure taken in regard to naval personnel was the arrest of a few key individuals. Among others, Raskolnikov, Roshal, and Remnev turned themselves in at the direction of the Kronstadt Soviet after the government on July 13 threatened a blockade of Kronstadt unless they did so.

54. Nevsky, *Katorga i ssylka*, No. 11-12 (96-97), 1932, p. 28.

55. A. Minchev, "Boevye dni," KL, No. 9, 1924, p. 9.

56. Rabinovich, PR, No. 6-7 (77-78), 1928, pp. 187-89.

57. B. Shumiatsky, "Shestoi s"ezd partii i rabochii klass," in *V dni velikoi proletarskoi revoliutsii* (Moscow: Ogiz, 1937), p. 93. The positions of Trotsky and Kamenev must have been made known through intermediaries since both were still in prison at the time of the Congress.

58. *Shestoi s"ezd*, p. 289.

59. Nevsky, *Katorga i ssylka*, No. 11-12 (96-97), 1932, pp. 28-30.

60. The only other reference to anything resembling a trial that I have been able to find is contained in Ilin-Zhenevsky, *Ot fevralia k zakhvatu vlasti*, p. 98.

61. The first issue of *Rabochii i soldat* appeared on July 23. Ordered closed by the Provisional Government on August 9, it was replaced by *Proletarii* (August 13), *Rabochii* (August 25), and *Rabochii put'* (September 3). The Central Committee resumed publication of *Pravda* on October 27, 1917, that is, immediately after the Bolshevik seizure of power. A. K. Belkov and B. P. Verevkin (eds.), *Bol'shevistskaia pechat': Sbornik materialov* (Moscow: Vysshaia partiinaia shkola, 1960), Vol. IV.

62. *Protokoly Tsentral'nogo komiteta RSDRP(b): Avgust 1917-fevral' 1918*, pp. 23-25.

63. Ibid., p. 23.

64. Ibid., p. 39.

VIII. Conclusion: The Party Divided

1. *Ocherki istorii Leningradskoi organizatsii KPSS*, p. 451.

2. *Sed'maia konferentsiia: Protokoly*, p. 201.

3. Elov, *3-5 iiulia*, p. 56.

4. See Nevsky's report on behalf of the Military Organization at a meeting of the Petersburg Committee on October 15. *Pervyi legal'nyi Peterburgskii komitet*, pp. 310-12.

5. Nevsky, *Katorga i ssylka*, No. 11-12 (96-97), 1932, p. 36.

Index

Abramovich, R. A., 173
Alexander Nevsky District, 26, 60
Alexandra, Empress, 13, 22, 24
Alexinsky, G., 193
All-Russian Conference of Bolshevik
　Military Organizations, 104, 106,
　107, 111-16, 120-25, 232, 233; *Biul-*
　leten' of, 113, 122, 123, 268
All-Russian Union of Towns, 21
All-Russian Union of Zemstvos, 21
Allies, 32, 108, 109. *See also* Entente
Anarchist-Communists: program of,
　61-64, 260; and Durnovo villa crises,
　64-66, 107-108, 116-17; and garrison,
　62, 63-64, 117, 138-39, 140, 145-46;
　and Kronstadt, 62, 80, 119, 151, 265;
　Bolsheviks and, 62-64, 66, 71, 73,
　100-102, 264, 266; Provisional Revo-
　lutionary Committee, 71, 100-102,
　107, 262, 264; and June 10 demon-
　stration, 71, 262; plan demonstration
　for June 14, 100-102; and June 18
　demonstration, 99, 106; role in ini-
　tiation of July uprising, 138-39, 140,
　145-46, 151, 152, 234, 274; in July
　days, 186, 187, 210, 215
Anarcho-Syndicalist-Communists,
　183, 187, 197, 282, 284
Anarcho-Syndicalists, 62, 260
Anisimov, V. A., 65, 203
April Conference. *See* Seventh
　(April) All-Russian Conference of
　RSDLP (b)

April crisis, 42-43, 49, Bolsheviks and,
　43-45, 46, 231
April theses, 38-41
Armored Car Division, 69, 147, 166,
　193, 212
Arosev, A. Ia., 113, 269
Arsky, N., 199
Asnin, Anarchist-Communist, 62, 64,
　108, 116, 117, 265
Avksentiev, N. D., 84, 213

Balabanoff, Angelica, 15
Baltic fleet, 190-91, 218. *See also* Kron-
　stadt
Baranovsky factory, 147
Beliakov, N. K., 129, 138, 233
Bleikhman, I. S., 62, 64, 99, 139, 152;
　exhorts First Machine Gun Regi-
　ment to overthrow Provisional
　Government, 145-46; in July days,
　160, 182
Bogdanov, B. O., 40, 81-82, 215; and
　June 18 demonstration, 97, 103, 105
Bogdatiev, S. Ia., 50; calls for over-
　throw of Provisional Government
　in April crisis, 45, 277; role in July
　days, 151, 185, 194; arrested, 218
Boky, G., 71, 74, 92, 212, 266
Bolshevik Central Committee, 3, 5, 6,
　229, 230; factions within, 5, 46, 56,
　77, 157; Russian Bureau, 18, 32, 33,
　34-35, 40; and April crisis, 43-44;
　elected at April Conference, 46; de-

291

DATE DUE	
DEC 11 2002	
GAYLORD	PRINTED IN U.S.A.